The Orator

The Orator

Guy Vander Jagt
On the Hustings

Paul E. Ried

Green Hill Publishers
Ottawa, Illinois

To Marjorie

Contents

Preface

I N THE FALL of 1982, Syracuse University granted me a semester's leave of absence with pay to study the campaign speaking of Congressman Guy Vander Jagt, representative of the Ninth District of Michigan and chairman of the National Republican Congressional Committee. It was through the good offices of the former executive director of the NRCC, Nancy Sinnott (now Dwight), and the director of public affairs of the NRCC, Rich Galen, that during the period from July 2, 1982, to January 2, 1983, I was given a desk in the committee's offices in the Eisenhower Center in Washington, D.C., as well as travel expenses to observe the congressman speaking first hand. These six months were important, exciting months in that they led up to the election of '82 and after, giving me a perspective on campaigns that few rhetorical critics ever enjoy.

I observed Vander Jagt in over forty public speaking situations where he played the leading role: seventeen of these were formal campaign speeches following breakfasts, luncheons, and dinners; five involved his discussion leadership either in conferences or in parliamentary business meetings; ten were interviews or question-and-answer sessions, several of which were recorded for television or radio. I also observed three "debates" or confrontational interviews he had with Congressman Tony Coelho, chairman of the Democratic Congressional Campaign Committee. By contrast, I saw him "stump" in a farmer's backyard at McGee's Corners, a crossroad in North Carolina, with children playing and dogs barking, and at a pig pickin' behind the VFW barn just a few miles away in Dunn, North Carolina.

ix

Some of the more memorable occasions for me were his speaking engagements at the black tie, seven-course Winter Dinner of the Gridiron Club (probably the most elite formal grouping of working journalists in the world), the December Freshman Orientation of the successful Republican congressional candidates of 1982, the Godfrey Sperling Breakfast on the day after the election, and the debates with Coelho on *Meet the Press*, on the *MacNeil-Lehrer Report*, and at the September 30th luncheon of the National Press Club in Washington, D.C. I saw him welcome Republican candidates to Washington just before their meeting with the president in the White House. I was in the East Room when one of these Republican candidates gained national television coverage and lost the support of his fellow candidates when he interrupted and publicly attacked the president. I attended Vander Jagt's campaign breakfast speech for Tom Bliley, his luncheon speech for Anne Bagnel, and his dinner speech for Kevin Miller in two states all in one day. I sat in on several closed meetings of the congressional leadership of the Republican party, and I accompanied Vander Jagt on his one-day blitz of Indianapolis for the campaign of Dan Burton. on August 23, 1982.

To enhance this almost continuous rhetorical investigation into Vander Jagt's political speaking, I traveled over eleven thousand air miles to Dallas, San Francisco, Chicago, New York City, Richmond, Indianapolis, Grand Rapids, and points all along the way. I also had complete freedom of access to speech materials filed in his office in the Rayburn Building and in the United States Archives.

A number of humorous incidents occurred as I followed him for three days on his own campaign trail in Michigan. I had, for example, the experience of watching him being given orders by several of his elderly constituents in a newspaper office in a very small central Michigan town. They gave him these directives as if they were teachers assigning lessons to a very young pupil. It was instructive to me that he listened carefully and fulfilled the assignments faithfully.

Several hours before, in Belding, Michigan, when I was asked on the spur of the moment to introduce him to twenty key business executives in the area, I found myself slipping into a campaign speech of my own, my first by the way, where I believe I nominated him for president of the United States in 1988! That was the point at which I realized I would have to draw back from the spirited nature of the campaign in order to regain some semblance of scholarly detachment.

I must confess I am still dazed from time to time as I recall flights on chartered single-engined airplanes, steak banquets, chicken salad luncheons, and conversations with people I had seen before only on television. I am still trying to find sanity in the dreamlike experience of speeding at eighty miles an hour (some say ninety) in a crowded limousine from Trevose, Pennsylvania, to Philadelphia with police escort to board a plane back to Washington for the congressman's "meeting with the president."

Anyone who has listened to and has attempted to improve the speaking of thousands of college students for over thirty years will certainly understand when I say I felt like a kid in a candy store at having the chance of following and listening to the man I believe to be the premier congressional campaign speaker in the United States today.

Many people deserve my thanks for helping me to complete this project, but some gave time and energy well beyond the call of duty. I owe a special thanks to my departmental chairman, Professor Cornell B. Blanding, and to the former dean of the College of Visual and Performing Arts at Syracuse University, Professor August L. Freundlich, for their firm support and for helping me to arrange my university responsibilities in such a way as to enable me to accept a leave of absence. I am also indebted to Dean Buron Blatt of the School of Education at Syracuse for his prompt and continuous encouragement through regular correspondence during the whole period I was in Washington.

I also want to recognize the assistance I received from Congressman Vander Jagt's staff, especially James M. Sparling, his administrative assistant, and Margaret L. Treanor, his personal secretary. The staff of the National Republican Congressional Committee was also supportive of my efforts and gave me complete freedom to go and come as I wished. I would like to thank and to mention by name my typist in Syracuse, New York, Diane C. Bonacci.

Crucial to the entire effort from beginning to end were the person to whom this volume is dedicated, my wife, Marjorie I. Ried, and the person about whom it is written, Guy Vander Jagt.

Paul E. Ried
September, 1983
Syracuse University

Introduction

T HE SUDDEN rebirth of the Republican party in the early 80s
has been a mystery for many—and not without good reasons.
Indeed, this was the party whose leader had to resign under fire in
1974. It was a political party which had not held control of the
Congress for over four years since 1932, two years in the late 40s and
two years in the early 50s. Furthermore, this was the party which the
mass media had successfully associated with stodgy conservatism,
white males over fifty, and individuals earning over fifty thousand
dollars a year. How could such a party sweep the country in the
election of 1980? How could such a party turn the Ninety-seventh
Congress into a working advertisement for the new federalism? Even
more amazing, how could President Reagan, in his seventies, so
benign and so pleased with old-fashioned American values, emerge
from semi-retirement and stand so effectively against the liberal
establishment?

Unquestionably, there are many causes; many events and
individuals can be counted in answering these questions. Some
nationally known political groups and figures spring quickly to
mind. Chief among them is the president of the United States, whose
effectiveness is embodied in his unofficial but fitting title, the
"Great Communicator." Others there are, too, who are not as well
known on the national level, but whose work deserves study and
analysis as having an indispensable part to play in the magnitude
and depth of the return of Americans to the Republican party. One
of these is the Honorable Guy Vander Jagt, nine-term congressman
from the Ninth District in Michigan and five-term chairman of the

National Republican Congressional Committee, the political arm of Republicans in the House of Representatives.

Although he continues to be given more and more coverage by the national media and is on the verge of achieving a national identity, his work is still generally unknown to the average American. Those, however, who are politically active on a regular basis, particularly those caught up in the turbulence of party politics in Washington, D.C., recognize his importance to the revival of Republican influence on the national scene. When most political pundits and many politicians were writing the Republican party off as a ghost of past glories, Vander Jagt was setting to work to give the GOP new life, a new beginning. He took what was almost a defunct political organization, the National Republican Congressional Committee, and turned it into what is recognized today as the "best political shop in the country." This he did in half a decade.

Even as the White House became Democratic in the mid-70s, Vander Jagt's voice was heard as a constant call to arms which rallied Republicans and eventually stirred grassroots America "to stay the course," after having accepted "the new beginning." His work as a campaigner throughout the 70s added a steady and reliable congressional strength to the Republican party which was made immediately available when Ronald Reagan ran for and won the presidency of the United States. After 1980, this congressional strength and the White House, working in concert, changed the overall direction of American government; together they prevented a Democratic landslide in 1982 and the Democratic domination of the legislative agenda of the Ninety-eighth Congress.

Vander Jagt's part in maintaining a Republican presence on the national scene through the years of trial and hardship was not a curious historical accident. The man who was designated the keynote speaker of the National Republican Convention in July of 1980 in Detroit had already devoted his entire professional life to a preparation for the role of political communicator. "As long as I can remember," even as a student in high school, he said, "I defined my career as wanting to share ideas, emotions, and convictions with the minds, hearts, and souls of other people." This commitment to communication was evidenced in each stage of his career's development: in his education, in his short but successful careers in the ministry and the law, in his professional experiences in radio

xiv

and TV, and in his tenures as a state senator and as a United States congressman.

What did he learn over these years? How did he put his knowledge and skill to use to strengthen the NRCC? How did he galvanize grassroots support for the Republican party? How did he use his power as a party spokesman? These questions serve as guides to the five critical essays in the first part of this work. Specifically, the first essay raises the question: What happened on the way to the polls in the 80s? This section delineates the congressman's role in GOP victories in the early 80s. The second essay details salient aspects of his campaign speeches for Republican candidates for office. Here his need for live response in speech communication is emphasized by the question: How much do responses really count? The third essay asks: Does a party spokesman have to speak on all occasions? The anwer is yes, and the occasions are spelled out in terms of the amount of his personal involvement with them. The fourth essay answers the question: How does he do it? How does he develop, design, and deliver ideas to others? The fifth essay, incorporating biographical materials, takes up the question: How did he learn?

The second part of this volume is made up of a collection of Vander Jagt's speeches selected as representative of three major periods in his thirty years of public speaking: speeches from the 80s, speeches from the 70s, and speeches from his early years.

Vander Jagt's object in these speeches, it has already been noted, is to reach, to touch, people, to close the distance between other human beings and himself. Manuscripts and written notes, he feels, represent a barrier to achieving this goal. Since his college days, in an attempt to avoid these obstructions, he has never written a speech ahead of time. Consequently, his early speeches recorded here stem almost totally from documents typed from notes which he wrote or dictated after he delivered the speeches.

In 1973, however, Margaret Treanor, his personal secretary, started to see to it that his speeches were taped and regularly transcribed word for word. Most of his speeches she transcribed herself. Her faithful service in this way accounts for the high verbal reliability of almost all of the speeches which are included in this volume. What is written here is what he said. The fact that the speeches are so free of verbalized pauses, start-stops, and glitches of various kinds is a result not of her editing of them, but of Vander Jagt's errorless delivery. Treanor typed what she heard on the tapes.

Of course, all that transpires during a Vander Jagt speech is beyond complete replication, especially in black and white. It remains for the reader to enter into the spirit of these occasions with imagination and with a willingness to suspend all initial tendencies to reject ideas cast in political contexts which, for most, are completely removed from common experience. In order to help the reader reconstruct these occasions, brief attempts have been made to set the scene so that what is inaccessible firsthand may be experienced vicariously. These introductions note the general characteristics of the audience and the occasion and, in some instances, the congressman's personal recollections of his development and design of ideas for delivery. Notes are also included where they are needed to explain otherwise unintelligible references to people and events in the live speech situation.

If Vander Jagt's speeches and the essays which precede them do nothing else for the reader, they should point up the enlarged scope of communication in modern politics. There are certainly excellent cases to be made on both sides of the political aisle in American government, but somehow it seems that Democrats have lost the ability to frame positive ideas for a national audience. FDR, John F. Kennedy, and Hubert Humphrey are voices of the past. Among Republicans, on the other hand, there seems to be a renewed effort to elevate their communicators. In fact, the resurgence of the Republican party seems to be built on the ability of its members to speak and to listen, to communicate.

Vander Jagt has set the pace in this regard for his fellow Republicans in the Congress. He is more and more surrounded by highly articulate and forceful communicators who are not afraid to be thought of as that—communicators. These colleagues, to say nothing of the overwhelming power of the president and his staff, along with Vander Jagt himself, all prove that the effective public speaker is neither a shadow of ancient Athens nor a relic of the republic that once was Rome. Today, as in the past, the orator who can bring the full power of a strong personality to bear on a good idea still represents a potent force in American politics. So successful have Republicans been in accomplishing this feat that they have virtually reversed the country's direction—all in less than a decade. What follows is a significant part of that story.

1

What Happened On the Way to the Polls in the 80s?

T HE NATIONAL elections of 1980 and 1982 were of great political significance. In November of 1980, the almost unbroken half-century of the Democratic party's control of the Senate was brought to an end, and the outline of a majority coalition of conservative Republicans, moderate Republicans, and conservative Southern Democrats took on a clearly recognizable form in the House of Representatives. For the first time since a few years after World War II, and before that, since 1932, conservatives had received the support of the American people to change the direction of government, to shift the emphasis in governance from federal to state and local levels and to increase incentives for greater investment and production in the private sectors of the economy. Americans, indeed, had voted Republican "for a change."

Although this situation was altered somewhat in the 1982 midterm election when twenty-six of the thirty-three House seats gained in 1980 were canceled out by Republican losses, the more general conservative populist movement around the country was not appreciably modified either in purpose or intensity. President Reagan and Republicans had lost a clearly defined majority coalition in the House, but they had held the Senate, and they had received the general, if tacit, support of Americans for the change in direction instituted two years earlier. When the freshman Republican class of House members in the Ninety-seventh Congress met for their last dinner together, those among them who had not

1

been returned to office in 1982 proudly proclaimed their place in a Congress of real change, in a reversal of five decades of Democratic control of the House of Representatives. They further acknowledged that, despite the reduction in the number of House Republicans, the chance of a continued long-range diminution of what had been progressively expanding federal activities still remained.[1] Some historians agreed that what they had done to effect this change in the first two years of the Reagan administration constituted a major historical watershed in American political developments:

> Prof. Richard P. Nathan of Princeton, comparing the first two years of the Reagan presidency to the early Roosevelt presidency, called this a "landmark" administration. "FDR's policies inaugurated nearly four decades of activism and growth in the operations of the national government," Professor Nathan said in a paper. "I believe the Reagan presidency has inaugurated a similarly long period of austerity in the domestic policies of the national government.[2]

It was felt generally that, even if the Reagan government should fail to survive future elections and Democrats should reestablish their control of the Senate, the conservative mood of the American public seemed to make a return to the liberal policies of the past most unlikely. A consciousness was growing among Americans that the years of affluence which followed World War II and the unquestioned military superiority of the United States were things of the past. Americans were tooling up to produce more with less, having realized the "party was over"[3] and having begun a "return to the basics."[4]

This movement, called traditionalism by some and fundamentalism by others, found practical political expression in support of prayer in the classroom, the pro-life or anti-abortion movement, the pro-family movement, increased military preparedness, and, of most immediate concern, the easing of taxes and regulations on both individuals and businesses. November of 1980, reflecting this rising force in society, it has been noted, had dealt a staggering blow to the liberals' control of the federal government.[5] Liberals all felt the shock wave as Republican conservatives swept into power, and highly visible and important Democratic names were dropped from the congressional rolls, names like John Brademus, Frank Church, Birch Bayh, and George McGovern. The fear of reducing American

2

politics to a one-party system was once again revived. This time, it was the Democrats' turn to worry; in 1974, it had been the Republicans'.

That Americans were willing to give these new directions in government sufficient time to take effect was established by their patience in the face of severe recession and high unemployment in November of 1982. These bleak economic conditions and the "iron law of politics" (that the party which wins the White House always loses seats in the following off-year election) could not blunt the force of the change in direction which was under way. In the '82 elections, it has been noted, Republicans avoided a Democratic landslide, saved their majority in the Senate, and maintained some slim possibility of eking out, on major issues at least, a predominant coalition in the House. This would not have been accomplished without the recognition and the reinforcement of a reservoir of good will in the country which was given to key Republican leaders in Washington. The give-and-take between the voters and the Republican leadership in October of 1982 tells this story clearly.

Before the election, keen political observers were expecting a Democratic landslide, but they were also intrigued that it had not already begun. Mr. Charles McDowell of the *Richmond-Times Dispatch* voiced his puzzlement on national educational television when he said that he was fascinated that a Democratic brushfire had not burst into flame despite the incendiary fact that the "number one topic of conversation" in the United States was the economic problem of unemployment.[6] A little later in the month of October, Albert Shanker, president of the American Federation of Teachers, in his weekly advertisement, was asking the same question:

> Election Day is only nine days away, but the American people haven't made up their minds. Polls show that they're more worried about unemployment than anything else, and, according to one survey (published in *Time* this week), 61% say they personally are economically worse off than when President Reagan took office. *Yet* only 33% in that poll blamed "Reagan and his policies," and 52% of those queried said they expected to vote for their current Congressman . . . although many couldn't recall that person's name or party affiliation.
>
> How can this be? With over 11 million people in our country unemployed—about 17 million if you count those who have given up looking for jobs and those who have only been able to find part-time work—the response should be, "Throw the rascals out!" That's what most people in their right minds would expect.[7]

In another commentary, published on the same day, Haynes Johnson pointed out that the "dogs" were not "barking":

> Consider the situation. Here is the country, demonstrably in its weakest economic condition in decades, with real suffering being experienced for the first time by millions of Americans entering the ranks of the new poor. Yet no massive political protest appears to be forming.
> Consider also that two years after his presidential election, Ronald Reagan has alienated just about every significant bloc of voters necessary to form an American political majority....
> These are ... generalizations, but they are based on conversations with people in all corners of the country.
> Yet, there are no signs of protest.[8]

In the issue of *Psychology Today* published just before the election, Daniel Yankelovich added a social scientist's observation to the effect that, although Americans were tightening their belts economically, they were not apparently going to blame or to attack Republicans in the upcoming election:

> For many months the President's critics have marveled at his seeming immunity from the public's ire on economic problems. The recession continues, the budget remains grievously unbalanced, unemployment is growing, most Americans cannot get affordable mortgages on new homes and are worried about money and the economy. Yet, against all the normal rules of political life, 67 percent of Americans seem to exempt the President from the kind of excoriating blame that finally ruined the Carter Presidency. To be sure, the President's confidence rating in the polls rises and falls with great regularity. But these day-to-day fluctuations should not be given undue weight. What counts more tellingly is the President's gift for exempting himself from blame for the country's most serious economic problems.[9]

The patience of some of these commentators seemed to be wearing thinner than the patience of the American public. While they conceded the dogs were not barking, they felt that the howls were imminent, and this feeling had been encouraged in the middle of October by signs that the electorate was moving ever more rapidly from support of the president and the Republicans to support of the Democrats. The mass media were framing their descriptions of economic problems in such a way as to emphasize an insecurity which Democrats were contending was a general and deep-seated fear among Americans. Whether this emphasis was accurate or not, some voters were apparently beginning to accept it as valid. Patrick Caddell, pollster for Democrats, had written for the October 17 issue of the *Washington Post*, "If they play their cards right, the Democrats could win 40 or more House seats and have a genuine, if still remote, chance of regaining Senate control."[10] He went on to list the problems that could build to a landslide:

> In short, with aggressive Democratic attacks, the Republicans could easily be overrun by a confluence of massive unemployment, anxiety over cuts in Social Security and other social programs, anger at tax breaks for the rich, near Depression conditions in the industrial and farm belts, hostility to Reagan from women, minorities, environmentalists and the poor everywhere, concern about nuclear arms and much else.[11]

Two weeks later, another article appeared in the *Washington Post* which suggested that the polls completed in the middle of October, at the time the Caddell article was printed, did indeed reveal an imminent voter swing to Democrats:

> A week ago, Republicans were fearful that a trend was developing that might not only push their House losses above 30 seats but also yield the Democrats the five-seat gain that would end GOP control of the Senate.
> Between Oct. 8, when the announcement came that unemployment had reached a post-Depression high of 10.1 percent, and Oct. 18, when pollsters were able to measure public reaction to the president's Oct. 13 speech on the economy, Republican candidates sagged and Democrats surged.
> Polls in all but a couple of the 13 Republican-held Senate seats dipped into the danger range for the incumbents.[12]

And, indeed, a *Washington Post*-ABC News poll had been completed and publicized as front-page news in the October 14 edition of the *Post:*

> By almost 2 to 1, voters feel there is a greater danger in Republicans going too far in helping the rich and cutting needed government services than in Democrats going too far in keeping costly, wasteful and out-of-date services. This perception of the Democrats as the lesser of two evils, along with the strong majority belief that President Reagan's programs are not working, continues to give the Democrats a 60 to 40 pecent lead among likely voters in the congressional elections less than three weeks away.[13]

5

Polls conducted by the National Republican Congressional Committee between October 16 and October 20 gave further evidence that the unemployment figures, published on the 8th, were trying the voters' patience and were spelling potential disaster for Republicans. The generic vote was 61 percent to 39 percent in favor of Democrats. President Reagan's job approval was at a new low of 48 percent approval and 47 percent disapproval, and the slogan "Stay the Course" was only effecting modest gains.[14] The predictions, then, of academicians such as Edward Tufte of Yale University that there would be heavy Republican losses of forty or more House seats were being borne out in polls conducted all across the political board.[15]

It was at this point in mid-October that Congressman Guy Vander Jagt, chairman of the National Republican Congressional Committee, met with the leadership of the committee. After hard discussion, they decided to give additional financial support to incumbents, to soften the Republican message for network TV advertising, and, of greatest importance, to give full financial backing a media blitz over the last two weeks before the election, including the president's five-minute spots on the last weekend of the campaign. The president was also encouraged to take a more "active role as the November date approached."[16]

President Reagan's nationally televised speech explaining the economic problems facing Americans was aired in prime time on October 13.[17] The day following, Vander Jagt appeared on the *MacNeil-Lehrer Report* to support Republican policies as the "hope of the future" for Americans. In a technical sense, these two appearances on national television marked the eve of the two-week media campaign blitz designed to forestall the impending landslide. From that point on, the president and the congressman appeared prominently in the mass media. Of course, the president was given regular daily coverage in all the media. Vander Jagt was featured in *Newsweek*[18] on October 25 and NBC's *Meet the Press*[19] on October 31. The rest of his time, during these last two weeks before the election, Vander Jagt spent campaigning in Michigan. October the 30th found him debating his Democratic opponent in the Muskegon Community College Overbrook Theatre,[20] but he always kept in close touch with the NRCC offices in Washington. He argued strongly by phone, as he had earlier in person,[21] that large sums of money be used to ensure the TV saturation of President Reagan's five-minute spot advertisement on the last few days before the election. His one regret, he said later, was the fact that he had not argued more strongly that thirty minutes of prime TV time be bought for use on the eve of the election either by the president or by himself.[22]

Although there is no absolute method of demonstrating that this media blitz over the last two weeks of the campaign saved the Republicans from a Democratic landslide and the loss of sixty or more House seats, it probably did. As a follow-up to the October 16 to 20 polls, another NRCC poll was taken on October 31. According to Linda DiVall, survey research director of the NRCC, this was done to "catch last-minute vote shifting in the electorate and to determine the causes of that shift."[23] The changes were as follows: the generic vote had shifted from 61 percent Democratic and 39 percent Republican to 55 percent Democratic and 45 percent Republican; President Reagan's job approval moved from 48 percent approval and 47 percent disapproval to 54 percent approval and 40 percent disapproval; and acceptance/rejection of the Republican slogan, "Stay the Course," in GOP vote intention changed from 50 percent-45 percent to 54 percent-40 percent.

This information reveals a shift clearly in the Republican direction, and it was probably due to the speaking and writing of Republican leaders in the mass media. On the basis of the results of his daily tracking polls, Richard Wirthlin said: "If the election had been held some ten days before it was, my guess is that we would have lost more seats in the House and we could have lost in the Senate."[24] He went on to add: "It is my strong belief that if he [President Reagan] had not taken the very active, visible role that he did in the last 12 to 14 days of the campaign, Republican losses could have been considerably higher."[25]

The efforts of the president, members of the White House staff, and Congressman Vander Jagt with his NRCC support, from October 14 on, were certainly geared to stopping the Democratic drift from breaking loose completely as an avalanche to overwhelm Republicans. In an interview with Congressman Vander Jagt after the election,[26] it was apparent that he had recognized from the publishing of the *Washington Post*-ABC News poll on October 14 that there was a distinct possibility of a late-breaking Democratic landslide, even though he maintained an optimistic confidence in his public statements to the contrary up until the election itself. When questioned about the apparent contradiction between his last-minute public statements and his growing private fears, he reconciled the difference by insisting that his avowed partisanship and his importance to party morale were of greater significance than his accuracy as a predictor of political events. True to the position of the advocate, he was more concerned with self-fulfilling prophecy and what should be than he was with scientific probability and what in fact would be. Until the unemployment figures moved into double digits in early October, however, he was completely convinced Republicans would break history by adding to their number in the House.

Seen in this perspective, the loss of twenty-six House seats in the midterm election of '82 became an achievement and not a disaster for Republicans;[27] it represented a less-than-average loss of seats in an off-year election. Since 1906, nonpresidential election years show for the party in the White House an average loss of thirty-six seats; since 1946, thirty-one.[28] Add to that the fact that the economy had not completely bottomed out of one of its most difficult recessions, and it becomes abundantly clear that Republicans had avoided by a hair the obliteration of a devastating Democratic victory.

It was John Chancellor of NBC, on the morning of November 3, after the election returns were almost completely in, who said in effect that the political landslide which threatened Republicans never materialized. This observation introduced a well-balanced view of the situation. While partisan reactions and interpretations of the vote varied widely, no mandate in either direction was given. Certainly, no objective observer could conclude that the election results meant stay the course without deviation. On the other hand, no one could declare that a mandate had been given to return to the past. Staying the course and reversing the course both lost to the idea that the course should be adjusted whenever necessary.

The point to this view of the '82 election is simply this: the two-way communication which had developed between Republican leaders and the electorate, explains what happened at the polls in the early 80s. A broadly based but clearcut message from Americans to their leaders in 1980 had brought Ronald Reagan out of semi-retirement in California where he had been cutting radio tapes, and it had also revived the political arms of Republicans in both the House and the Senate. Although not so clear, this message remained effective through 1982.

Early on, in 1974, Congressman Vander Jagt had been elevated to the position of chairman of the National Republican Congressional Committee, an office that provided him with a forum through which the impact of his speeches was greatly enlarged. This added substantially to the speed of the conservative movement as it spread among Americans. When in 1980 and, again, in 1982, Vander Jagt and Reagan were accorded the privilege of speaking from a national platform, the political potential of conservative America became a reality. President Reagan and his supporters, later his White House staff, and chairman Vander Jagt with the staff of the NRCC, turned the full power of the speaker's platform, network television, and the press to the task of giving the conservatives their first real voice in national politics since 1932. The message which had started in grassroots America had gone full circle.

It was by ascending to the chairmanship of the NRCC that Congressman Vander Jagt achieved the status of a national Republican spokesman. He proceeded to associate himself so closely with the committee that it gradually became an organizational extension of his own personality. Although he disclaimed such an influence,[29] the development of his own image as a partisan campaign orator, the sword of the Republican party, paralleled point by point the emergence of the NRCC as a crack political force on the national scene. It could be added, quoting Leon Shull, director of Americans for Democratic Action, that the liberal Democratic movement, so much a part of the United States since Franklin D. Roosevelt became president in 1932, began its retreat in 1974.[30] This was the year that Vander Jagt assumed the chairmanship of the committee.

The National Republican Congressional Committee is the political arm of Republicans in the House of Representatives. Its offices are located in the Dwight D. Eisenhower National Republican Center, 320 First Street, S.E., diagonally across from the Cannon Building, two blocks east of the Rayburn Building, and just an easy ten-minute walk from the Capitol itself. Its overall program includes all of those specific, pragmatic functions associated with

9

furthering the political aims of Republican members of the House. It raises money; it manages campaigns of challengers as well as incumbents (wherever it is necessary or wherever it would help); it runs a Republican Information Network, making Washington happenings immediately and regularly available to GOP centers all over the country; it publishes regular campaign newsletters; it arranges for the writing and distribution of press releases; it conducts national surveys or polls to assess voter trends; it produces television and radio campaign advertisements and radio actualities; and it conducts candidate seminars and workshops. It also schedules and provides advance preparation in Washington and on tour for the campaign speeches of its chairman.

Although administratively autonomous, the NRCC cooperates regularly with the Republican National Committee (RNC) and the National Republican Senatorial Committee (NRSC). The RNC is associated most closely with the executive branch of government and is housed with the NRCC in the Eisenhower Center. The NRSC is the NRCC's sister committee on the Senate side of the Capitol. These three political organizations often share information and funds as they engage in combined efforts to achieve mutually beneficial goals.

The work of the NRCC is supervised by an executive committee which is composed of one congressman from every state which has Republican representation in the House. A representative group from the executive committee oversees the committee by meeting on a regular basis to review the work it has accomplished and to devise general policy. The day-to-day responsibilities of management, however, are attended to by full-time staff members in the Executive and Legal Division of the NRCC.[31] They regulate operations in four other divisions: Finance and Administration, Campaign, Public Affairs, and Communications.

Although this committee has been in existence since the year following the Civil War, it has only been within the last decade of technological advances that the full impact of its potential has been felt. Its ability to reach out across the country and to conduct speedy financial and informational transactions has been increased exponentially due to the very recent advances in communication, computers, and word processors. Direct mailing techniques have been advanced to a science.

As a chairman of the NRCC, Congressman Vander Jagt has been the spearhead of these developments.

He has presided over an increase in contributions to the NRCC from 25,000 donors giving a total of $900,000 in 1974 to 1.7 million donors giving a total of $34 million in 1981. The committee used the figure of $37.5 million as a working budget in 1982. From January 1, 1981, to mid-November, 1982, close to $60 million had been raised by the NRCC.[32] Vander Jagt also argued for and ultimately succeeded in obtaining a fundraising letter from President Ford which turned out to be the "most successful fundraising letter ever written, dollar for dollar."[33] In less than a year after the letter was first mailed on October 20, 1975, the $2.25 million it cost brought a return of $13 million. One other "first" achieved on April 7, 1981, was the biggest single money-raising event in the history of American politics. The Republican Senate-House Dinner at the Washington Hilton Hotel, sponsored by the NRCC and the NRSC jointly, hosted 3,000 people who gave $3.2 million. Many political events, fundraising letters, and television advertising campaigns have been pacesetters, bringing in greater amounts of money and accounting for greater numbers of party supporters than ever before.

These astounding financial achievements were in part a result of Vander Jagt's early and cooperative planning in June and July of 1975 with the NRCC's brand new executive director and brand new director of finance and administration, Steven F. Stockmeyer and Wyatt A. Stewart III, respectively. It must be remembered that they were planning together at a difficult time for Republicans. They were facing a 1975 budget which they could not meet, and they had no hope of help from a nearly broke Republican National Committee. The National Republican Senatorial Committee had a staff of three who were struggling barely to survive. The closing of the Eisenhower Center was a very real possibility.

They proceeded, however, to generate the Ford fundraising letter and to bring together as competent a group of people as existed in any political organization in the country. Vander Jagt hired strictly on merit, not political connections, and he cultivated employee initiative with personal encouragement and praise.[34] His standard mode of organizational communication was the evocation of the strengths of the persons whom he hired, questioning, explaining, and listening. This, along with his dogged and plucky

11

advocacy in pursuing the objectives of the NRCC with others in Washington, accounts for the success of the committee and, indirectly, the heights achieved by the Republican party in the early eighties. No other person associated with the committee had the confidence, political connections, and the communicative skills necessary to achieve what Vander Jagt achieved. Stockmeyer believed that the work of Vander Jagt through the NRCC was a key factor in the gradual rebirth of Republican influence over the 70s.[35]

The general methods of operation and fundraising which were so successful for the NRCC were shared with Bill Brock, chairman of the Republican National Committee, when Stewart consulted with the RNC staff on administrative and financial matters. With this early help, Brock turned the RNC into another Republican political force which added greatly to the common effort to bring more Republicans to Washington.

The National Republican Senatorial Committee also owes a debt of thanks to these early efforts of Vander Jagt and the NRCC. After having been introduced as having "put together...one of the most effective campaign organizations this city [Washington, D.C.] has ever seen," the chairman of the NRSC, Senator Robert Packwood, said:

> After all of the accolades that Ed [Meese] has given you about our committee, the Senatorial Campaign Committee, we would not be where we are today but for Guy. Our committee six years ago for all practical purposes did not exist. In the 1976 elections, we only had enough money to give $400,000, total, to all of our candidates. And in 1977, having seen what the Congressional Campaign Committee did, we wanted to emulate them in raising money by direct mail, and I borrowed, I was chairman of the committee then, I borrowed $75,000 from Guy's committee.[36]

This $75,000 was used as seed money for operations which grew and accounted for the increased strength of the NRSC in its successful political support of Republicans in the Senate. In 1982, Richard Richards, chairman of the RNC, was able to say that the RNC raised more money with the NRCC and the NRSC than ever before and that cooperation among them was at an all-time high.[37]

It is generally recognized by political analysts in Washington that, as of 1982, the NRCC remained the "best political shop in the business."[38] Certainly, increased financial support had been converted into stronger Republican representation in Congress. After the catastrophic loss of almost fifty seats in '74, Republicans broke about even in '76, gained eleven in '78, and added a whopping total of thirty-three in '80. The results of the 1982 elections, it has been pointed out, were indecisive. But, given the economic circumstances surrounding that election, Republican losses of twenty-six in all were relatively modest.

It was Tony Coelho, chairman of the Democratic Congressional Campaign Committee, who said the money and know-how of the NRCC saved for Republicans some ten to twelve seats in 1982.[39] The NRCC was so superior to its counterpart in the Democratic party that Coelho confessed that he was trying to emulate "with no reservations" what the NRCC had done.[40] He went on to congratulate chairman Vander Jagt:

> Before I answer the question, I just want to take this opportunity to thank Guy for his kind remarks. I do have great admiration for Guy and the job that he has done. I think he's done an absolutely fantastic job for the Republican Committee and has done something that I'm really interested in doing, in making the party a factor again in politics. It is so critical that we do that. That's my goal for House Democrats, and, if I can just do half the job that he has done, in half the time, we'll get there, and we'll do it quick! I intend to do it quick! I intend to do it a lot faster than that, Guy! But, he has been a great example to follow.[41]

The success of the NRCC and its staff was given special recognition by the press as "the most sophisticated campaign operation in America,"[42] as part of a "disciplined" effort run with "plain professional smarts,"[43] and as "far ahead of the Democrats in mastering the new style and technology of politics."[44]

This last note points up the NRCC's advances in developing the art of televised political advertisements. These ads were being produced at cost in its own studios in the Eisenhower Center as early as 1978. The first attempts made by the NRCC were done with film, but production shifted to three-quarter-inch videotape in 1980 and one-inch in 1982. The technical quality of the ads improved dramatically over these years.

Maintaining its early lead, the NRCC has remained the largest producer of political advertisements in the world. Prior to the 1980

13

elections, for example, the committee poured $3.5 million into an unprecedented national advertising campaign and approximately another $1 million into three hundred TV and five hundred radio commercials. To point up the comparison between the progress of Republicans and of Democrats on this matter, it wasn't until 1982 that Mr. and Mrs. Averell Harriman loaned some $400,000 to the Democratic Congressional Campaign Committee "to buy a building on Capitol Hill, to be used as a radio and television studio."[45]

Most of the NRCC advertisements featured individual candidates, and their distribution was controlled by the staffs of the congressmen and challengers for whom they were made. Some ads, however, were produced for national distribution to support Republicans generally. The ones in 1980 were built around the theme, "Vote Republican for a Change," and they were extremely effective. Approximately 37 percent of the voters who voted Republican, it was found in Gallup exit polls, did so "for a change."[46]

Two ads won awards for their impact on the political scene. One made use of an actor who looked very much like the Democratic majority leader of the House, Congressman Thomas P. (Tip) O'Neill, Jr., and it portrayed him driving a car which ran out of gas, much to his surprise and chagrin. It clearly alluded to the lack of forethought and planning by Democrats over the many years in which they controlled the Congress. It was nominated for a Cleo Award, and did, in fact, win the 1981 Francis W. Hatch Award for Political Commercials made by the Advertising Club of Greater Boston. Another ad starred James A. Willders, Jr., known as "Bruzzy," who attacked the Democratic party for its mismanagement of the economy.[47] It won the 1981 Andy Award of Excellence.

The year 1982 saw the production of another three hundred TV political ads supporting the general campaign theme, "Stay the course," first phrased by Bailey, Deardourff and Associates. It was picked up and repeated regularly by President Reagan in his campaign swings across the country for House and Senate candidates. While effective in conveying the idea clearly, it was less successful than the 1980 theme in turning out the Republican vote.

In addition to ads, radio actualities were forwarded to radio stations all over the country every day. These are brief statements by a congressman about current legislation which are taped by phone and which are transmitted immediately to stations in the appropriate congressional district.

The NRCC has also developed one of the most sophisticated candidate training programs ever contemplated in politics. Its objectives have been accomplished through regular seminars and workshops which have been offered both in Washington, D.C., and in districts around the country. Since 1976, videotaping of candidates' speeches has been used more and more to improve their presentational skills, typical of the more recent emphasis on the overall personal resources of the candidate in campaigning. From July of '81 to September of '82, twelve training workshops were conducted for 285 candidates, 144 of whom eventually appeared on general election ballots. Most of the people in these workshops who did not run for office became more involved in the political process, nonetheless, by volunteering to work in local campaign offices.[48]

As chairman of the NRCC, Congressman Vander Jagt was at the forefront of all of these developments. He led in bringing the NRCC from a relatively small and innocuous sounding board for Republican ideology to a first-rate organization at the cutting edge of political change. To suggest, however, that this achievement was his major contribution to the broader movement toward a more conservative America would be to overlook his even more important role as a party spokesman, a speaker who could make use of the modern, high-tech mass media as well as direct, skin-to-skin modes of public speaking to live audiences on their home grounds all around the country. In both of these efforts, the NRCC accorded him full financial and technical support through its Public Affairs and Campaign Divisions, and the persuasive campaigns which resulted round out this tale of what really happened on the way to the polls in the early eighties. The responses to Vander Jagt's speaking and his own reactions in turn serve as the basis for the next essay.

2

How Much Do Responses Really Count?

FROM DECEMBER 1974 to December 1980, Congressman Guy Vander Jagt's influence among Republicans grew to such an extent that he decided to contest the House leadership of his party with the minority whip, Robert Michel of Illinois. Although Michel ultimately won the election and became minority leader, Vander Jagt made a remarkably close race of it. The vote was 103 to 87. This very creditable show of power was in large part the result of his having traveled almost 800,000 miles during his six years as chairman of the NRCC to give more than a thousand speeches on behalf of Republican candidates in all fifty states of the Union. In the last two months of the 1980 campaign, he traveled almost continuously to give campaign speeches for over sixty of his fellow congressional candidates.[1] Vander Jagt, unchallenged in his own home district in Michigan, had complete freedom to speak for whomever he wished, whenever he wished.

All of these experiences, both as a campaign speaker and as a partisan politician, moved the press to portray him in his bid for minority leader in the House as the "orator,"[2] "Mr. Outside,"[3] the "Sword,"[4] and "Mr. Speaker."[5] Michel was characterized respectively as the "tactician," "Mr. Inside," the "Oilcan," and "Mr. Nice Guy."

The very fact that Vander Jagt had become known as the chief party spokesman for congressional candidates moved his opposition to sharp measures. The House agenda which had included ten-minute speeches from both candidates on the floor to their fellow Republicans was altered to exclude them, and the campaign speech Vander Jagt had been carefully planning for weeks was never given. Neglecting a defense of his right to speak, Vander Jagt was instead busily at work on his campaign speech. In this, he made his opponent's case by giving Michel the chance to prove that the parliamentary tactician on the House floor could effectively silence the orator.

Indeed, Vander Jagt's reputation as a speaker seemed a liability when Republican House members finally decided in favor of Michel:

> Rep-elect Duncan Hunter of California, one of the 52 freshmen Vander Jagt helped to victory through his NRCC work, interrupted a Vander Jagt discussion with reporters after the vote to tell it his own way.
> "We still regard him as a shining star of the Republican party," said Hunter, who admitted he voted for Michel. "Perhaps he did too good a job" in his campaign work, Hunter said. "He was converting people to Republicans every time he talked. We need him out on the stump."[6]

This thought was echoed by others, one of whom was both a fellow Republican and a Michigander, Carl D. Pursell of Plymouth:

> Pursell said House Republicans need a leader who is a "legislative professional" such as Michel, a technician who can pull together coalitions to help pass GOP programs in the Democrat-dominated House.
> Vander Jagt, on the other hand, "can be a plus externally" by continuing as chairman of the National Republican Congressional Committee, Pursell said. That job gives wide visibility to Vander Jagt's highly lauded speech-making prowess.[7]

His very special talents as a campaign speaker had been recognized early by his colleagues in Washington and were clearly responsible for his having been chosen to give the keynote speech at the Republican National Convention in 1980:

> The decision to give the coveted assignment to Vander Jagt was made during a telephone conversation this week between Reagan and GOP national chairman Bill Brock.
> According to one account, Brock asked Reagan whom he wanted for keynoter, and Reagan replied "the best speaker in the United States." When Brock mentioned Vander Jagt's name, Reagan readily agreed.[8]

17

Brock's suggestion was undoubtedly given impetus by Don Shea's memorandum to him praising Vander Jagt's speech at the National Prayer Breakfast in early February:

> I told Jim Frierson of my reactions to Guy Vander Jagt's message or address at last week's National Prayer Breakfast. Jim thought it would be appropriate if I communicated my unsolicited thoughts to you.
>
> *Very* seldom have I been as deeply impressed by a speech both in content and delivery. Guy treated a highly personal subject—one's own relation to Christ—in a way that was strikingly meaningful without being in any way unctuous. He spoke wholly without notes, had amazing rapport and response with a diversified audience, with truly, in my experience, unmatched voice and eloquence. Jimmy Carter [who was in attendance and spoke after Vander Jagt] began his remarks by saying, graciously and accurately, that he could scarcely touch Guy's message or delivery. Vander Jagt received a really moving standing ovation of very notable duration.[9]

The many responses he received to his National Prayer Breakfast speech, from both Democrats and Republicans, were all highly laudatory. As in Shea's case, for a large number of people, the speech was a singular experience. Congressman James Hanley, as yet another example, a Democrat from upstate New York, praised the speech as "the best prayer breakfast sermon" he had ever heard.[10]

This same kind of enthusiastic response was also given to his keynote speech. First, they came as forty-plus rounds of applause immediately and live from Republican delegates on the floor of the Joe Louis Arena in Detroit. Their reactions were echoed in written form for weeks through letters which poured in from individual citizens representing all parts of the country. Some five hundred copies of this speech were requested by private citizens and were sent to them from his congressional office, while the national offices of the Republican party answered many other inquiries.[11] The keynote was also printed in *Congress Today*,[12] a publication of the NRCC.

As late as February 24, 1982, a year and a half after the keynote had been delivered, a retired college professor wrote:

> I must take this occasion to express my deepest appreciation for the immense pleasure I experienced while listening to your keynote address delivered at the last Republican convention. Having studied the oratorical skills in a French school when I was young, I truly appreciated listening to you who, evidently, have reached the pinnacle

18

of this forgotten art. You not only effected an unusual rapprochement between politics and music, which is a tour de force, in itself, but you brought me an unforgettable moment of rare intellectual pleasure that only the great artists can give us. The entire delivery was superb. It was "magnifique." In fact, at the end of such rare eloquence, I had to resist the urge to stand up and applaud while shouting: Bravo! Encore! Encore! But my sedate entourage, though equally appreciative, would perhaps have frowned upon my exuberance....So I sat there, motionless, savoring it, while the tonality of your address was still lingering in my ears, and my mind vividly recalling my own feeble efforts to acquire those oratorical skills when I was young, long, long ago. It was an unforgettable experience. Sometimes I believe we are slowly forgetting the enchanting delights that only the pleasures of the mind can bring us. And so, thank you, and I hope to hear more of you in the future.[13]

The *Chicago Tribune*[14] and a number of Michigan newspapers[15] gave space to the keynote; but, with only one exception, eastern first-line papers did not give it coverage.[16] Instead, they seemed to dismiss the speech as being of little importance beside the Ford-Bush race for the vice-presidential nomination. And, indeed, if a keynote address is a convention-opening speech which sets the tone for all that follows in a meeting of party members, Vander Jagt's speech was not, in fact, the keynote address. As it turned out, the real keynote address was given by former President Ford who asked to be first on the program to address the convention. Through a series of postponements, Vander Jagt's speech gradually slipped to the third day of the convention and became an introduction to Ronald Reagan's announcement of George Bush as his running mate on the Republican ticket.

Although the excellence of the keynote seemed to be taken for granted by the party's leadership, it remained an event secondary in importance to political forces within the GOP which were vying for control of the selection of the vice-presidential nominee. The mass media, sensing this shift in emphasis, found their way into the middle of these nomination maneuvers and moved away from covering or analyzing the effects of Vander Jagt's presentation. The one exception was NBC's John Chancellor, who interviewed the keynoter after the speech to inquire into his methods of speech preparation and his general educational background.

It needs to be said, too, that Vander Jagt himself was a finalist for the vice-presidential nomination. Theodore H. White pointed out correctly that in the last few hours before Reagan's choice was finally announced, Vander Jagt and Congressman Jack Kemp were both viewed by the press and the FBI as having hot telephone numbers.[17] But, as his speech was overlooked by the media in favor of the race between Ford and Bush, so his candidacy for vice president was lost in that very same squeeze.

There seemed to be wide differences between the reactions of the mass media and grassroots America to Vander Jagt's speech. Perhaps the best assessment of this difference came in the following eyewitness account:

> There are not many men alive who could hold an audience as raucous as a national political convention by recitations from the Midnight Ride of Paul Revere or Ralph Waldo Emerson's: "When duty whispers low 'Thou must,' the youth replies 'I can.'"
>
> But the Rev. and Hon. Guy Vander Jagt did, as the keynote speaker of the 1980 Republican National Convention.... For he recalled that Ronald Reagan had to win out over the establishment: the Washington establishment, as well as the media establishment—which he was able to do, said Vander Jagt, "because he has the love of the people."
>
> (Not all of the people, to be sure. For at the edge of the Joe Louis Arena, in the best seats in the press gallery, sat Mr. Benjamin C. Bradlee and several of his subordinates of the *Washington Post*. Mr. Bradlee apparently thought Vander Jagt was funny in his poetic and patriotic references—during which Bradlee laughed—as did All the Editor's Men. But there was no such laughter from the delegates section—where the audience is comprised of people who are elected by the public, rather than hired at the pleasure of Big Businessmen like Mr. Bradlee.)...
>
> Congressman Vander Jagt may not have impressed some of the media aristocracy very much, but he left a great many delegates to the Republican National Convention with an indelible impression, as well as thoughts about his future.[18]

This keen observation on the responses to Vander Jagt's keynote points up the special appeal he has for the popular audience. It might also be observed that he responds in kind; he needs and aggressively seeks the fresh reactions found in the immediacy of grassroots contact. He wants to touch human beings where they live. This special appeal brings him back time and time again to live speech situations, to campaign communication where speaker and listener both have immediate access to each other. As will be explained later, the very rare chemistry which develops between himself and living, breathing audiences makes the Vander Jagt campaign speech for many a one-of-a-kind experience.[19]

He realized the benefits of his years of live campaigning in a symbolic Reagan-Bush rally with Republican congressmen on the steps of the United States Capitol in September of 1980. It was "a dream come true," he was reported as saying, and it was a milestone on the road to a GOP unity of the executive and legislative branches of government:

> Vander Jagt, chairman of the Republican National Congressional Committee... was one of seven speakers at the rally, and the only one to be interrupted several times by applause from the audience.
> Introduced as "the man who has spent more time in airplanes than any Republican congressional candidate, Vander Jagt said of the rally, "this is an unprecedented move—the opportunity to hear from the government in waiting. It is the opportunity to say we are proud of our presidential nominee and proud to be running with him. United we can make America work. We can show dreams can and do come true."[20]

After the victorious '80 elections, the Ripon Society bestowed its venerable leadership award on Vander Jagt, along with the former Republican National Committee chairman, Bill Brock, and Senator John Heinz of Pennsylvania, chairman of the National Senatorial Republican Committee, for having engineered the Reagan-Republican landslide:

> Vander Jagt, Brock—now U.S. trade representative—and Heinz are credited with having masterminded the national strategy that brought their party, as Vander Jagt said last night, "from the courthouse to the White House," and to a majority in the Senate. The architects of success walked away from the podium cradling shiny silver bowls filled with jelly beans.
> "I accept this award on behalf of the American people," said Vander Jagt grandly from the podium, "who for the first time since 1952, voted Republican '...For a change.' "[21]

Testimonials to the congressman's efforts as a campaign speaker appeared regularly in the letters he received, in the introductions of him as a speaker on the banquet circuit, and in his meetings with colleagues in Washington. A few examples taken from the many give the typical flavor of these remarks and, of course, attest to his very special role in recent Republican good fortune. It was a former president who wrote:

> You should be very proud of the superb job you did as the keynote speaker at our Republican Convention in Detroit. I was tremendously impressed as millions were by your presentation. Quite honestly, I am envious of your platform excellence but more importantly I am so happy to see that you are receiving...deserved recognition....I also know your recognition and prestige will grow and expand in the days ahead because of your outstanding performance in Detroit. Your opportunities in the future are unlimited, so keep moving forward.[22]

The congressman from the Eighth District of Virginia, in an executive meeting of the NRCC, said, "If we do get a Republican majority [in November of 1982] it will be due to our chairman's work."[23] The only Republican freshman to have unseated a Democratic incumbent in the 1982 House elections said, Guy Vander Jagt is the "best speaker in the country," and he said this before the whole membership of the Republican Congressional Leadership Council without qualification of any kind.[24] The respect given to his political speaking is not limited to Washington, D.C. A state senator from Virginia said, "Although little known to the general public, Guy Vander Jagt is one of the key architects of the Republican comeback at the grassroots level."[25]

These, of course, are responses from Republicans. He has also generated response from the Democratic side of the divide:

> U.S. News & World Report reported in its Washington Whispers this week: "House Democratic leaders will borrow a leaf from their Republican rivals next year and target a handful of senior GOP lawmakers for defeat at the polls. Prime early candidates for election blitzes: Minority Leader Robert Michel of Illinois, GOP Whip Trent Lott of Mississippi and Michigan's Guy Vander Jagt, House Republican campaign chairman."[26]

And, indeed, Mr. Charles Manatt, Democratic National Committee chairman, was urging Michigan Democrats working in Washington to realize that " 'you have a No. 1 responsibility of getting this man [Vander Jagt] fully busy saving his own seat,' instead of campaigning around the country for other Republican candidates."[27]

His effective campaign speaking for others had not gone unnoticed for he was "credited with whittling the Democratic majority in the U.S. House of Representatives by eleven in 1978, and by another thirty-three"[28] in 1980. However, his work for others had had no apparent detrimental effect on his ability to win votes for himself. The only time his own winning percentage in the Ninth District of Michigan fell significantly below two-thirds of the popular vote was in the 1974 election, just after the Watergate incident and Ford's subsequent pardoning of Nixon. Then, he received 56.6 percent of the popular vote.[29]

When he was first elected to Congress in 1966, there were twelve Republicans and seven Democrats in the Michigan delegation to the House of Representatives in Washington. In 1974, these numbers were exactly reversed; in 1980, they had remained unchanged, twelve to seven in favor of Democrats. Vander Jagt's popularity, however, steadily increased over these years to the election in 1980 when he had no Democratic opponent, the "first Republican in fifty years to run for Congress in Michigan without major party opposition."[30]

Certainly, his growing national prominence accounted for a part of this unusual circumstance, but he was forced to campaign hard again in 1982 when his opponent used his success as chairman of the NRCC as an argument against him. Jerry Warner, prosecuting attorney of Muskegon, repeated throughout the campaign the argument that Vander Jagt had built too big a name for himself in Washington as a GOP leader to have given enough time to representing the Ninth District of Michigan. Included here is a word-for-word transcription of Vander Jagt's perfect response to this most imperfect attack:

> And as to national leadership, well, I work about thirty hours a week on District business, about thirty hours a week on legislative matters, and about thirty hours a week on national leadership. I know very well that that adds up to ninety hours, and that's how many hours I work a week. And the hours on national leadership do not come from the hours that I give to the District. They come from my wife, Carol, and my daughter, Ginny, and my own free time. And I am glad to do it because those thirty hours a week of national leadership make ten times more effective the sixty hours a week I give to my congressional district fifty-two weeks a year.
>
> I guess I owe you a thank you, Jerry. My own polls showed me that when this campaign began only 16 percent of the people had any idea

that I had any national leadership position, but upon hearing it, 72 percent have the common sense to say that it is wonderful for them and for their communities because they know that that makes it possible for me to serve them better.[31]

It does to some degree seem paradoxical that Vander Jagt has accomplished so much as a campaigner for his party and yet has not established for himself a national image. He has teetered from time to time on the brink of acquiring a national identity with the American people, but he has not achieved the clearcut and instantaneous recognition which the average citizen accords a political headliner. Although it has been known for years in Washington, D.C., that he has had great influence, it is only recently that he has been recognized with some regularity in the public print and on network TV question-and-answer shows. This notice, however, has been associated almost entirely with his work in the National Republican Congressional Committee, and the media usually represent him as a political partisan who carries out the policies of others. A communicator, not a thought leader who can establish policy himself, he speaks for others, they imply. This image seems by definition to undercut his potential as a superstar.

There are other factors which have worked against his emergence as a national political figure. His penchant for person-to-person contact in grassroots stumping leads to local spheres of influence but lacks the broad arena of visibility associated with tube-oriented communication. His one real opportunity to test himself over a three-network hookup with a broadly based national audience, his keynote presentation, it has been noted, was overshadowed by more well-known personalities who were battling each other within the Republican party.

The media, as ever, were held spellbound by this high-level, hard-hitting fratricide. The fall of an authority figure, especially when precipitated or executed by another authority figure in the same ideological family, is sure to attract media coverage. But just as journalists are transfixed by civil war, they are absolutely without interest, unfazed, when a family remains unified, when a Republican congressman, for example, shows loyalty to a Republican president. Vander Jagt has consistently supported President Reagan, and, what is more, he is loath to criticize religious

24

institutions, the military, and his congressional Republican colleagues, thereby virtually eliminating for himself all of these surefire ways of becoming newsworthy in the eyes of journalists.

The slightest criticism of the president, even as a joke, calls forth national press. In August of 1981, in a journalist's session in his congressional office, it was observed that the Republican party equaled the Democratic party in popularity polls for the first time in years, but that the support of older women had fallen off as a result of their fear that President Reagan would march the United States straight into a world conflict. Vander Jagt quipped that they were really deserting the Republican party because they could remember Reagan's old movies. This immediately became national news.[32] The hundreds of times Vander Jagt has expressed his admiration of and support for the president in speeches around the country are rarely noted even by local papers, never in national ones.

The only quotation of Vander Jagt by Steven V. Roberts in his article on the internal party conflicts among Republicans was one in which the congressman was made to seem critical of the president:

> "When the Republicans got in," said Representative Guy Vander Jagt of Michigan, chairman of the National Republican Congressional Committee, "the image of the Republicans favoring the rich certainly resurfaced. And Reagan contributed to that, appearancewise, with the new china and all those other things. Many blue-collar people said, 'The Republicans really don't care about us.' "[33]

Mr. Roberts picked up on Vander Jagt's negative preface to a positive defense of the Reagan policies by reporting the negative idea without tying it to the positive idea it prefaced. He recounted Vander Jagt's recognition that the White House "china" among "other things" contributed to the appearance of the president as having given special advantages to the rich. What Roberts did not say was that Vander Jagt believed that such a picture of the president constituted an entirely erroneous basis for a totally negative view of the administration's political programs. The congressman's belief that people are sometimes misled by unimportant negative symbols to overlook important positive realities, such as Republican programs designed to help low-income groups, was not reported.

Almost always, Vander Jagt speaks with respect for traditional values and for authority figures—as do most conservatives. He also aims at the heart of his listeners as well as their minds. Reporters, however, seem to be more interested in politicians who unemotionally break with tradition, who, by intellectual analysis, attack the *status quo* to prepare the way for new ideas. Conservatives are hard put to attract the sympathetic interest of media professionals who seem themselves to hold more liberal points of view.[34] When conservatives are noticed, they are depicted as boring, or lazy, or, at the least, not willing to do the really hard work of hammering out laws which make for a deep-rooted social change.

Another factor which should be noted is the sheer number of congressmen in the House. Each member of the House of Representatives accompanies 434 others when they all arrive in Washington for two-year terms. Unless they are re-elected over many terms or have special responsibilities which are at the center of political turmoil, what they say is lost in the deluge of speeches made by their many colleagues. By the time the average citizen catches up with an individual congressman's contributions, that congressman may have long since been replaced by someone else. It is only after congressmen have elaborated their ideas over many years that these ideas are registered with the media and conveyed to a national audience. Senators, by not having so many colleagues and by having longer terms in office, do less electioneering and more speaking to current issues which, in turn, means they have more visibility in national affairs.[35]

Over and above all of these causal factors which have produced the anomaly of a national party spokesman without a national identity stands the congressman's philosophy of communication, his desire to share "ideas, emotions, and convictions" with others, with their "minds," their "hearts," and their "souls."[36] His image as a speaker means only as much to him as his skill in conveying his ideas to others who come to hear him speak. When faced with a choice of playing to a broader mass audience or to those immediately in front of him, he never neglects the audience immediately on hand. He places the immediate listener in as honored a position as the delayed or shadow responses of an unseen or distant listener. In his keynote address, he was mindful of both kinds of audience, the TV audience and the delegates listening in person, but he was not so concerned with speaking to the whole national spectrum of political views that he forgot the party faithful who were present to gain a partisan's inspiration.

26

The fact that Vander Jagt invests his credibility in what the Republican party stands for with Republican audiences enhances his image as a campaigner for other Republicans. He is not expected to show the balanced judgment and the reflective openmindedness of a contender for national office. His sights are aimed on those who can respond with immediacy and with liveliness, and his view is appropriately partisan or limited to one side of the political spectrum. When, for example, he spoke on the floor of the House of Representatives in support of the president's reform or "reconciliation" tax bill on August 19, 1982, he did so as a Republican in support of his leader. He wrote to his colleagues on August 12:

> Our national opinion polls show that the greatest single factor, *by far*, in determining voter intention in Congressional races across the country is President approval rating. Not since FDR has a political leader so clearly dominated the country or had such an enormous potential for impacting on the outcome of Congressional races. If President Reagan's approval rating goes up 5 or 6 points, additional seats will fall in the Republican column. If his approval rating goes down, we lose ground.
>
> The polls also showed that the greatest single factor in the President's approval rating is people's perception of the President as a strong and effective leader. The President has made it clear that he believes the tax measure is essential to economic recovery. The defeat of a policy made crucial by his decision and in which the President has staked so much personal prestige would obviously not enhance his leadership image. Defeat by the members of the President's own party might well be devastating to his leadership image.
>
> The outcome of this fall's Congressional elections will have historic consequences that will shape America for many decades to come. With 79 days to go before those elections, we are like a football team in the fourth quarter with the outcome still hanging in the balance. Had I been the quarterback, it is possible that I might have called a different play. But the fact of the matter is the play has been called by our quarterback and, as a member of the team, I personally feel the only course I have is to execute that play as best I can rather than join "the other team" in throwing my own quarterback for a loss.
>
> That's how I reached the decision I did and that is why I intend to vote for the reconciliation tax bill. I hope you will too.[37]

As chairman of the National Republican Congressional Committee, he has always voiced optimism about the election of Republican candidates to the House of Representatives. He defied the "iron law of politics," already noted as the law which states that the party which wins the White House always loses seats in the following off-year election. He did this by adducing reasons why Republicans would break historical precedent and would add to their number in the House in '82. It has already been reported that he continued to support this contention even when he learned from polls in the middle of October that there existed the real possibility of a Democratic landslide and the consequent loss of fifty to seventy House seats.

His determination to maintain the party's united front, despite developments which could damage it, has drawn criticism from political analysts in Washington, newspaper journalists for the most part. Mistaken election predictions and a constant search for a good face to put on Republican foibles were satirized in a genial, fun-loving way at the Winter Dinner of the Gridiron Club after the '82 election results were tallied. The Gridiron chorus sang the "Vander Jagt Song" to a tune from *South Pacific*, the first verse of which went as follows:

> I'm as corn-y as Cong-ress in August,
> My fore-casts as flaky as pie in the sky,
> I'm the e-lite when it comes to defeat,
> I'm that won-derful Van-der Jagt Guy.[38]

Behind the joking here, an attempt was made to find, or create, a very small chink in the Vander Jagt armor which liberal partisans would like to exaggerate. Carl T. Rowan, for example, in a May '82 article accused him of buying the reelection of Republicans by the hypocrisy of dressing old "Dame GOP" in such a way as to sneak her by voters unrecognized with high-tech cosmetics, clothes and camera work.[39]

Another journalist, however, an editorial writer on the *Washington Post*, described his admitted partisanship as a "refreshing candor." In an age when so many people are pretending to a nonpartisanship in public affairs, Vander Jagt has not cloaked his partisan sentiment in statements about merits of the case and independence of judgment regardless of political party. His nerve and imagination in an open contention for power offer a new vitality to the two-party system in American politics. They also increase his credibility as a campaigner with Republican audiences.

A philosophy of communication like Vander Jagt's which stresses a given place, the moment, and people who can be seen and felt in three dimensions leads directly to tailor-made, hand-and-eye coordinated, human contact which mass production cannot replicate. It also makes possible the fullest kind of experience in communication. All forms of symbolization can be brought to bear. Reactions can range over the whole spectrum of possible responses including immediate and close contact between listener and speaker. But such a relationship is impossible to experience vicariously. No written explanation can ever capture for a reader the total exchange which occurs, and this is especially true in Vander Jagt's case as he fires the imaginations and arouses the passions of large, expectant audiences of fervent party supporters.

Even if this experience cannot be felt vicariously, a description of the various stages through which a Vander Jagt campaign speech goes can serve to illuminate, in part at least, the momentum of responses as they flow freely back and forth and as they build between the speaker and his audience.

It must be kept in mind that Vander Jagt is more than the average congressman. As chairman of the NRCC, he is one of a handful of Republicans in Washington with recognized, tangible influence. The responsibilities which accompany his special status in the party carry him all over the country to schools, to conventions, to meetings of political action committees, to prayer breakfasts, and, of most importance, to rallies and fundraising dinners for Republicans running for election to the House of Representatives. In this last instance, where he makes his greatest contribution to the party, he is invariably called upon to galvanize Republican workers to greater effort by paying tribute to their candidates for office. His importance in Washington and his broad array of contacts from traveling around the country lend a tremendous strength to his credentials as he undertakes this task.

The fact that he has made the effort to visit personally, coming perhaps hundreds of miles, to shake hands and to speak face to face with loyal Republicans gains for him tremendous respect. He is honoring each and every person present, and they sense that. Here is a man of great responsibilities who has taken his precious time and his not unlimited energy to speak personally to them. The adrenalin inevitably flows when one of the chosen from the golden city has appeared, almost godlike, not simply on television, but live and among the living, just downtown in the local hotel or auditorium or conference center. And what is even more impressive, he seems to be enjoying every minute of it.

His ethical appeal is further enhanced by the obvious intensity of his faith, not just in the candidate and the party, but in the belief that talent and hard work do indeed produce results, that a well-prepared speech, for example, can have an appreciable effect on the thoughts and feelings of others. And, in a broader sense, his absolutely unshakable belief that an individual personality can have an impact on a community fulfills completely the expectations of an anxious, waiting group of Republicans who have been in the process of attempting to have just such an impact.

He can be seen at the head table listening intently to party leaders, talking little, and eating only sparingly before his speech. He is always the picture of good humor and interested concern. This image rounds out the ethical appeal he has for his audiences; a flood of good will ensues. It becomes an almost total response to his personal power which derives from his strength of character and his overwhelming credentials as a veteran campaigner. These qualities are usually given special reference by the candidate who always seems to introduce Vander Jagt as the "best speaker" the Congress has to offer. Typically, he responds by praising the introduction and by thanking all of the people at the head table, *each by name,* and any others in the audience whose work and name deserve mention.

Within the first sixty seconds, it has dawned on everybody present that the congressman has come prepared. He not only knows the key Republicans in the district, he knows the candidate, the candidate's opposition, and many of the people in his audience by both name and official responsibilities. It is also readily apparent that he has planned ahead in other ways. He knows what he is going to say, and he wastes no time in getting to it. He compliments his audience finally and completely, then, by moving without gimmicks or worn phrases from brief but highly effective introductory courtesies to his purpose, the praise of the candidate, the candidate's supporters, and the party to which they all belong.

There is no doubt about his intent; his object is to link the candidate to the party and to argue the case for both in the upcoming elections. At the very outset, the point is made that the relationship between the candidate and the party is mutually beneficial. Just as the candidate benefits from the support of the party, the party benefits from having this specific candidate as its representative. He cites those concrete achievements of the candidate which deserve merit, often comparing them with the corresponding deficiencies of the opposition, both those of the individual opponent and those of the Democratic party generally. In this, the political world is clearly divided between the right people and the wrong people as he affirms the strengths of Republicans and denies those of Democrats.

His speeches then assume the directive design of the advocate as he moves to a clearly logical appeal in his presentation. He states his positive proposition early and explicitly: the candidate should be elected to office. He proceeds to support this statement with reasons which assume solidly traditional American values and which are based on evidence growing out of his knowledge of the background of the candidate. In short, he highlights a simple proposition and proves it. He then offers the candidate as evidence of the high quality of candidates generally in the Republican camp which, in turn, is a reason why Republicans should do well as a party in congressional elections. He broadens his initial position to include the support of the party and all Republicans around the entire nation. Once again, he submits reasons and evidence for this wider acceptance of Republican goals and strategies.

His listeners are sometimes surprised and always pleased when they are provided with good reasons and sound evidence by their spokesman. Regularly, politicians who are reputed for their speaking prowess are expected to be somewhat high-flown or grandiloquent in their delivery and not too thoughtful about their subjects or the issues involved. Stereotypes of a bombastic or an overly orotund style are sometimes given so much press that the quality of the speaker's thinking is either overlooked or forgotten. As a result, people mislead themselves into believing that eloquent speakers are likable lightweights with little substance or logical appeal for the educated audience.

This kind of superficial reaction to Vander Jagt's reputation as a speaker has led a number of his political opponents into embarrassing surprises. He always subordinates his delivery to his content, his ethical appeal to a logical appeal. As will be pointed out in another essay, his logical appeal is his primary asset in speaking, his first strength as a campaigner. Unthinking opponents, those who have accepted him as this stereotype of the orator, have underestimated him and, in that process, have been absolutely staggered by the logical, well-supported force of his arguments. Among those who have felt his strength in head-to-head debate are former congressmen John McFall, Wayne Hayes, John Brademus, and James Corman.

Congressman Jim Wright in 1972, a Texas Democrat who was later to be elected majority leader of the House, astutely observed the strength of Vander Jagt's arguments when he recorded the following:

> In debate on the Water Pollution Bill on the House floor in March, 1972, the Public Works Committee had successfully fought off as many as twenty proffered amendments, some offered by influential veteran practitioners of the parliamentary skill, including one by George Mahon, chairman of the powerful Appropriations Committee. Then Guy Vander Jagt, Michigan Republican, pleaded so forcefully for an amendment requiring study of a process of recycling wastes that it was overwhelmingly adopted. The power of Vander Jagt's plea that day was simply irresistible.[40]

Indeed, Vander Jagt devotes the main portion of his campaign speeches to streamlining his arguments and his supporting evidence in such a way as to give his ideas the most potency with the least apparent effort. These logical proofs which he power-packs into his speeches are drawn from a wide and interesting variety of sources. He draws upon statistical surveys, scientific experiments and demonstrations, the testimony of prominent national figures, TV broadcasters, and leaders in the worlds of space exploration, sports, and folksinging. He uses historical illustrations, personal anecdotes, and concrete examples taken directly from his own immediate and professional experiences. He is a master of analogies, comparisons, and contrasts, using the first mainly as it is best used in debate, to refute the arguments of others, and employing the second two in affirming his own.

His most salient method of establishing his case is the powerful psychological technique of repetition. He is able to approach an idea from so many interesting angles that the redundancy is seldom noticed. Often his repetition of logical proof is so interesting it is mistaken for an emotional appeal.

Then, too, he intersperses proofs with a light touch. His personal warmth, good will, and humor, bubbling out when this happens, soften his partisan image considerably, tempering his zeal with a modest, self-effacing manner. More often than not, when he jokes, the joke is on himself. He combined a statement of party loyalty with this sense of humor when he described for an audience a conversation he had had with his wife after hearing the results of the 1976 election of the majority leader in the House:

> As I was walking to my car, I learned that Jim Wright, that relatively moderate Democrat from Texas, had just defeated the ultra-liberal Democrat from California, Phil Burton, by one vote, as the new majority leader of the House of Representatives. Now my wife, Carol, has had a ten-year admiration for Jim Wright. She just thinks he's a wonderful man and a great American. And, as I got into the car, I said, "Carol, I just heard, guess what, much to everybody's surprise, Jim Wright defeated Phil Burton for majority leader by one vote!"
>
> She said, "Oh, gee, isn't that wonderful. That's just tremendous. Why—Jim Wright's a great American—I just can't think of better news to the country."
>
> I said, "Hold on here a minute, Carol, I'm not so sure how wonderful that is. After all, Phil Burton would be a heck of a lot easier target for me to hit than Jim Wright is going to be."
>
> She said, "Oh, excuse me, Guy. I'm sorry. For a second there, I was only thinking of our country."
>
> Now, when you can get your wife brainwashed into apologizing for thinking of America instead of the Republican party, you're pretty partisan indeed. I could have explained to her that whatever is good for the Republican party is good for America, but I didn't, and that's another time and another speech.[41]

It is as logical proofs build the strength of his proposition that the less enthusiastic, the most cynical, among his audience are caught up in the spirit of party loyalty and the exuberance of the occasion. These logical proofs, wedged together neatly and delivered simply, without embellishment, constitute the appeal to which the more diffident listeners respond when, for the first time, they turn their chairs from tables to face the speaker. While a few will not admit his personal appeal, there is no escape from the force of his logic.

The atmosphere takes on a keener sense of satisfaction. Bursts of applause and, at points, laughter become more resounding. Comments like "Hey, this guy is something else *again*," with replies like "He is *really* good," are common when the reasons offered for a more hopeful Republican future sink in and take hold of the audience.

This extended clearing of the intellectual thicket is the crucial turning point in the campaigner's presentation. It sweeps up the more reluctant listeners along with the others who are already involved as it prepares the way for an ascent to loftier heights where he directs a frontal assault on their emotions and their deeper sensitivities.

Invariably, Vander Jagt's bridge from a closely reasoned case to an emotional conclusion is based on poems or human interest stories handcrafted to fit the audience and his theme. The emotional power inherent in the poetry he recites or the situation he describes seems somehow inadvertent and takes the audience almost by surprise. His delivery is simple, without dramatic flourish, and his wording is plain, almost dry. He gives his audience little time to recover from the sensational surge of the moment. In a word or two, he concludes and sits down. The quiet crackles into the crescendos of a standing ovation. More often than not, tears stream down cheeks at every table in the banquet hall.

Two of these recent "goose-pimple" conclusions which have captured the hearts of his audience are his recitation of *Opportunity* by Edward Rowland Sill and his relating of President Reagan's story of the heroic gallantry of an American pilot toward a crewman as their B-17 fell from the sky over Germany in World War II. The emotional impact of the latter of these was registered when Rich Galen, director of public affairs of the NRCC, recounted his fascination at watching a seasoned political consultant surreptitiously wipe tears from his chin as he heard the story for the third time![42]

Early in his career, Vander Jagt aroused these same deep feelings. His conclusion to his student effort entitled "Bonn Report" was renowned in Michigan for lending to the speech a very special power which literally "moved a thousand audiences to tears."[43]

The fact that many believe Vander Jagt to be the premier political campaigner on the American scene today probably hinges on his inimitable skill in making this transition from a logical to an emotional appeal in such a way as to lift an audience out of itself, to help it transcend time and place to glimpse for a minute the broader vision of a new and better universe.

Unless hurried by the time restraints of a campaign schedule, Vander Jagt remains at the head table for as long as it takes to receive and to respond to inevitable expressions of appreciation. The adulation which moves the party faithful to press in upon him, to shake his hand, and often to recommit themselves to party service seems in these moments overwhelming. Responses of this sort cannot be compared adequately with headcounts of a statistical survey of television watchers or magazine readers. The millions, for example, who heard his nationally televised keynote address, may seem astronomical when contrasted with the thousands who have heard the campaigner in person, but those bonds of trust forged over a dinner table when the congressman personally stretched minds, wrenched hearts, and shook hands seem more likely to endure with many farther reaching effects. The person-to-person influences which radiate from the banquet hall on these occasions have to be more heartfelt and mind-binding than those emanating from dots dancing across the screening of an electronic exhortation on television.

Responses, then, really do count, but they come in many forms. And each form has an importance relative to the others. In Vander Jagt's case, the form of greatest significance is that form which demands an immediate response and yet another response in return: the live situation where party enthusiasts seek recognition and inspiration. He appreciates the responses of his colleagues and admits to encouraging the attacks of his liberal opponents by unabashedly advocating conservative policies. Indeed, he would also court a national image and the broadened responses it would bring, but, where a decision must be made, he chooses to speak to and through his immediate, if local, listeners. He seeks the long-term, vigorous response of people who care.

These are his rewards, the heartfelt responses of living, breathing people who want to shake his hand and talk back, if only to say thanks. Ultimately, these are the responses he seeks. If television helps him to achieve such responses, he uses it, and, when personal contacts help him and the party to use television more effectively, they are doubly rewarding. But, it is the live and immediate response which really counts and which brings him back time and again to campaign for his fellow candidates and for the Republican party.

3

Does a Party Spokesman Have to Speak on All Occasions?

M ODERN SPEECH theorists have taught us that speakers must listen and listeners must speak if mutually beneficial communication is to take place. The reversal of roles in this fashion, surely, has alway been implicit in the political communications of a democratic republic. Speakers or political figures who usually initiate communication are expected to represent the views of their constituents. In order to realize this goal, they must listen regularly to their constituents or "followers," and, by the same token, constituents must speak regularly to their representatives of "leaders."

The role of speaking, it should also be noted, does not necessarily mean assuming a position of strength in relationships; nor does the role of listening mean weakness. When a speaker raises an honest question, or describes or explains a situation, the listeners (or listener) are placed in a position of superiority or strength since the speaker by nondirection has offered the listeners the initiative (or the freedom) to answer the question or to judge the facts for themselves. The speaker can legitimately work from a position of weakness in communication, if it is felt that achieving the best outcome in a relationship means evoking the strength of listeners and arranging the situation so that they do the speaking.

Theoretically, it is possible for a person to maintain a nondirective stance toward an idea for a lifetime, but for people who are politically active this approach is limited by the time it takes to vote. Sooner or later, political communication resolves itself to an obligatory yes or no. A citizen, politician or not, can sidestep an issue temporarily by abstaining from voting, but when majorities and minorities are eventually calculated, abstentions do not count. They translate as a bland neutrality or as political zeros. Adaptive action, then, in both speaking and listening is absolutely essential in political communication, and it resolves itself ultimately into a clearcut, simple yes or no.[1]

Congressman Vander Jagt recognizes this fact in his life as a political communicator, but he chooses to extend the process by which he reaches his final decisions, both on his positions on the issues and on his votes, for as long as he possibly can. His slow transformation from a nondirective, open inquiry into the facts of a matter, through an indirective analysis of problems and weighing of alternative answers, to the directive, closed position of the advocate, affirming or denying a specific program or policy, carries him over many forms and modes of political communication. Indirection, here, refers to an intermediary stage in the development of his ideas as he moves from nondirection to direction in his logical designs for speaking. Nondirective inquiry and description aim at locating problems which need solution. Directive advocacy implies that a solution to a problem has already been chosen. Indirection refers to designs which help to establish priorities among problems as well as priorities among their solutions.

The various occasions for his political communication may be organized, along with their accompanying media, from the most informal, interpersonal, almost intrapersonal, levels of communication to the most formal, structured, extrapersonal or high-tech levels. They might be grouped and ranged from one extreme to the other as follows: (1) most personal, private conversations where two or three people are involved in closet negotiations without any definitely recognized time limits; (2) informal small group discussions and personal interviews; (3) planned group or committee conferences where discussion leadership is required for business to be conducted in an efficient manner; (4) question-and-answer dialogue or enlarged (fishbowled) conversations in which the speaker reacts to members of a larger audience or constituency such as professional journalists; (5) stump speaking to medium-sized audiences in less formal circumstances—e.g., an outdoor, open-air environment; (6) formal public speaking situations where time limits are set as on the floor of the House of Representatives and as in after-dinner campaign speeches; (7) more ceremonial and very formally arranged public relations where the press, radio, or television is involved and where space and time are severely monitored. Vander Jagt's occasions for political communication range, then, from situations with personal give-and-take requiring little or no direct preparation to mechanized, highly impersonal situations which demand a large amount of direct preparation.

Just as each of these situations presents special problems to the communicator, each situation represents special difficulties which must be recognized by the student of communication who attempts to engage in rhetorical criticism. The two most informal, intimate situations, for example, are the most difficult to observe since the observer always seems to some extent an intruder. When terrible or delicate truths are likely to be discussed, the observer, especially one with pencil poised or tape recorder ready, subverts the occasion. It ceases to be a private conversation; the persons communicating automatically assume a more public stance.[2]

On the other hand, as an example of highly structured mechanized communication, the TV ad represents a completely different set of difficulties. While it is much easier accurately to describe and analyze the message, it is virtually impossible to determine exactly how deeply how many people are affected by it. The people who think, talk, and take action as a result of the message may finally form a network of communications which covers the whole country over a very long period of time. This network utterly defies completely accurate description and measurement.

Despite the limitations facing the rhetorical critic, a study of Vander Jagt's approaches to these various levels of communication proves productive of a number of insights concerning political speaking and listening.

In situations where the informal one-on-one and small group conversations of the congressman have been open to observation, he is first and foremost a listener, welcoming all suggestions, a tactful friend who helps others express ideas without guilt or fear of reprisal. His communicative design on this level is almost always nondirective, sometimes indirective, and seldom, if ever, directive in character. He encourages others to take the initiative in communication, and he gives his complete attention as a listener.

On a mid-September '82 campaign tour through Virginia and North Carolina, after a long day which included three formal after-meal speeches, one at breakfast in Richmond, Virginia, one at lunch in Gastonia, North Carolina, and one at dinner back in Virginia, in Roanoke, he sat with three young Republicans in the Ad Lib Restaurant of the Roanoke Hotel. They were critiquing the speaking which they had heard at the banquet. Two people at the table joined issue not too gently about the different speaking styles of Kevin Miller and Ray Garland, both of whom had taken part in the after-dinner ceremonies that evening. Miller had introduced Garland, and Garland had introduced Vander Jagt, who gave the main address. Miller and Garland, it should be said, were the winner and loser respectively of the Virginia Republican congressional primary election held earlier in May, and the Miller supporter and the Garland supporter at the table were disagreeing not just on issues relating to effective speaking but on the personality traits and the political tactics of the candidates as well.[3]

Vander Jagt edged into the conversation skillfully to soften the differences which had developed and to observe the fact finally that when you make a friend in politics, you lose an enemy. His implication was that it is always necessary to view enemies as future friends and to adjust regularly to events which produce altered political alignments of both people and parties. Notice that he had introduced a third idea designed to mediate the two others. He also confided that he had forgotten this axiom himself when he was unable to control his own long-standing and deep resentment of one particular congressional colleague who had always left him feeling angry and disgusted. Time and time again, he said, he tried to overcome these feelings of revulsion, but failed, at which point he had to accept, however reluctantly, the permanent loss of a friend and the making of an enemy. This self-deprecation seemed to be motivated by an attempt to assuage any feeling of embarrassment that his young Republican friends might have had following his suggestion that they should avoid bitter argument among themselves.

One young woman in this group was also strongly set against attempts by the Congress to rescind the abortion laws. The individual should be able to decide for herself what happens to her own body, she maintained. He replied by asking if she thought individuals should be permitted to decide for themselves whether their taxes should be used to pay for abortions desired and procured by others? "Is it fair to ask people who do not believe in abortion to help finance it with their tax dollars when you believe it unfair to ask women to have babies they do not want?" The answer to a different question came back immediately: "It's cheaper to pay for an abortion than it is to pay for the upbringing of a child who, with or without a parent, is on welfare for twenty-one years." He smiled and replied, "That's a good point."[4]

In a nondirective use of questions, he elicits from others their strongest feelings and arguments. This approach, exemplified with these young Republicans in Virginia, tends to be his standard, initial approach in personal phone calls, conversations with individuals before and after more formal speeches before large audiences, and in private conversations in his congressional office. He raises questions, offers lines of thinking for the reactions of others, all the time listening intently, encouraging, and reacting in an open and sympathetic way. He also purposely uses nondirective designs to aid him in audience analysis. This searching out of the beliefs and feelings of others provides him with information which has a direct impact upon his own thinking and ultimately upon the design and content of his speeches. It also helps him to avoid taking premature positions on key issues without first ascertaining which arguments will be needed for whom as the ensuing dialogue or debate develops.

He tends not to take the initiative unless he is fulfilling his role as a congressman, and, then, he does so in an indirective way. This is especially true in conversations before or after formal speeches when he leads others into discussions of the common problems he and they face in such areas as managing meetings, political activities, financial conditions, markets, and economic questions generally. Usually, he ends up listening.

Regularly, too, he is supportive of others by attempting to raise their spirits. On one occasion, the son of a former congressional colleague dropped into his office in the Rayburn Building to show a friend a congressman's office. As they were studying the awards on the walls and the mementos around the office, Vander Jagt asked,

"What are you doing, these days?" "Looking for a job," he replied. "I heard you had graduated and that you made the dean's list." "Yes," the young man said, "but it was only in the last semester." Vander Jagt smiled back optimistically, "But what could be a better time to finish on a high note?"[5]

The flavor of his willingness to encourage others, to help them to share their strengths, their information and their views, comes through clearly in his conference leadership in committee meetings, and, to a lesser extent, in his enlarged question-and-answer sessions either with members of an audience after a speech or with professionals who interview him in his capacity as chairman of the National Republican Congressional Committee.

Prime examples of his skill in this role as a conference or discussion leader occur when he leads a meeting of the executive committee of the NRCC. In a one-hour meeting with ten congressmen and seven staff members, he elicited reactions from all of the congressmen and most of the staff. He got four formal reports from staff members on the state of the committee's finances, public relations, a disinformation project,[6] and campaigns around the country. He encouraged and got extended reactions to these reports. In each case, he demonstrated visual approval of what was being said by giving each speaker his undivided attention. When his brown eyes fixed a speaker, his concentration was total and apparent to everyone present. That he was supportive and optimistic was absolutely clear in his verbal reactions to their contributions. He made comments such as: "In view of the obstacles, the dinner was a tremendous success." "Wyatt could be a millionaire out of politics and in the business world." "That's good news!" "Joe, can you come to the White House to give this briefing?" "Terrific report!" "There's heroic duty behind that last report." "Thank you; just fine." "Terrific job!" And, always encouraging more participation, his most frequent reaction was, "Any questions?"

Giving form to the meeting, he introduced it by comparing the scheduled reports to a "meal's main courses" and by referring to his own contribution as a final "icing on the cake" or simply, "the bubbles." He was, with this statement, previewing the conclusion to this meeting when everyone would be taking the elevator down to the first floor of the Eisenhower Center, to the new entrance[7] which was only recently built for the NRCC. The new door was celebrated with a bottle of champagne, real bubbles to see and taste, and to remember. Niceties such as these account in part for the fact that Vander Jagt has so many "admirers with long memories."[8]

In his six years as chairman, there has never been a split vote in meetings of the NRCC. Votes have always been unanimous. This almost unbelievable consensus is due largely to the fact that Vander Jagt has prepared for meetings by drawing others out in conversation ahead of time. In this way, he has been able to anticipate disagreements and to allot in committee meetings the time necessary to work them out. He has an intuitive sense, too, of movement and rhythm in group action and can program the agenda in such a way as to give the more important questions the most time. He brings participants into the proceedings at moments most conducive to their help in producing quality ideas and the achievement of general assent to them.[9]

Just a month after the celebration of the new entrance to the Republican office building on First Street, S.E., the leadership of the National Republican Congressional Committee met again in H227 of the Capitol. With eighty-three days left before the November elections, the meeting represented the last full membership meeting where a total picture of the '82 prospects for Republicans could be assessed. Vander Jagt introduced the all-morning meeting by describing his own schedule of speeches as a continuous support of the belief that November 2, 1982, would break history by adding, not losing, Republican seats in the House of Representatives. He compared his own stand with the less optimistic statements of others in the party.

After the staff reports, he went around the room, congressman by congressman, state by state,[10] getting descriptions of the Republican campaigns, the opposition, and chances for success. The reports were far more optimistic than anyone expected and moved him to ask for more help in making Republican chances clear to the public.

More and more over the years, he has opened himself up to the give-and-take of question-and-answer dialogue with others. His enthusiasm for this kind of occasion shows through in his giving more detailed information on specific subjects and in his essaying a broader range of subjects. After a presentation at a breakfast of the

42

National Consumer Finance Association,[11] for example, he offered to answer *any* question from the audience. "If you want to ask me when a congressman gets up in the morning, go right ahead." While the sixty-five businessmen attending applauded his thirty-minute speech, after the eighteen-minute question-and-answer period, he received a standing ovation, and all of this at 9:15 A.M. before the audience's long, hard program of meetings stretching across the entire day.

In this instance, as in many others, he also encouraged members of the audience to relate examples and anecdotes which further elaborated the points he was making. He entertains mini-speeches as well as questions from audiences. He even goes so far as to recommend from time to time a question-answer period without his formal remarks, anticipating these speeches or statements. While his preparation is less demanding on such occasions, he prepares himself well on subjects which are current and which are of special interest to the audience involved. For the NCFA, for example, he refreshed his memory on state credit laws, bankruptcy laws, and amendments in Congress related to these matters.[12]

On his swing through Virginia and North Carolina for Republican candidates on September 17 and 18 in '82, he prepared for questions on social security, national security, and the tobacco industry. Different candidates had been under different kinds of attacks and, consequently, had different needs. In Raleigh and Smithfield, he needed to bring to bear his understanding of how the new eight-cent tobacco tax got through the Congress. In Gastonia, social security was the subject, and the depth of Republican support of it was the issue. At each stop along the way, however, the same key bits of information concerning national security were needed, and each repetition helped him to make additional economies in the wording and the delivery of these facts in preparation for more formal occasions later.

The ideas being developed and refined in Virginia and North Carolina were echoed in other press conferences, including a subsequent conference at the Washington, D.C. Press Club on September 30, 1982, just two weeks later:

> ... the cigarette tax is a volatile political issue, particularly in states like North Carolina and Virginia and other tobacco-growing states. I

personally believe that it ought to be a tremendous asset for the Republican party because, yes, an increase in cigarette tax from eight to sixteen cents was in the original Senate finance bill. The Democrats, as it came to the House Ways and Means Committee, which is two-to-one Democrat, could easily have taken it out. They didn't. They agreed they couldn't agree on anything and sent it straight to the conference. Then, at four o'clock in the morning, on Sunday morning, after days of conferences, Senator Dole questioned the Joint Economic Committee staff and said, "Is it true we have a one-point-seven billion dollar surplus? We've got one-point-seven billion more than we need?" They said, "Yes." And then he said, "Is it true that the 1983 increase in cigarette taxes from eight to sixteen cents would be about one-point-seven billion?" And the committee staff answered, "Yes." He said, "Then I propose that we eliminate the cigarette increase for 1983." And Chairman Rostenkowski said, "You are defenseless. We've got you on this one because if we recede, there is nothing we can talk about. And in our Democrat caucus the vote was almost unanimous that the tax stay, so it's there." Land sakes a livin', if anybody in the South is upset about that tax, they can ask the Democrat chairman of the Ways and Means Committee.[13]

Repetition of materials from one occasion to another is his rule, not his exception, and it should be clear, too, that materials used in presentations on one level of formality he adapts quickly and effectively to those on other levels. Differences are those of degree, not kind. The more formal the occasion, the more time, effort, and skill Vander Jagt applies to fit the idea to the occasion, but the idea remains basically the same. Direct preparation, then becomes more important as time and space restraints are imposed upon the speaker and his listeners.[14]

The level of formality increases once again when Vander Jagt moves from question-and-answer public dialogue to stump campaign speaking. The stump speech is the least formal of all formal speaking occasions, but it, nevertheless, calls for a prepared presentation which is sustained over a long period of time, unbroken by questions or by mini-statements from the listeners. It is the primary testing ground for Vander Jagt's new materials and ideas. Usually, it occurs in quite ordinary places: a backyard with a platform or a soapbox, a field behind a barn in the open air, a bandstand, a gymnasium, any place not normally associated with public speaking. This form of political communication might be thought of as grassroots speaking as it was known throughout the Nineteenth Century.

Vander Jagt spoke on two such occasions back-to-back at McGee's Corners in Smithfield, North Carolina, and at the VFW Center barn in Dunn, North Carolina, on September 18, 1982. In both cases, he was campaigning for his friend and fellow Republican, Red McDaniel, a war hero who spent six years in Vietnam as a POW and who later served for a time as commanding officer of the U.S.S. *Lexington.*

At McGee's Corners, forty-five adults and ten children had gathered together in the farmyard of a staunch McDaniel supporter who had used his own money to hire migrant workers to paint signs for McDaniel's campaign and to supply hot dogs and cokes for this specific occasion. Children were playing in the grass, and balloons were flying (some were popping) when the congressman in his dark gray suit emerged from Red's campaign van into the 80° heat to speak for twenty minutes in support of the candidate. He argued before that broken circle of farmers in the strongest terms that McDaniel would cut government controls and support a stronger military. He said, further, that of over two hundred candidates for whom he had campaigned in the last year and a half, Red McDaniel was "the best."

Three hours later at Dunn, he used as a speaker's podium a second-story porch recently constructed of two-by-fours and attached to the VFW barn which stood just on the edge of town. In the mouth-watering smoke of roasted pig, he spoke to over two hundred well-fed people who stood in the field behind the barn. He repeated the speech of tribute he had given at McGee's Corners with some additional evidence supporting McDaniel's qualifications for representing Republicans from North Carolina. Especially effective was a cameo listing from memory of all of the military medals and awards McDaniel had been given. He concluded with a promise to repeal the tobacco tax in the House if the people of the Third District would send Red McDaniel to Congress.

With this second stump speech, he had moved into the nebulous gray area between interpersonal and extrapersonal political speaking. At McGee's Corners, he spoke without a public address system, without a lectern or any mechanical device at all. His contact with the audience ws immediate, skin-to-skin, and McDaniel's supporters had direct access to the speaker for personal reactions and handshaking. In Dunn, a P.A. system had been set up to amplify his voice, and he was not a part of his audience. He was above and removed from it. Instead of standing among his listeners, he had now moved from the pure "stump" to the speaker's stand and had edged subtly into a more formal, more extrapersonal occasion for speaking. He was whisked away immediately after the speech to a chartered plane to fly back to Washington for an 8:00 P.M. reception and, therefore, only party officers and dignitaries had the opportunity to approach and to make personal contact with him.

The more formalized "stump" or after-dinner speech to a large audience in a ballroom or banquet hall is the standard occasion for a Vander Jagt campaign speech.[15] This form of speaking accounts most for Vander Jagt's reputation as a campaigner. It has been the focus of a great part of this work, especially in the previous essay and, again, in the collection of his speeches which forms the second half of this volume. So much space has been devoted to it elsewhere that no further elaboration is required here. In passing, however, it is interesting to note again how regularly he is called upon to deliver this kind of speech. A typical month of speeches, found in his datebook schedule of speeches in October of 1977, suggests the frequency with which he delivers this particular kind of speech:

2 Sun.	Garden Grove, Calif.	Nationally televised "Hour of Power" with Dr. Robert H. Schuller
5 Wed.	Washington, D.C.	Republican National Committee Advisory Council
6 Thurs.	Birmingham, Ala.	Associated Industries of Alabama
7 Fri.	Dearborn, Mich.	Michigan Medical Society Joint Practice Comm.
11 Tues.	Washington, D.C.	The Society of the Plastics Industry, Inc.
20 Thurs.	Grand Rapids, Mich.	The Lotus Club
22 Sat. A.M.	Atlanta, Ga.	National Federation of Republican Women

22 Sat. P.M.	Northfield, Vt.	Vermont State Fundraising Dinner
24 Mon. A.M.	Houston, Tex.	National Paint and Coating Association
24 Mon. P.M.	Indianapolis, Ind.	Indiana Medical Association PAC
27 Thurs.	Miami, Fla.	National Machine Tool Builders Association
28 Fri.	Salt Lake City, Utah	Western States Republican Conference
29 Sat.	Moorhead, Minn.	Tribute to Congressman Stangeland (fundraiser)

Notice that only one of these engagements, the very first, did not involve an inspirational, partisan speech of advocacy to a large, live audience of business and professional people and/or Republicans. Although he worked especially hard in the mid-70s to bring more people into the Republican party and more Republicans into PACs,[16] this schedule is not atypical of other months in his other years as a campaigner.

This kind of campaign speech, it has been noted, is that for which Vander Jagt is best known, but he is also at home in the even more restricted or standardized form of public speaking which exists on the floor of the House and which has, in recent years, been C-Spanned around the country by cable TV. Here, too, Vander Jagt's advocacy on public issues has been recognized through coverage by the national TV networks in 1972, 1976, 1979, and yet again in his more highly publicized House floor defense of President Reagan's tax reform bill on August 19, 1982.

On March 29, 1972, he argued successfully that the Environmental Protection Agency should "encourage the development in areas of resources management . . . the recycling of pollutants into resources, thereby producing income rather than just incurring operating costs."[17] Here he brought to the question before the House his long experience and great success in meeting the problem of water pollution in Lake Michigan.[18] On February 3, 1976, and July 1, 1976, he spoke for suspending "the imposition of

47

Federal penalties" for noncompliance of day-care centers with new standards that the Congress had not to that point carefully processed.[19] Again, on March 30th of the same year, he supported the Federal Election Commission's independence from congressional veto in regulating the public financing of congressional campaigns. He noted that H2536, the bill to destroy that independence by supporting "the right of either House to veto a regulation coming from the FEC," was very much "like putting the rabbits in charge of guarding the cabbage patch."[20] He also argued that the bill blatantly favored one special interest group: big labor.

It was on June 28, 1979, that he spoke in favor of greater tax relief to American industries which were attempting to increase the domestic production of oil. Supporting the Shannon amendment which imposed further taxes on American oil interests was, he said, to support the victimization of the U.S. by OPEC:

> I am convinced that historians some centuries from now, musing on the glory that once was America, will become convinced and pinpoint Thursday afternoon, June 28, 1979, as the day that we decided to commit national suicide. At the very least, I am convinced that the befuddled historians will be desperately trying to figure out why—why in the world Uncle Sam, at the very moment he was threatened by OPEC, reached into the congressional holster and withdrew a six-gun and aimed it not at OPEC, but shot his own leg and limped off a cripple forever.[21]

When, in 1982, he defended the president's tax reform bill where small tax increases in nonessential items were proposed, he did so feeling that he was in no way retreating from the position that the tax cuts passed the year before would hasten economic recovery. He argued that some tax increases, not associated with the individual's income tax, would help reduce the national deficits and interest rates:

> I believe in the incentives that we enacted last year and I believe that they will work. And that is why I support this measure. No. 1, to protect the tax incentives that remain in place, but, No. 2, those incentives have not worked up until now because they could not get through the barrier of high interest to the business community so that they could respond to it. The starch-stopper pill on the market today stops the starch from reaching the system of the body and high interest rates have prevented

our incentives from reaching the investment community of this country. So let us do what we can to reduce interest rates and unleash our incentives and put America back to work again.[22]

In these last two forms of public address, Vander Jagt compressed his ideas to meet the special time restraints imposed by the occasions. This is especially true in House debates as he makes constant use of analogy to cement points quickly and vividly. It is also apparent that many of his ideas in legislative debate slide out of and slip back into his campaign speaking on the banquet circuit.

He uses, in these more formal situations, the ideas which have been gradually developing through constant experimentation and evaluation in his more informal speaking experiences. In these more formal situations, his arguments and supporting materials are streamlined and power-packed to gain the maximum possible potency in the minimum possible time. Operating on Cicero's famous maxim, he says "much in little."

Of all of the speaking occasions which face Guy Vander Jagt (and all political communicators), the most far-reaching and sought after is the one in which the message is magnified and broadcast by the mass media. Mechanizing the message in this way, either by print or telecommunications, saves the speaker great amounts of time and energy and makes possible a more broadly based political organization and a more continuous sense of democratic process in an advanced and highly complex society. These advantages of the mass media far outweigh the difficulties involved in their use.[23]

Adapting to this twentieth-century development in communications, Vander Jagt has recognized it as the most highly formalized and the most public form of political speaking. No matter how great the illusion that these media are warmly personal and immediately sensitive to their listeners, he regards them as the most extrapersonal, ceremonial form of communication, demanding of him his most extensive preparation. Published and televised presentations, interviews, discussions, press conferences, and formal speeches (or essays) all require the quintessence of effective communication. The best ideas in their best style must be presented on these occasions regardless of the loose informality of the type of format being followed.

49

Although Dennis Wholey, as a prime example, gave the impression of a sympathetic interviewer in a private conversation with the congressman late at night on the PBS network,[24] both recognized the fact that their communication was being viewed by a far-ranging audience across the nation and that reactions would come by telephone from friends and enemies alike. Vander Jagt's statements would be scrutinized from every possible angle for inaccuracies, misinterpretations, contradictions, and general lapses in logic.

The sense of the campaign, of advocacy, becomes even sharper for Vander Jagt as he approaches the mass media. Being prepared for these situations means being able to argue his case in the best possible manner. Sooner or later, explanations are interpreted as arguments, and information is viewed as evidence either by people in the viewing or reading audience, or by interviewers who are presumably with him in person to stimulate his ideas.

In all mass communication situations, he is on display as a representative of Republican thinking, and his is the responsibility of communicating this thinking with clarity and force. In this sense, no national political figure in the United States can ignore the communication of an idea in favor of its quality alone, and Vander Jagt has pointed out repeatedly that people will not beat a path to anyone's door to buy a brand new mousetrap until they realize the advantages it will provide over other traps on the market.

While Vander Jagt finds his greatest personal satisfaction in the live-audience speaking situation, he admits the preeminence of the mass media in modern political effectiveness. This is why it was during his tenure as chairman of the NRCC that it became the largest producer of TV and radio political advertisements in the country, if not the world.[25] This is why he included in his education, as will be noted in the treatment of his early preparation for a career in communication, reporting the news on television and radio. This is why he argues regularly that a greater percentage of the NRCC's resources be devoted to making Republican ideas visible in the mass media.[26] And, as is logical, this is why he believes the mass media require the best of what he has developed in other less formal situations. If he only gets five minutes on *Meet the Press* or ten seconds in a news segment[27] late in the evening, the time he does earn on these programs has to count for more than it does in any other mode.

50

His interest in the mass media extends to the written form as noted in his regular contributions to *Eighty-Two*, a regularly printed newsletter produced by the NRCC which was sent in 1982 "to congressional candidates, GOP House Members, Members' district offices and Members' Campaign headquarters," and to "officers and members" of other Republican groups around the country.[28] It contained practical advice for the management of congressional campaigns, including in each issue a "Chairman's Message." In these columns, Vander Jagt's ideas were reduced to the barest minimum of space with maximum effect:

> The miracles of modern news reporting are a commonplace to today's congressional campaigns. The new technology puts greater demands on candidates than ever before. But it also presents greater opportunities for reaching voters.
> News media want to serve the public, just as you do. Good news reporting reaches people "where they live"—in more ways than one. "Make the news," and you will reach thousands of people at once. If you address what your constituents care about most, you will be a newsworthy candidate.[29]

When all of the mass media situations in which Vander Jagt communicates are considered, his TV and radio appearances are the most remarkable. He brings to bear on them a lifetime of preparation as a public speaker. One morning he breezed into the NRCC offices at 9:15 with two 1½-minute spots written by the White House staff and sent to him at 8:30 that same morning. Without manuscript, teleprompter, or any notes at all, he completed the two spots to within three seconds of perfection on the first takes without one single glitch, hitch, or start-stop in his delivery. In a half hour, he had pounded three minutes of someone else's copy into his head, word for word, for a final "take."[30]

This same letter-perfect delivery characterizes his television campaign spots which, once again, repeat bits and pieces of his time-tested, surefire materials from speaking to live audiences. In the 1982 campaign in Michigan, he used his Ronald Reagan, Red McDaniel, David Brinkley, and Tip O'Neill references in combination for a five-minute spot, and, singly, as one-minute spots. He also cut several one-minute spots into thirty-second spots, all again on the first take.[31]

His use of the NRCC radio and TV facilities in producing

campaign spots every two years has sharpened his ability to work with these media to the point where he was requested by representatives from the Mutual Broadcasting System to replace the retiring Paul Harvey with regular radio political commentary.[32] He began, indeed, to cut weekly radio tapes for MBS in March of 1983.

Employing his communication skills, then, at all levels or occasions for speaking and listening, the party spokesman has gradually over the years come to symbolize the hub of a multipronged public relations effort for congressional Republicans. Each time he makes a personal appearance on behalf of a Republican candidate, the NRCC's resources are summoned to extend the chairman's influence on all levels through all kinds of media to the whole district.

A classic example of this simultaneous consolidation of communication at all levels is revealed in the campaigner's eight-hour blitz of Indianapolis, Indiana, on August 23, 1982, to support Dan Burton, Republican nominee in the Sixth Congressional District. An advance team from the committee spent several days setting up the series of closely packed events which were sequenced to get the most coverage possible for the time and money spent. Vander Jagt's primary obligation was to speak formally at a fundraising luncheon at the Columbia Club, but there were other audiences and other media. He gave televised interviews at the Homesteading and Redevelopment Center in downtown Indianapolis; he was quoted in the afternoon edition of the *Indianapolis News;*[33] he was interviewed personally in the offices of the editorial writers of the *News* and of the *Indianapolis Star;* he answered the questions of leading political reporters in the Presidential Suite at the Columbia Club, and he chatted privately[34] with three congressional candidates, Burton, Ralph Van Natta, and Mike Carroll. He also accompanied them and their staffs as they toured the redevelopment area around Monument Circle. At each street corner, he spoke with people who stopped to inquire into the point behind the tour. He met each of these occasions as if it were his first of the day.

His work as a party spokesman, it has been established, ranges across all the important modes of political communication, and his tendencies to prepare diligently, to use the directive approach of the advocate, and to rely on proven arguments become more pronounced as he moves toward extrapersonal forms of communication and more formal occasions. The reverse holds; he tends to be more nondirective and more willing to test new ideas and different supporting materials in more informal situations where interpersonal contact is the rule.

Again, we ask the question posed at the outset here. Does a party spokesman have to speak on all occasions? The answer is yes; the more of each occasion, the better. If the needs of all levels of communication can be met at one moment in time, or on one tour, or in one "take," ever so much more the better, perhaps the best.

4

How Does He Do It?

C ONGRESSMAN Guy Vander Jagt, it has been noted, faces a great variety of speech situations in the fulfillment of his regular political responsibilities. In the previous essay, these situations were sorted out and categorized from the least formal to the most formal. It was also concluded that he gives greater preparation to ideas on formal occasions than he does on more informal occasions. This is not unexpected as the formal situation imposes severe time restraints on the actual delivery of the idea, and this restriction demands of the speaker more time in preparation.

He also tends to be progressively more directive in his designing of ideas as he moves from informal to formal occasions. In informal, personal kinds of communication, he tends to be more non-directive: to listen, to inquire. His method of preparing ideas progresses regularly from these open-minded positions to a closed, fixed stand, or advocacy, in more public, extrapersonal situations. He seeks information before he undertakes the value orientation of the advocate, and his campaign speeches are, therefore, carefully worked out in an initial search for facts.

His development of ideas and the collection of supporting materials with which he elaborates them have generally originated in his special assignments in committee work, hearings, and legislative discussion and debate. Typical subjects of his speeches from the late sixties to 1971 reveal his committee service in astronautical science and the conservation of natural resources: space and lunar probes,[1] tributes to astronauts,[2] recognition of Earth Day,[3] and agricultural environmentalism.[4] Shortly after 1971, his concerns were tailored to his work on the House Committee on

Foreign Affairs: tributes to foreign service officers,[5] free enterprise abroad,[6] and the U.N.[7] More recently, he has used his position as chairman of the NRCC to guide his development of ideas. In 1974, when he assumed this new role, he began to sharpen Republican lines of argument to defend the party's policies and prospects. Some ideas he drew from individual Republicans; others were developed jointly with his colleagues through conversations and group discussion. The results of this practice appear clearly in "Wake Up, America!"[8] "Count Your Blessings,"[9] "A New Beginning,"[10] and "The Three Rs."[11]

In addition to speaking out of his immediate interests and contacts as a legislator and a political organizer, his own experiences, his reading, and his reflections over a lifetime provide a constant source of materials, some of which have reappeared time and time again over his thirty years of speaking. When he listens to friends and colleagues, he seems to be constantly absorbing ideas and stories to be put to use later, sometimes much later, on the more formal public levels of communication. This is especially true in social gatherings. Often, he admits, his wife is more intense and communicative on these occasions than he is. He, all the while, seems to be weighing ideas for their possible uses in future speaking engagements, working them into place even before an evening with friends has ended.

The ideas which find their way into his more formal presentations have undergone a long and involved screening process. He works and reworks an idea by speaking it aloud many times, not simply to friends, but to himself, often memorizing it in the process. One story may very well be sharpened and condensed over months before it satisfies his own critical standards and before it slips into his public communication. Even then, each time he delivers it publicly, he checks to eliminate any extraneous words, misleading syntactical arrangements, and confusions based on changed circumstances.

This slow, evolutionary form of idea processing is perfectly consistent with his conservative mental set. On the basis of careful observation and reflection, he inquires into the past to find answers to problems in the present and anchors his moves into the future squarely upon them. He generalized his feelings about this practice when he was describing the Muskegon Waste Management System:

"One of the reasons that the new idea is so very strong," he said, "is that it isn't a new idea at all. It's an old idea with a new twist."[12] His creative contribution comes, then, in giving more traditional American values a unique and lively turn for contemporary audiences.

The congressman is the classical model of conservative respect for things as they are. He seldom burns his bridges or breaks with an established idea to affirm completely new ones. He revises his ideas gradually by pieces and parts, transforming the old idea by easy stages. There is so much overlap in his thinking, zigzagging back and forth across old and new ideas, that it is not until his speaking is observed in perspective over a long period of time that a regular emergence of new and different ideas becomes clear.

He gives total concentration to the development of ideas, and his dogged willingness to stay with an idea, to repeat it, to rework it and to anguish over it, accounts in large part for the apparent effortlessness and fluency of his speaking. At first glance, it is not clear how concentrated and how steady his preparations for speaking are. Thriving on his responsibilities to audiences, he gives the impression that what it is he is doing is fun, not work, but the fact of the matter is that he has disciplined himself to work long hours on speeches and he makes each minute count. This sense of discipline dates to his earliest attempts as a public speaker:

> The first principle that I enunciate in the speech "The Price of the Best," which has been a guiding light to me, is the conviction that within reason a person can achieve most anything he wants, if he is willing to work hard enough to get it. I believe that my own speech career is an example of that maxim. People today often compliment me on what a gifted speaker I am. "How I wish I could speak so naturally and so easily," they will say, or "How I wish I had been given the gift of public speaking which you have." In my opinion, that is pure tommyrot. The vast majority of people are far more gifted with natural speaking ability than I. Even now, after thirty years of my working almost daily at the task of learning how to speak effectively, most of my colleagues in the Congress can give a far better spontaneous speech than I. I often find myself envying the far greater natural speaking gifts of my colleagues. If I have a leg up on some of them, it is because I have learned better than they how to prepare a speech and then take the time to pour into it the preparation that is so necessary to a good speech.[13]

Although he has moved from one subject area to another in his speaking career, his general themes have centered upon a conservative interpretation of American life. He has stressed the conservation of natural resources, the limitation of government, the strengthening of the military, the freeing of the individual, and the unleashing of free enterprise in trade and business. These ideas have become associated with recent conservative trends and are consonant with the Republican platform of 1980: tax cuts, restraints on federal spending, stronger enforcement of civil rights laws, stimulated foreign trade, aid to inner cities through enterprise zones and urban jobs, and a self-sufficiency in energy.[14]

Tying these Republican views together in the early 80s, he kept the analogy of the ship of state always in mind. He thought of the forty-eight years before 1980 as a setting of the ship's course which was leading the state into dangerous waters, climaxing in the Carter years with disastrous inflation, high interest rates, and the weakest kind of indecision in American foreign policy. He saw the election of 1980 as giving President Reagan and Congress the signal to implement a reversal of this course. It would take time, he felt, to slow the ship, divert it from economic icebergs, stop it, and, finally to turn it around and get underway in the opposite direction. But this was the mandate of the elections in 1980, he believed, when the American people accepted the slogan, "Vote Republican for a Change."

The theme of the Republican party in 1982, "Stay the Course," was his theme, too. Staying with the change of direction long enough for it to have some effect demanded patience and fortitude. Turning a giant ship of state around creates turmoil and requires time, and time was what he felt Republicans were buying to help the ship emerge from the confusion of this course reversal. He repeated this point time and time again as he campaigned for himself in Michigan and as he spoke for other Republicans in their campaigns.

He wrestled with different ways to express this idea. In March of 1982, he commented that a story he had heard in college had been haunting him.[15] A novice mountain climber had hired a guide in southern France to instruct him on his first climb. After the first day of their ascent, they stopped at one of the huts built on the mountain for climbers to rest the night. In the morning when they awoke, the young climber was frightened by claps of thunder and bolts of lightning. When he expressed his alarm to the guide, the guide hastened to observe, "But, my friend, it always storms at daybreak in the Pyrenees." Although Vander Jagt did not use this particular story in any of his speeches when he needed to illustrate the stresses and strains attendant upon a major change in the direction of government, he was mentally testing it against other analogies that he was using, e.g., "stopping a team of wild horses," and "getting medicine out of a bottle and into a very sick patient." These analogies were regularly used to relieve the stress which the slowness of the change placed upon the patience of his audiences as well as explain to them the complications of the process itself.[16]

This portrait of political change was at the very core of the Republican planning for the election of 1982. A strategy for debate was formulated and distributed to all of the Republican candidates for office. It was stated as a proposition and then put in strategic and rhetorical forms which were stripped down and put on three-by-five cards for memorization by the candidates. The strategic version was put on one side of the card, and the rhetorical version was put on the other:

THE REPUBLICAN PROPOSITION
FOR THE 1982 ELECTION
STRATEGIC VERSION

IF IT'S A PAST POLICY, IT'S DEMOCRATIC
...AND BAD.

IF IT'S A PRESENT PAIN, IT'S DEMOCRATIC
...AND BAD.

IF IT'S A PRESENT POLICY, IT'S REPUBLICAN
...AND GOOD.

IF IT'S A FUTURE BENEFIT, IT'S REPUBLICAN
...AND GOOD.

RHETORICAL VERSION

DEMOCRATIC POLICIES OF THE PAST ARE RESPONSIBLE
FOR THE PAIN OF THE PRESENT. THE DEMOCRATS STILL
EMBRACE THE TAX AND TAX, SPEND AND SPEND POLICIES
WHICH HAVE PREVAILED FOR DECADES AND WHICH WOULD
CONSIGN US TO STILL MORE INFLATION, RECESSION, AND
NATIONAL DECLINE.

REPUBLICAN POLICIES ARE BEGINNING TO CHANGE
AMERICA AND, GIVEN A CHANCE TO WORK, WILL LEAD
TO A FUTURE OF GREATER OPPORTUNITY, PROSPERITY
AND SECURITY FOR ALL OF US.

Basically, this proposition was developed in discussions among the members of the executive committee of the NRCC, but, according to Congressman Newt Gingrich, Mr. Bill Roesing gave it its first wording.[17] The proposition was not intended to carry the full burden of the candidate's give-and-take in confrontations with opponents. Its purpose was to lay out an either-or pattern of thinking which would assure each candidate of a basic strategy and an initial statement of that strategy in the face of attacks from Democratic opponents. The ultimate success of individual campaigns would necessarily depend upon the thinking and speaking skills of the candidates as they moved beyond these basic guidelines.

In marshaling his supporting materials for this proposition, Vander Jagt drew from a vast storehouse of ideas developed over years of experience and kept in several file drawers indexed by subject in his congressional office in the Rayburn House Office Building. These materials include brochures, letters, news clippings, poetry, tapes of old speeches, magazine stories, and hand-written notes. Scattered throughout these are examples or stories or "nuggets" which have seen service with many different topics on many different occasions. One such story about jelly beans came from the conclusion of a speech given by the Senate majority leader, Howard Baker, when he and Vander Jagt shared a speaker's platform early in 1981.

Before I stop, I'd like to give you one brief insight, maybe, a personal vignette that you might enjoy. The president has recommenced the business of having regular leadership meetings as well, and they're beginning to be very useful. . . . But the little vignette I want to show you for a moment—if you'll conjure up the image on Tuesday morning at 8:30—when all of us in the leadership went to the White House to an event advertised as a breakfast meeting. When we got there, there was no breakfast! That was a good start. There was a small sweet roll and coffee or tea, which gives you some measure of the frugality of this administration. But on the center of the cabinet table, and, you know, the cabinet room is a long, magnificent space in the West Wing of the White House, was a large bowl of jelly beans. I refer to it as the ceremonial bowl of jelly beans because, in addition to the large bowl of jelly beans in the center of the table which remained untouched, was a smaller bowl of jelly beans which the president passed around the table twice in the manner of administering the sacraments. And you would be amazed to see men and women at that table who had not thought of having jelly beans before breakfast choosing with enthusiasm among those assorted colors of the California imported jelly beans.[18]

This story became for Vander Jagt a standard illustration of the president's popularity as it appeared in a warmly human way. He used it time and time again in 1981 and 1982 to reinforce the idea that President Reagan's leadership ability was very much underrated and that this ability would prove to be an important reason why Republicans would add to their number in Congress.

Other forms of supporting materials located in the Vander Jagt files are quotations, analogies, and statistics, all of which regularly find their way into his speeches. While he is known for eloquence in delivery, the one much overlooked but the really most important ingredient in his effectiveness as a speaker is his use of a wide variety of supporting materials. Through these he establishes his logical appeal with audiences. Very recently, he has made increased use of newcaster's statements, allusions to modern music and TV figures, and sports analogies. Although he occasionally refers to specific football and basketball games, he almost always calls up baseball when he seeks a more general sports analogy. Other standard examples and analogies are derived from space exploration, nuclear power, scholastic achievement, and military tactics.

His files are replete with a record of suggestions and statements from other speakers, colleagues, and friends, e.g., Red McDaniel's *Scars & Stripes*,[19] speeches by the former congressman Tennyson

Guyer[20] and former Governor George Romney of Michigan,[21] and selections from the speeches and letters of such figures as Kenneth McFarland,[22] former President Richard Nixon,[23] Congressman Ed Bethune,[24] and Congressman Robert H. Michel.[25]

He added the following story to his repertoire from a speech by President Ronald Reagan:

> Once each year the House prayer breakfast group joins with the Senate breakfast group to have a National Presidential Prayer Breakfast. That is attended by the president, the Joint Chiefs of Staff, the Cabinet, and leaders from all over the world, three or four thousand strong. This year was a particularly moving experience. The prayer breakfast this year was closed by a few remarks from the newly inaugurated President of the United States. The meeting was taking place in a dramatic foreshadowing at the Washington Hilton Hotel. And President Reagan rose to speak and he said, "I don't want to give a speech this morning; I just want to tell you a story."
>
> He told a story about an unknown author that was walking along a seashore, and as he walked along the seashore he was walking at the side of his Lord. And [as] they walked along together, along the seashore, there opened up in the sky above him the experiences of his life in panoramic form, one after the other. When they came to the end of the seashore and his life's experiences up to that point, the author paused and looked back at the two sets of footprints in the sand. And he noticed that every once in a while there was only one set of footprints. And upon looking further, he noticed that wherever there was only one set of footprints it happened to correspond to a time in his life of great trial and tribulation and distress and trouble.
>
> He said, "Lord, you promised that if I would walk with you, you would always stay at my side, you would never leave me, you would always be with me. Why, then, did you run away whenever the going got toughest and I needed you the most?" The Lord smiled and said, "Oh, my son, I did not run away from you, I did not desert you. Where you see one set of footprints in the sand, it was there that I reached out and carried you in my arms."
>
> The president then concluded with these two sentences: "I know that in the days ahead there will be times when there is only one set of footprints in my life. If I did not believe that with all my heart, I could not face the awesome challenges ahead." Little did he realize when he spoke those words, how very soon there indeed would be one set of footprints in his life.[26]

Most of these all-purpose sources of ideas form the general background for speeches, but they are not consulted as much as they once were due to his greater reliance upon specifically prepared materials provided for him from speech to speech by his support staff. With each formal speech situation, Congressman Vander Jagt is given specific information about key issues, the listeners, and the location where he has been invited to speak in the form of "backgrounders." These are developed for him by staff members in his own congressional office if the speech is to be given in his own district in Michigan and by staff members in the National Republican Congressional Committee if the speech is made for congressional condidates or for the Republican party's general interests elsewhere.

A backgrounder basically provides up-to-date facts about the state, the city, and the community where he is to speak. The interests, beliefs, knowledge, emotional sensitivities, and the general activities of the people there, as well as the latest local problems, public issues, and sources of pride are included. If the region's professional or collegiate basketball team is winning and in the limelight, this becomes grist for the congressman's mill. If there are to be party dignitaries and local opinion leaders in attendance at any point in the visit, these are noted with biographical specifics wherever possible. If political rifts in the Republican party have developed, they are detailed ahead of time. Even the physical makeup and surroundings of the occasion are charted, including acoustical and visual peculiarities of the room or location where he is to speak. Media plans, interviews, press conferences, and candidate discussions are all included in the time schedule. They are planned and often walked through ahead of time by an advance team from his NRCC staff.

The information in backgrounders comes from a variety of places. General sources give facts and figures about the state, geographical location, and political history of districts and congressmen. The most helpful of these are *The Almanac of American Politics,* edited yearly by Michael Barone and Grant Ujifusa, and *Politics in America: Members of Congress in Washington and at Home,* also edited yearly by Alan Ehrenhatt (editor) and Robert E. Healy (associate editor). For specific and human interest background information, contacts with key Republicans in the district and state involved are made by phone and, if there is time, by mail. Certainly the person who invites Vander Jagt to speak is questioned with an eye toward "inside" information which may have a special bearing on what should or should not be said. Staff members also may have a special knowledge of the area to be visited, and they are called upon to share it.

The congressman also appreciates the staff's opinions on lines of thinking which might be included, ideas, and stories which might be applicable to the region. These are provided, not just in the written materials which are given to him before the trip, but in private conversations with staff on planes, cars, and in hotel rooms until the actual time when he faces the audience itself.

Although he may not make immediate use of any of the materials provided, the backgrounders are usually lengthy and detailed. As a case in point, the backgrounders prepared for Vander Jagt's speaking tour for fourteen candidates from October 11 to October 18, 1982, starting in Billings, Montana, and ending in Philadelphia, Pennsylvania, and touching down at Denver, Tucson, Las Vegas, San Francisco, Palm Beach, Tampa, Miami, and Atlanta, extended to two full loose-leaf notebooks approximating a two-volume book!

His own preparation time is built into the schedule as each speech situation is given individual attention. This holds even in cases where he is giving approximately the same kind of speech. In speeches of tribute for candidates in various districts, he obviously needs to recognize differences among the candidates so that he can develop reasons and supporting evidence which accord with these differences. This means building substantially different presentations from one stop to another. Even in instances where the major portion of his speech consists of boiler plate, the first five or ten minutes which are devoted to praise of the candidate are brand new and will never be used again.

Always, Vander Jagt's first fear is that he will not find time in the schedule for preparation. His need to prepare is especially acute because he does not use notes in the delivery of speeches. In addition. however, and of greater importance, his reputation as an accomplished campaigner forces him to take pains to fulfill the high expectations of his audiences. When he is introduced regularly as the pride of all public speakers, he feels an obligation to produce well beyond what people would consider an effective and eloquent message. This sense of responsibility makes him his own toughest critic.

The desire to surpass himself with each succeeding speech

produces in him a panic of preparation when he actually anguishes over ideas and their expression. On October 6, 1982, for example, after speaking to the National Chamber of Commerce at its conference kickoff breakfast in Washington from eight-thirty to nine in the morning, he was scheduled to welcome Republican challenger candidates who were to be at the White House Executive Offices for a briefing on the nation's unemployment problem by the White House staff at ten. As he only had forty-five minutes available to him for preparation of his second speech, he literally careened from the banquet hall, the Hall of Flags in the chamber's national offices, to a coffee room off the Patio where he sequestered himself for the full forty-five minutes.

What he did during this time is typical of what he does in preparation for all speaking engagements. He walked and talked his way through what would be a brief speech of welcome as many times as he could, phrasing, and rephrasing the ideas each time. He used every single minute until he had to leave to travel the distance between the National Chamber of Commerce offices to the White House offices. He gestured; he played with vocal inflections; he varied his rate of speaking. He moved constantly from one end of the room to the other as he experimented with the sequencing of ideas and the choice and arrangement of words. He prepared the speech by literally speaking himself into a state of readiness.[27]

This last thought is the key to his development of ideas. A speech is to be spoken, not written. If a speech is written and read, it becomes an "essay on its hind legs." It loses its identity as a living, moving form of communication. A speech, prepared his way, on the other hand, enables the speaker to take full advantage of interpersonal contact. Vander Jagt maintains that kind of contact completely, without manuscript or notes, without distractions of any kind. This freedom permits him to bring to bear on others the full force of his personality, and it derives from his extensive and thorough preparation.

In a very real sense, his personality is his preparation. As a conservative, and in some ways a puritan, he gives meticulous observance to promises made, to being punctual at all times, and to meeting obligations of all sorts with an almost religious fervor. Former President Ford referred to him as "the moral conscience" of Congress[28] with good reason. His background in the ministry and

64

the law makes itself felt in his total commitment to a gentleman's sense of contracts and agreements and specifically to those in his professional life as a speaker whether there are twenty or twenty thousand people in his audience.

Early in a speech to chiropractors, Congressman Vander Jagt received a standing ovation of such duration that the master of ceremonies moved to the speaker's lectern and, with an air of finality, presented him with a plaque to celebrate the group's approval of his voting record in the Congress. In so doing, he cut the speaker off after his introduction and just before he was about to launch into the body of his presentation.

Anyone in the audience would have thought that the congressman's overall design was nondirective because his five-minute introduction made the point that he could not in all justice urge his audience to become involved in politics since they were already deeply involved. He used a boxer's analogy to clarify this involvement when he said that they, like Sugar Ray Robinson, pound for pound, were the toughest competitors for their point of view in Washington. He also alluded to his mobile campaign tours through the Ninth District in Michigan where in each town, a line of people would be waiting to talk to him, and, for every eighteen people who wanted to criticize or complain, there were two who wished to thank him. One of these two, he said, would inevitably turn out to be a chiropractor.

To judge, then, from this factual description of his audience's involvement in political action, it would have seemed to the average listener that his design was relatively nondirective, that he was in a relatively detached, nonargumentative mood. Anyone familiar with his usual design as a campaigner would have been surprised that he had not taken his standard directive approach, the approach of the advocate. That same well-informed auditor would not have been in the least perturbed to find, as was actually the case, that the speaker had twenty more minutes of speech planned, and that the point to be made in those twenty minutes, never delivered, would have been a directive one, that Republicans, with the help of professional groups like chiropractors, should break history by gaining House seats in 1982.

If creativity is making something out of nothing, Vander Jagt is not creative. It is clear that he creates out of many things. He always arrives in a public speaking situation fully prepared with a positive contention and armed with reasons and plenty of evidence. As one of the flag bearers of the Republican party, he is used to the debate situation and to cross-examination by hostile journalists, so he has learned over the years that advocacy is his best defense.

The directive approach in politics has only recently returned to fashion. For thirty years after World War II, affluent Americans had freedom from economic hardship and were relieved of the necessity of ordering priorities strictly on the basis of merit. During these years, relatively few political programs were constructed around positive reasons; almost every program carried to the American public for approval was based on a problem or a need. In all good humor, it seems, Americans acepted a problem as a good reason for approving any attempt aimed at solving it. Since the austerities of the 70s, however, brought on in part by the consequences of instituting specific government programs in this way, it has become increasingly apparent that a description of need is not a reason for accepting anything. Negative circumstances, in and of themselves, do not constitute positive reasons for any one specific program. For example, recognizing the existence of problems in the United States is no reason to immigrate to Mexico. Many problems provoke many answers, but each answer must be judged on its own merits, not on the relative severity of the problem it is supposed to solve.

With this in mind, it is not hard to understand why, since World War II, reporters investigating problems have been given a greater hearing than advocates arguing a specific program or point of view. Gradually, however, over the last few years, the softer scientific approach in politics toward understanding social and economic problems has given way to the harder rhetorical necessity of advocating programs with well-reasoned arguments.

In this newer age, the late 70s and the early 80s, Vander Jagt's skills of advocacy, not to mention President Reagan's, have become more appreciated and more sought out by others. Indeed, to describe the political advocate is to describe the campaigning of Guy Vander Jagt. He is the modern prototype of the advocate. As a campaigner, he must be recognized as always speaking from strength, as taking the initiative in communication to establish Republican answers to social and economic problems. This he does by supporting specific programs and policies with good reasons and evidence.

At the moment a speaker offers reasons for a proposition or a program concerning the future, he or she has entered the realm of values. Reasons imply values; the better the reasons, the more valuable the proposition they support. Strength in communication, then, means offering the best program, i.e., that program which is grounded on the greater values inherent in the best reasons.

This is not to say that good reasons should be divorced from evidence. In fact, the reverse is true. Effective advocates base their reasons upon evidence, but when a piece of evidence stands alone, it has no value. It takes on human value only when it is associated with the advocate's reasons. When, for example, an individual's weight is observed to decrease with exercise, this fact, in and of itself, is neither good nor bad. If a speaker argues, however, that people should take exercise because it will decrease weight, the speaker has infused weight loss with value. The fact that weight loss and exercise are related positively can then be used as evidence to substantiate the speaker's reasoning. If, on the other hand, the speaker were to stop short of values, simply to expose for others the relationship between weight loss and exercise, the design would be nondirective explanation, a design in communication which represents the exact opposite of advocacy.

The advocate's case progresses from a positive proposition to good reasons to supportive evidence. This exactly describes Vander Jagt's logical design in his campaign speaking. His introductions and conclusions add substantially to his case, but they remain secondary to his reasoning and evidence.[29] His speeches of the 80s are all characterized in this way. The keynote address at the Republican convention in July of 1980 remains the most celebrated instance of this particular design.

Over and above an investment in values, the directive design of advocacy requires of the speaker a considerable amount of courage. Putting one's values on display exposes the ego to public attack, and the social pressures following a defeat in such cases can be debilitating. Further, a person who is known as a willing advocate, a debater, becomes a target for each and every Young Turk who wishes to publicize a competing group or idea. This design, then, not only courts attack but makes the speaker vulnerable to the loss of an image of judicial balance and calm dignity, both of which are crucial to leadership on the national level.[30]

Indeed, it also takes courage to undertake propositions of value for future policy. When a speaker recommends that a particular policy or plan should be accepted, an idea is being projected into the future. Such projections are always suspect. The only thing that is known with certainty about the future is the fact that nothing can be known with absolute certainty about the future. What *was* can be established in fact by empirical demonstration. What *should be* is always a probability, tenuous and open to debate. The road to security in communication, then, is to describe and analyze what has already happened. Determining the facts of the past follows rules which make the process relatively safe. Projecting a plan into the future means wrestling with an unknown environment as well as allowing for the weaknesses of the human beings upon whom such plans depend.

These are risks which no amount of preparation can eliminate completely, and taking them demands of the individual a kind of courage which extends beyond the plain, old-fashioned courage it takes to give a speech. Vander Jagt contended that Republicans should break historical precedent by adding to their number in 1982 because they had Reagan, resources, and the edge in redistricting.[31] He also argued that Americans should have voted for Ronald Reagan because he could provide greatness, unity, and a new beginning for America.[32] He even said that something good should happen to Americans because the United States has an abiding faith in God.[33] In each instance, he was clearly taking risks!

The process of formulating and defending value judgments for the future betterment of the community calls for a long-term optimism as well as courage. Making a positive statement about the future attests to an individual's willingness to live into the future and to invest time and energy in planning for it, and, in the case of the public speaker, to repeat those plans time and time again to different audiences. The advocate believes that there is a good life or the possibility of one and that it can be achieved and maintained.

This kind of idealism may repel the cynic as childlike, but it is crucial to advocacy. Without it, the advocate becomes too enmeshed in detail, absolute accuracy, and the fine-spun qualifications of scrutinizing reality. Speaking to others in support of a program for the future requires, first and foremost, that their imagination be aroused and brought to bear on the idea being developed. An accurate, detailed, well-qualified view of the environment does not fulfill that aim. Instead, the advocate must take a global approach with as few qualifications as possible and with a visionary's taste for dreams if interest and action are to be generated.

To be inspired to action, an audience's feelings must be stimulated. Optimism aids this reaction; pessimism drowns it in fear and depression. No speaker ever knew this better than Guy Vander Jagt. His speeches are filled with optimism, so much so that he could be criticized for not often enough giving speeches in which analysis of the problem is primary and for giving too many where answers are entertained without due concern for necessary qualifications. Certainly, in his recent political speaking, he has emphasized answers and their reasons in his persuasive design, but in his student years and in some early speeches and sermons, he used less directive designs, ranging from nondirective description and causation to the more indirective design of problem solving.[34]

What in fact has occurred in the persuasive designs he has employed over the years can be observed through his shifting of supporting materials from establishing problems to supporting reasons for his central theme or proposition. In his keynote address at the Republican Convention in July of '80, as an example, he certainly viewed Carter's program as a problem, but instead of pointing it up as a discrete first main idea and following with the Republican alternative as a solution to it and as a second main idea, thereby setting up a more indirect two-step sequence from problem to solution, what he did was to begin by emphasizing the Republican program in his initial statement of the proposition: Americans should support Ronald Reagan. Then, he used the Reagan-Carter differences as a giant comparison of the strong and the weak or the good and the bad to support the reasons he adduced to establish that proposition. Starting in this fashion immediately with the proposition is a more directive design than the indirective design of setting up a problem before undertaking the proposition in the form of a solution or an answer to it. President Jimmy Carter recognized the chief difficulty with indirection of this sort when he analyzed his own speaking: "I present an engineer's solution. Lay out the problem, lay out the possible solutions and then present a proposed answer. The trouble is that by the time I get to the answer, most people have quit listening."[35]

Giving a positive proposition emphasis reveals great optimism, but nowhere is Vander Jagt's optimism more pronounced than in his speech "Count Your Blessings." Even in the Watergate years, he told his audiences they should indeed count their blessings, and his conclusion to that speech, in poetic form, symbolized most vividly his irrepressibly optimistic and strongly constructive attitude as a speaker.

The last characteristic of the advocate which Congressman Vander Jagt embodies in his speaking is physical strength. Just making the trips necessary to maintain a speaking schedule of more than one hundred formal occasions each year demands a magnificent physical constitution. Beyond this, great stamina is necessary to sustain the high energy level required of campaign advocacy. In the low profile, detached, nondirective designs, the informality appropriate to the situation is reinforced by an easy, no-sale, subdued delivery which employs bodily positions, movements, and gestures which do not demand or symbolize strength, e.g., sitting, a quiet voice, casual dress, open palm gestures, and movements, if any, away from or parallel to the audience. The reverse holds with the more directive designs. In order to create a unity of design and delivery, the speaker stands, dresses formally, maintains eye contact, uses emphatic gestures, pushes the voice to enlarged conversation, and moves or leans aggressively and often toward an audience. This type of delivery requires more actual energy output from a speaker. The advocate in this sense might be thought of as charging an audience by sheer mental and physical vitality in order to inculcate values, to inspire in others the vision and the will to act firmly and positively in support of the proposition.

Only more directive designs can move people to greater achievement. A speaker cannot carry an audience to the mountain top by describing scenery. It takes more energy, more consolidation, more preparation, as well as the design of the advocate to inspire listeners to action.

The difficulties in fulfilling the advocate's role are compounded by a number of critical factors. When an audience is heterogeneous, particularly if it contains both friends and enemies, it creates a problem for the partisan. The advocate's ideal audience is the audience the congressman seeks: a strongly homogeneous audience, large, courteous, and friendly.[36] When enemies or important members of the opposition enter the picture, the full force of advocacy becomes blunted. Thoughtful qualifications, which antagonism necessitates, tend to dampen enthusiasm and force a more deliberate pace in the logical progression of ideas. They also produce hitches in the actual rate of delivery, destroying the mood. The broad allusions to statistical evidence and supporting materials are limited by a greater need for accuracy of detail and precision in the use of words. Special care must be taken to avoid extravagance of imagery and emotional appeals since an opponent, it is recognized, can have a field day with an emotional appeal or an anecdote which is inaccurate or overdone even by the very slightest bit.

On one occasion, Vander Jagt permitted himself to get boxed into a campaign situation where he knew many of these audience indicators were wrong. He spoke to the National Association of Home Builders at its 38th Annual Convention and Exposition in Las Vegas on January 23, 1982, at a time when many home builders of long-standing were going bankrupt. Their hostility was starting to show, but there were many friends in the audience, too, as he had been especially effective arguing for legislation in the Congress helpful to home builders. This mixed audience was further complicated by the presence of Congressman Tony Coelho of California, chairman of the Democratic Congressional Campaign Committee. It was also the one situation he can remember in which he had not carefully prepared himself. He despaired for weeks after the poor performance he made.[37] He spent far too much time, he felt, qualifying his ideas, rewording them, stopping and starting, trying to be gentlemanly, stumbling over courtesies, and, to top it all, assuming the conciliatory and hypocritical attitude of an honest broker instead of taking the role of the partisan in open and honest debate.

Another situational factor which makes a key difference to Congressman Vander Jagt's advocacy is the medium of television. The TV screen adds a dimension which has to be taken into account. As a "cool" medium, that is, a medium of communication which permits the listener greater detachment, it limits the degree of emotional involvement which should accompany advocacy. Here the "hotter" characteristics of the advocate tend to wash out. A medium which supports dramatic entertainment, particularly light hearted comedy, does not encourage a value-oriented, heroic,

71

optimistic show of rhetorical strength. Talk shows are the rule. Lounges and chairs, conversation, and free association encourage in speakers the rhetorical design of nondirection.

Further, campaigning with his own constituents in his own congressional district in Michigan means that substantial adaptations are demanded of Vander Jagt. It is a different experience to take his mobile van into a county courthouse parking lot where twenty people are lined up to talk to him, voters to criticize perhaps, but, nevertheless, honoring him by their presence.[38] When he is speaking for Republican candidates elsewhere in the country, he sweeps into a hotel where the ballroom is filled with Republicans who are not his constituents and who are honored by his presence. In the first case, he is the supplicant; in the second, the conquering hero. A hero with nothing to gain, can touch a lot more hearts than a campaigner who is seeking votes. At home, he devotes a great deal of time to explanation and inquiry, more nondirective approaches in communication.

Since design appears in the tactical clustering of ideas in the body of a presentation, it has little to do with the makeup of Vander Jagt's introductions and conclusions. His usual introduction, it has been noted, includes an expression of thanks and hearty compliments for the speaker who has introduced him and for his listeners generally. These comments are always appropriately gracious and set a mood of optimism and good will. Wherever possible, he draws parallels between his experiences and those of his listeners. When he spoke to the National Rural Electric Cooperative Association in Houston, Texas, he was alert to the history of rural electric cooperatives because, years earlier, the sponsor for his weekly half-hour television program called "What Goes On Here?" was the Rural Electric Cooperative of Michigan. Appropriately, he noted, "I learned that I don't believe a rural America would have made it without you, and I know that I wouldn't have made it to the House of Representatives without you."[39]

His conclusions are almost always of the "goose pimple" variety, emotionally charged and ringing. They are invariably effective, cementing the theme of the presentation as they move the heart. These, like his introductions, however, remain subsidiary to his logically structured arguments. Vander Jagt's delivery of these conclusions is always quiet and subdued, enhancing the emotional

72

impact. He never permits himself the luxury of becoming emotionally involved in his own concluding appeals. Although his delivery of speeches never draws attention to itself, it deserves to be addressed in a slightly more extended manner here.

Senator Howard Baker, majority leader in the Senate, who followed Congressman Vander Jagt as a speaker at the Frozen Food Association Conference in Washington, D.C., described his colleague's speaking through an allusion to his father-in-law, Senator Everett Dirksen:

> Good morning, ladies and gentlemen, I'm delighted to be here. I'm always a little intimidated when I follow on after Guy Vander Jagt. I stood in the hall, and I listened to the marvelous delivery and the exquisite enunciation that Guy brings to his presentation. And I was reminded, speaking of Senator Dirksen, who was my wife's father, I'm reminded of the story that someone once told when he was interviewed on a program and said, "Senator, is it true, is it true that you rehearse your speeches at great length, that you prepare them carefully and deliver them methodically and meticulously? Is it true that you choose your words, that you choose your words for their exact accuracy and content?" And he said, "No, I choose my words for how they taste." And, Guy, you have delivered, I'm sure, an excellent presentation this morning, but it sounded absolutely delicious from the other part of the room.[40]

Characterizing Vander Jagt as possessing a "delicious" delivery is certainly a poetic way of depicting the congressman's manner of presenting ideas, and it is true that his listeners do savor his ideas. However, his choice and arrangements of words, his verbal skills, his vocal and visual behavior, and his own visceral being are, in reality, plain and economical; in a word, conservative. He conserves time and energy both for his listener and for himself by preparing diligently for each individual speech situation. This continual and concentrated preparation allows his ideas to shine through the delivery effortlessly with instant and lively clarity, each sentence falling in just the right way on just the right side. His voice and gestures are rigidly controlled to highlight his ideas. He assiduously avoids drawing attention to himself. He dresses in the fashion of a conservative businessman and cultivates a spare, judicious use of dramatic animation. Always underplayed, his emotional appeals are never couched in purple patches nor embellished by extravagant movements and gestures. He remains confortably natural with or without a speaker's lectern, but he never relies on it for physical or psychological support.

This kind of subdued and concentrated efficiency of effort combined with a clear, crisp wording produces a buoyancy and lilt in his delivery which is raised to eloquence by near flawless diction. Mispronounced words, starts and stops, blockings, untimely pauses and gestures, and solecisms of any sort occur so rarely that they are virtually nonexistent.

The wonder of his broadcaster's kind of flawless delivery is that he uses no notes or manuscript of any sort. If he uses poetry, statistics, or quotations, he commits them to memory. In a sense, he delivers speeches from a mental script. So as not to parade his almost total recall, he often pretends to read quotations from blank sheets of paper. As a student debater he made a practice of shuffling blank three-by-five cards so as not to appear conspicuous as a show off.[41] One opponent who had not heard him speak before picked up these cards to verify some statistical evidence Vander Jagt had used in the debate. Seeing the blank cards, he proceeded to accuse Vander Jagt of falsifying evidence and was surprised a second time to find that each detail of these statistical data was accurate! Being able to function in this way makes Vander Jagt oblivious to TV cameras, public address systems, microphones, and speaker's lecterns.

As he moves from the speaker's platform and formal public speaking to the more informal interview situation or to question-and-answer periods with larger audiences, he needs less direct preparation time. He may use those materials which he has so meticulously prepared when he answers specific questions, but there is no need to sequence the ideas as different questions from different people make a cumulative flow or rhythm in presentation impossible. In addition, moving from the podium to the coffee table permits a more informal atmosphere which creates less need for a strict control of the elements of delivery.

The informal situation also gives the congressman an opportunity to point up his interest visually as a listener. He gives absolute and complete attention to others, seemingly absorbing every possible ounce of the weight of their ideas, This was clearly evidenced in the *MacNeil-Lehrer Report* on October 14, 1982, when he and Congressman Tony Coelho appeared together to discuss the prospects of their respective parties in the forthcoming election. His attention, when he was caught listening by the TV cameras, was riveted to others as they spoke. A pleasant and sympathetic facial expression conveyed an open attempt to understand and appreciate what was being said. This was in sharp contrast to Coelho's grim, hooded, or hand-covered countenance.

He demonstrated just as much interest when he listened to a farmer, an elderly retired couple, two businessmen, and the managing editor of the *Howard City Record* in Michigan, all of whom were crowded into the *Record*'s office on October 19, five days after his appearance on *MacNeil-Lehrer*. His attitude was respectful and attentive, and their requests for help as well as their points of view he accepted cheerfully.[42]

By way of summary, then, Vander Jagt's methods in the development, design, and delivery of ideas are classically conservative. He puts the idea first, immersing himself in background sources, conversations, and correspondence of all sorts to find the most appropriate materials for given audiences on specific occasions. As he moves from the informal, interpersonal levels of communication to the formal, extrapersonal levels, he becomes more demanding of himself. His preparation becomes more intense, his position on issues becomes more firmly fixed, and his tactics become more directive in their persuasive design.

Originality he views as a challenge to make what is universal and timeless up-to-date and of immediate practical value in solving modern problems. He never abandons the old without testing it against the new. Just as he has made an art form of breathing new life into old ideas in his speaking, so he has sought out and helped to effect a new beginning for the Grand Old Party. How has he done this? How has he earned his unique and vital role as the premier congressional campaigner in the Republican party? He has done it by the repetition of the simple and homely virtues in speechmaking, by the thorough and painstaking development and design of his ideas, and by a straightforward, plainly conservative approach to their delivery.

5

How Did He Learn?

I T SHOULD be readily apparent that the Honorable Guy Vander
Jagt is unique in contemporary politics. He is not only a trial
lawyer who has sought political influence in public affairs; he is a
professional commentator, having worked as a broadcaster in
commercial television and as a disc jockey on radio. Beyond these
excellent but relatively standard credentials, he is a Protestant
minister who has committed himself to a necessary goodness in
American life, a belief which has surfaced in his speeches in many
ways, the most celebrated of which is his repeated reference to Alexis
de Tocqueville's explanation of American greatness through
goodness. It was Tocqueville, it is recalled, who wrote in the early
1800s that America is great because America is good. This three-
dimensional background, the law, the mass media, and the church,
sets Vander Jagt aside from almost all other congressmen.

His very special and distinctive characteristic, however, is that
he has unabashedly embraced the career of public speaking to
achieve both his educational and professional objectives. He
maintains complete equanimity when someone introduces him as
"the best speaker I ever heard," or when he is asked "to show them
how a real speaker does it." In a modest, direct way, he proceeds to
live up to the most grandiose introductions, proving time and time
again how truly exciting the act of communication can be. And so, it
has been pointed out, he has built a reputation as Congress's finest,
and, as such, he has become a national spokesman for the
Republican party.

He gained this recognition by purposely devoting a lifetime to
the mastery of skills necessary to superiority in public speaking. He

has refined these skills, as already suggested, in every major type of platform in contemporary American life: forensic debate in the courtroom, homiletics from the pulpit, radio and television presentation, legislative speaking on the floor of Congress, and ceremonial speaking on special occasions where tribute needs to be given or where Republican audiences need a "view from the mountain top" as an inspiration to greater efforts in achieving their political goals. The question as to how he got his start toward these achievements still remains to be addressed.

His interest in communication was evident as early as the fourth grade when by "talking to friends" he edged out a classmate by one vote for class leader.[1] This tendency toward active participation in student affairs continued when he went to Cadillac High School. He was president of the Hi-Y, president of the Westminster Fellowship, vice-president of the Senior Class, vice-president of the Cadillac Youth Center, co-salutatorian, and co-editor of his high school newspaper. He took part in dramatic productions and speech contests, and he sought out and received special help and encouragement in these efforts from his teacher of speech, Mr. Matt Van Oostenberg.

By the time he graduated from high school, he had already filled a pulpit in Tustin, Michigan. He explained his unusual circumstance in an interview on "Hour of Power":

I had attended between my junior and senior year in high school a church summer camp. It was a real mountaintop experience for me. So when I got back home and our minister said he was overburdened with a second church that he had to take care of, and would I please take it over from him, still in the glow of that mountaintop experience, I said, "Yes, I would become the preacher of that little church in Tustin, Michigan." And my very first sermon, my very first Sunday, I had just turned seventeen. They were so proud because they turned out everybody, and they had the biggest congregation of all time, and it was eighteen people!"[2]

He was speaking in public before he was driving an automobile. Since he had no driver's license when he started preaching, his father drove him to church, waited outside in the car, and drove him home again. After a month in his new role, when the young preacher felt more confident with his congregation, he permitted his father to come into the church, to participate in the service, and to listen to the sermon.[3] By the end of his year in Tustin, he was preaching to a congregation of eighty people each Sunday.

His life's goal had already crystallized when he matriculated at Hope College in September 1949. At the age of eighteen, he decided to build a career as a public speaker. He spoke with the chairman of the Department of Speech, Dr. William Schrier, and said that he wanted to share his "ideas, emotions, and convictions" with others, with their "minds," their "hearts," and their "souls." He wanted, he said, to be a "great speaker." Professor Schrier, an experienced speech teacher, responded appropriately but carefully, trying not to undercut youthful enthusiasm, when he told his energetic young charge that this was putting the cart before the horse. He said in effect that when great problems are confronted by persons of great ability, *sometimes* great speeches emerge. Greatness in communication is a happy by-product of achieving other goals; it is not an end in and of itself.[4]

As the student was willing to do almost anything to succeed as a speaker, the teacher accepted him on the student's terms. And the student convinced his teacher. Shortly before Vander Jagt's graduation in 1953, Schrier announced to his wife in all seriousness, "Guy may someday be president of the United States."[5]

In his freshman and sophomore years, young Vander Jagt won first prize in the Men's Extempore Peace Contest in the Michigan Intercollegiate Speech League, first place in a debate tournament in Grove City, Pennsylvania, and was made secretary of Phi Tau Nu fraternity and representative to the Student Council from the Emersonian Fraternity. In addition, he took every opportunity to "share ideas with others" in an extracurricular, off-campus way. He got a job as a disc jockey at WHTC radio in Holland. He was the master of ceremonies at the Tulip Festival. He toasted the May Day Queen, and he gave speeches to junior high and high school groups in the area. In a letter home, he wrote:

> The talk on politics at the junior high school went over very well. There was a question-and-answer period after, and the group was largely Republican, so they really tried to put me on the spot. After I left, they all remarked, "Isn't it too bad that such a good speaker has to be a Democrat."[6]

78

In the spring of his freshman year, he gave a Memorial Day address in Cadillac and the commencement address at Gerrish-Higgins High School in Roscommon, Michigan.[7]

During his last two years in college, Guy Vander Jagt continued to speak in the community, to represent the student body as its president,[8] and to give award-winning orations. As he looked back over his four-year record in collegiate competition, he never entered an extempore speaking contest where speakers were ranked that he did not finish in first place. Even more unusual, he was the state champion debater in the Michigan Intercollegiate Speech League debate finals in his sophomore, junior, and senior years. As a freshman, he placed second with a total of 119 merit points. The state champion that year won with 120 merit points. Vander Jagt's overall record as a student speaker is probably, to this day, without equal in collegiate competition.

His first formal oration in manuscript form in college competition was "The Price of the Best." He was only a junior, but Professor Schrier felt he was ready for the toughest competition and entered him in the annual Old Line Oratorical Contest. Those students who won state championships competed in the finals which were always held at Northwestern University in Evanston, Illinois. These were the closest thing to a national championship in existence. While he made the finals, he recalls, "It was the only time in...intercollegiate competition in oratory that I failed to finish first."[9] He placed third.

His next student speech resulted from his experience over the summer of 1952, between his junior and senior years, in Bonn, Germany, as the community ambassador from Holland, Michigan, with the Experiment in International Living. The title, "Life with Lizi," refers to his adopted sister, Lizi, in the family with whom he stayed in Bonn. The speech was condensed for competition in the National Peace Oratory Contest as the "Bonn Report."

Finally, his third student oration was a tribute to John Marshall which won the Hearst Newspaper Oratorical Contest National Finals. In total, this speech earned $1,900: $50 for the district contest, $100 for the regional, $250 for the state final, $500 for the national divisional, and $1,000 for the national contest first-place ranking. Indeed, this was a substantial sum in 1953.

In each of these speeches, he worked closely with Professor Schrier, whose philosophy of rhetoric has structured the congressman's approach to the speech situation to this day. Basically, Schrier defined oratory as the art of "getting over a persuasive message to a specific audience."[10] He recognized only three different types of persuasive messages: the problem-solution type, the philosophical type, and the eulogy or speech of tribute. Ninety percent of all orations, he maintained, are of the first type. Exposition he did not include under the heading of persuasion, and speeches to inform, he felt, would not qualify for contest work in oratory. Sermons, except for those which are strictly expository, he believed, might be thought of as suitably "oratorical" in nature. His suggestions for producing an oration were for the most part Ciceronian.[11] Two attitudes which Schrier left indelibly etched on the young orator's mind were his complete faith in direct and intensive preparation and his preference for advocacy over exposition. Both remain key influences in the congressman's standard operation procedure in speaking, and they help to explain his special successes in political communication.

Vander Jagt's ready acceptance of his professor's judgments against exposition and in support of advocacy is explained in part by his own natural predilections. Even in his freshman studies, he had to work at expository writing. The "I'll-do-this-if-it-kills-me" attitude is readily apparent when his essay on "My Room" is compared to his essay in support of the proposition that Hope College should be viewed as the best college in the United States.[12] The former is a dull, plodding, and somewhat confusing description of his room, starting with an "average-sized pine door" and running from the north wall in a "clockwise direction" to the south hall. The west wall is somehow lost in between a corner and the door, leaving the reader contemplating points on the compass and number of walls. Advocacy came more easily, however. His case in support of Hope College is composed of a number of lively, well-supported reasons: the close bond between professor and student, the friendliness of the student body, and a salutary religious environment. The supporting materials are concrete, interesting, and clearly related to the reasons which they are intended to support. His reaction to these two different designs presaged a special lifetime affinity for the tools of the advocate, reasons and evidence, and, wherever possible, a ready avoidance of expository forms of expression.

After he was graduated from Hope College in June of 1953, Vander Jagt's career zigged and zagged across three different fields, the ministry, the mass media, and the law. He also traveled regularly back and forth between Michigan and the East Coast.

He went directly to Yale Divinity School and was there from September of 1953 to June of 1954. Then he returned to Cadillac, Michigan, for the summer, and started reporting the news at 6 P.M. and 11 P.M. for WWTV Channel 9. He began signing off as a newscaster with, "That's the top of the news from the top of Michigan," a news imprimatur similar to Fulton Lewis, Jr.'s, but different enough for him to make it his own. This statement, by the way, was literally true as the station's aerial was on the highest point of land in the Lower Peninsula of Michigan. In a sense, his name identity in that part of the state was based on his synthesis of two tops, the top of a hill and top of the news. He enjoyed what he was doing and decided to continue broadcasting through the fall of '54, but in January of 1955, he returned to Yale to resume his studies with Richard Niebuhr, Liston Pope, and William Sloane Coffin. He was especially attracted to the philosophy and teachings of Richard Niebuhr.

The school year 1955-1956 found him once again in Bonn, Germany, on a Rotary Fellowship, but he returned to Michigan in the summer of 1956. Since his mother was terminally ill with cancer, he was permitted by Yale to continue his work for credit at Western Seminary in Holland, Michigan, and to take his last required course for graduation from D. Ivan Dykstra, professor of philosophy at Hope College. He was graduated in June 1957.

The following fall, he filled the pulpit of the Cadillac Congregational Church and, at the same time, went back to his television broadcasting, working Monday through Friday at WWTV. He prepared his Sunday sermon from 8:30, Saturday morning, to midnight. His one chance in a lifetime to play golf often enough to improve his game was wedged in during the summer and fall months of this year. The path he chose and the necessary preparation to its following left no time for this kind of entertainment.

In January of 1958, he began traveling back and forth between Michigan and the East Coast again. He enrolled in law school at Georgetown University, and, always looking for another responsibility, became the public relations assistant for Robert McIntosh, former congressman from Port Huron, Michigan. He had arrived in Washington in the middle of winter with a suitcase, the Bible, and a copy of *The Brothers Karamazov*. He was so busy working all day and going to school in the evening that, when he left Washington in the summer to enroll in the law school at the University of Michigan, he returned with the same books, still reading in both of them. He had found, however, despite his early misgivings, that he thoroughly enjoyed reading the law and proceeded to formulate a plan for a future in politics.

By the fall of 1958, he was enrolled in Ann Arbor, was working as a radio disc jockey at WPAG, and was producing "What Goes On Here?" a weekly television program in Cadillac. In 1960, after two years at high speed, he completed his law degree and with that, he ended his work as a student. Reviewing that decade, he had been awarded a baccalaureate degree and two advanced degrees, and had established himself as a professional performer in radio and television.

For the next four years, Vander Jagt understudied Harold Sawyer, a leading lawyer with the law firm of Warner, Norcross & Judd in Grand Rapids. After he had graduated from the University of Michigan, he asked Judge Robert Dethmers, a fellow alumnus of Hope College, to give him the name of the law firm with the best trial lawyer in the country. Dethmers promptly introduced him to Sawyer. Years later, Sawyer was to follow his protégé into politics as a congressman representing the Fifth District in Michigan.

When George Romney was appointed secretary of HUD and William G. Milliken left his office as state senator to replace Romney, Vander Jagt went to Cadillac with his bride of a week, Carol Doorn Vander Jagt, to run for Milliken's former seat. Shortly after they arrived in Cadillac, a full-page advertisement was published favoring the other Republicans running in the primary, and his cousin's name appeared in support of another candidate! So, with his vigorous young wife and no more than two or three friends, he undertook the long, hard campaign from April to November of 1964. Building on his former contacts through his earlier television exposure and speeches in the community, he gradually overtook the competition and won his first and his most difficult political campaign. Subsequently, he was chosen by members of the press gallery as the outstanding freshman in the state senate.

The manner of much of his person-to-person campaign speaking in the first election was determined by his Democratic opponent, Dr. Eugene Gershon, an established doctor who owned a hospital and had overwhelming resources to pour into the campaign. Gershon said simply, "Guy, you are a young man with no money, and I can outspend you ten to one. I'll promise not to spend anything, if you don't, and let's debate together all over the district." This kind of gallantry, as well as a full schedule of debates with an earnest opponent, made his first election a unique experience for the young politician. After the results were in, the victorious Vander Jagts and the vanquished Gershons spent a two-day vacation together in New York City where Dr. Gershon bought Mr. Vander Jagt a new wardrobe of clothes for a delayed honeymoon in Europe. While speaking in Europe and later in the United States, Vander Jagt made constant use of this experience as a classic example of the good and generous sportsmanship possible in American politics.

Once again two years later, he ran for an open political seat when Robert P. Griffin left the Ninth Congressional District in Michigan to fill a vacancy in the United States Senate left open by the death of Patrick McNamara. He won this campaign by the "largest vote majority of any of the fifty-nine new Republican members."[13]

At this point in his career, his public speaking engagements as well as his day-to-day congressional business became subject to and dominated by his committee assignments. He was appointed to the Science and Astronautics Committee and the Government Operations Committee where he was placed on the Conservation and Natural Resources Subcommittee. These assignments, along with the special interests of his administrative assistant, Bernard "Bud" Nagelvoort, led him to champion issues related to ecology and the environment: space, water, fish, and the Sleeping Bear Dunes National Park in northern Michigan. In a real sense, Vander

Jagt was one of the congressional pioneers in the ecology movement when, early in the 1960s, he declared war on pollution. He thought of himself as witnessing for the environment when he urged President Nixon to make the 70s the decade of the environment. By the time Congress and the country made the environment an issue of first rank, however, he had moved on to different committee assignments and new subjects for his speeches.

In 1971, he became a member of the House Committee on Foreign Affairs and got specific assignments on subcommittees for State Department Organization and Foreign Operations for Africa and Europe. Subsequently, his speeches began to follow these newer interests, and his travels were broadened to include Africa and the Far East. President Nixon sent him abroad after the Chinese *entente* to explain the Nixon Doctrine in Japan, Taiwan, and South Korea. In this limited sense, and under the most difficult circumstances, he became a spokesman for America abroad. He spoke in countries ranging from the most closed communist satellite, Czechoslovakia, to the most open, Yugoslavia.

While on his 1973 trip to Korea with his wife, his notes were kept in letter form to their daughter, Virginia, who had remained in the United States. In his January letter to Ginny, the congressman lamented his scanty briefing and lack of information on the country he was visiting:

> No one can understand in our U.S. missions abroad, no matter how frankly you confess it, how little the average congressman knows of a strange country he's visiting for the first time. The theory was that I would have many hours on the plane on the way to the Orient to read the briefing materials on Japan, Korea, and Taiwan so I'd know something when I arrived. At the last minute, however, USIS discovered that whoever had prepared the Korean section had classified it and then had gone on vacation. Apparently the only one who can unclassify something is the someone who classified it, and he was unavailable so there was no Korea in my briefing book. So it was with extremely limited knowledge that I faced the questions of the Yale Club a few short hours after my arrival....

He went on to describe briefly the three main tenets of the Nixon Doctrine:

1. The U.S. will keep its commitments.
2. The U.S. will continue to provide a nuclear shield for non-nuclear nations threatened by a nuclear nation.
3. We look to the non-nuclear nation threatened in non-nuclear ways to provide the substantial measure of its own defense. Whatever that country can do for itself, we expect it to do. What it can't do, we would expect to continue to do. But we expect it to do more, wherever possible, through regional cooperation.

He concluded as follows:

> In a way, I was walking a narrow line. On the one hand, reassuring Korea that the U.S. commitment was as strong as ever and, on the other hand, telling them they had to do more because we were going to do less. But on the whole, I think the message got across clearly. It's easy to appreciate their concern. For as long as the farmer in the rice paddy can remember, he has heard U.S. planes zooming overhead and seen U.S. tanks rumbling down the highway. As long as he sees their presence, he feels secure that the U.S. will be at his side if the North Koreans spill over the border and try to seize South Korea by force. When he sees and hears the U.S. planes and tanks no more, how can he be sure they will come back when the enemy attacks? This is his concern.[14]

In 1974, change came rapidly in the fortunes of the Republican party. That year saw Watergate to a tragic conclusion. The disasters which began with Spiro Agnew's resignation in October of 1973 ended with Richard Nixon's farewell address in August of 1974. These events were not without their impact upon Congressman Vander Jagt. He suffered the anguish of any Republican with conscience, torn between staunch loyalty to the party's leader and a deep sense of justice and fair play. His fortunes seemed no better than the party's. He was in the hospital for several weeks with pneumonia, and he was plagued by self-doubt as he geared up for one of his most difficult campaigns since his very first for the state senate.

But he won his 1974 congressional campaign, and he was heartened by the appointment of his fellow congressman from Michigan, Gerald R. Ford, as the president of the United States. He became a part of the party's leadership in Washington when in December 1974 he ran for and won the chair of the National

Republican Congressional Committee, already described as the political arm of Republicans in the House of Representatives. Peter DuPont of Delaware, a liberal Republican, was running against John Rousselot, a John Birch Society Republican member from California. There was so much room down the middle that Vander Jagt was able to start late and edge his way to victory by one vote, shades of the fourth grade and the importance of "talking to friends." He was now included in weekly leadership meetings at the White House with President Ford. His committee assignment was also changed. He was assigned to the powerful Ways and Means Committee with responsibilities on the Subcommittee on Trade and the Subcommittee on Select Revenue Measures.

It was during the Ford years in the White House that Vander Jagt became a spokesman for the Republican party, a force on the political scene to be reckoned with, but this phase of his career has been treated in sufficient detail elsewhere. It remains only to point out that, while the range of subjects Congressman Vander Jagt had covered in his thirty-year career as a speaker cut across the full spectrum of political issues, certain key subjects emerged as especially important to him in specific time periods over those years. Experiences studying and discussing in the areas of concern in his congressional committee assignments were made the basis for his speaking. Recognizing the speakers's need to be well-informed, he always drew from these immediate interests in his choice of subjects and audiences. As a student in the early 50s, his primary concern was *war and peace,* and, reminiscent of Harry Emerson Fosdick, he suggested in a unique way that people should work as hard at peace in peacetime as people work at war in wartime, a bold message for the 50s and for a country flushed with victory after World War II.

In the late 50s and early 60s, *love, goodness,* and *positive thinking* became regular themes for him in pulpits in central Michigan. Association with the law firm of Warner, Norcross & Judd from 1960 to 1964 brought him face to face with *legal issues* and *forensic speaking,* arguing cases before the bar. During the late 60s, his emphasis as a political speaker shifted to *environmental concerns* such as space, water, and land development.

After the surprise *entente* with communist China in the early 70s, President Nixon called on him to serve as his representative abroad in the Far East. He also played a diplomatic role in Africa

86

and Europe, speaking in defense of the Nixon Doctrine which amounted to a lower profile in American *foreign policy.*

The year of 1974 was the turning point in his career. He was elected to the chairmanship of the NRCC, and he negotiated a move from the Committee on Foreign Affairs to the Committee on Ways and Means in the House of Representatives. These changes all converged upon him to produce another readjustment in his speaking career from foreign matters to *domestic politics.* This switch was established finally when he became the chief stump speaker for other congressional Republicans, both incumbents and challengers, over the years from 1975 to 1980. From 1976 on, he was recognized as a party spokesman, speaking at first for Gerald R. Ford and then for a Republican Congress. The only recent change in his speaking since the period from 1974 to 1980 has been his specific support of President Ronald Reagan. Persistently, since November 1980, he has contended Republicans in Congress would continue to gather strength in Washington by close cooperation with the White House.

Summarizing his speaking career in this fashion abbreviates many of the important issues in the history of American political life from the early 50s to the present. He seems always to be forecasting the future, moving in the creative vanguard of politicians seeking to answer new problems. True, his answers are based on traditional beliefs, but he revitalizes them with the latest developments and modern, up-to-date terminology. Politically and personally he is a conservative thinker, especially critical of excesses and waste in human talent and natural resources, unwilling to give up the best of the old ways in the process of taking up the new.

His speaking has evolved over the years from idealism to realism, from international issues to national issues, and from the religious to the political implications of problems which require congressional action. In the process, he has learned the languages of the academician, the minister, the lawyer, the ecologist, the diplomat, the politician, the economist, and the statesman. Understanding and using these languages through practical experience has produced a statesman-orator able to communicate creatively and clearly to his fellow citizens the most difficult issues of the day, and, as such, he has become a national force in affecting the course of contemporary political events.

How, then, did he learn the professional skills necessary to becoming one of a few select spokesmen for the Republican party? He recognized, first, that political democracy absolutely requires modern professional communicators to keep the public and policymakers in close touch. He then prepared himself in all of the major areas of modern political communication in order to assume such a role. He mastered every form of communication from the most personal face-to-face speaking to the most mechanical place-to-place types of the mass media. He is, indeed, a speaker for all occasions with any audience.

He prepared himself specifically for what he is: a political orator and a national spokesman for the Republican party. True to his purpose, he occupies that unchartered twilight zone between policymakers and the public. He translates each for the other, pointing out areas of common concern, guiding the public through areas of anxiety to keep them in communication with the tight core of thinkers who take immediate responsibility for leadership. Vander Jagt put this function perfectly when he wrote, "As long as I can remember, I defined my career as wanting to share ideas, emotions, and convictions with the minds, hearts, and souls of other people."

Speeches From the 80s

To the Freshman

Congressman Vander Jagt's responsibilities relating specifically to the business of the National Republican Congressional
Committee naturally included speeches to inspire groups central to
the party's success. He regularly spoke to Republican congressional
candidates when they met together in Washington, D.C. He
supported these candidates individually by speaking to their staffs
and close supporters at local fundraisers in their districts. He also
spoke often to business and professional groups. As chairman of the
NRCC, he addressed the committee members, staff, and
congressmen in discussions and special-occasion meetings
throughout the year. Examples of each of these speech situations are
included here in his speeches from the 80s.

In "To the Freshman," given on December 1, 1982, the
chairman spoke to the successful Republican candidates for House
seats when they first met as a group of freshmen congressmen-elect
at a reception and dinner in their honor at the Hyatt Regency Hotel
on Capitol Hill. There were twenty-five of the twenty-six winners
present; Congressman-elect Jack Swigert was too ill to attend. The
total of twenty-six was exactly half of the number of the freshman
class of 1980 so the occasion was characterized by mixed blessings.
Elated over their own good fortune, the freshmen who were there
were, nevertheless, thinking of those who were not so fortunate.
Vander Jagt was sensitive to this situation and introduced his speech
with videotapes of political ads of some of the most successful
candidates, drawing their thoughts back to the best of the
campaigns.

91

W EREN'T THEY terrific? If you think you enjoyed seeing those commercials tonight, wait until you see them again in two years.

I'm going to use the authority of the chairmanship tonight to rearrange the order of the program just a little bit. The program consisted of meeting the distinguished Republican leadership team. We've done that. Getting acquainted with one another, via the delightful television commercials; we've done that. Then you were supposed to introduce yourselves one at a time with a line or two about your family and campaign, and then I was supposed to close with a speech.

I have asked the staff to be sure that this dinner and your first day end on a high note, and I am very, very confident that your introductions of yourselves will be a far higher note than any words that I can possibly utter. So you're going to listen to me now and then introduce yourselves after I have made my speech, and, as a matter of fact, my old-time colleagues will be delighted to know that I don't really have a speech tonight. I think all of us have heard enough campaign speeches for the year 1982.

I do, however, want to share with you a few thoughts and congratulate you again on your victories and, once again, tell you how proud I am of each of you and how thankful and grateful I am that you won and that you succeeded. As I mentioned this noon, if all of you had lost instead of won, that pendulum would have swung back with a vengeance toward the old program of big spending and big government that created the economic misery that we're struggling with today. Because you won, we still have within our grasp the glittering, golden opportunity of continuing to move in this new direction until the day the programs bear fruit and, in 1984, we recapture what we lost and beyond and move toward that majority coalition that can lead this country for decades to come, leading us toward growth, opportunity, and prosperity and freedom for all our people.

You've come now to the, near the, end of your first day together as a class, and you have begun an association with a group that will be the most precious group in your lives and for all of the rest of your years. You, in the months and years ahead, will laugh together and cry together; you'll struggle together; you'll fail together; you'll succeed together.

You are, indeed, a very extraordinary class. As Ed Bethune said, given the conditions out there, you had to do it this year, as a Republican, to make it. The prevailing winds were not our way, and only the toughest and the best and the finest survived. Thank goodness, you were so fine.

It's a class that's a little bit older than the freshman classes of the past couple of elections. Four of you are in your thirties; nine of you are in your forties; ten of you are in your fifties; and there's one lucky guy who's still in his twenties. If you take the three or four babies aside, the average age of this class is fifty. I happen to believe that's a wonderful age.

This class is made up of nine state senators, two state representatives, a couple of former speakers of the house, a senate majority and senate minority leader, a circuit judge, a county executive, a couple of mayors, some businessmen (manufacturers, insurance, accounting, travel, electronics). There are two bankers, and, once you check the price of housing in this area, you might want to make the acquaintance of this kind of person. There are a couple of former congressional assistants. That's how Bob Michel, our Republican leader, got his start. We have a former broadcaster, a former Vietnam POW, a former astronaut.

It is, indeed, an incredible class, and you did have to be very good to make it here in 1982, and I am totally convinced that in your midst tonight are a couple of future U.S. senators, maybe a governor or two, and certainly a member of some president's cabinet down the road, and, who knows, perhaps in your midst, very possibly, there is one who is starting that road tonight that will take him all the way some day, or her, to 1600 Pennsylvania Avenue.

This has been a week for me of enormously mixed emotions. It has been a week of great sadness and gladness, a week of deep joy and sorrow. The gladness, and the joy, is sharing vicariously the thrill of your wins and the incredible stories of how you won and what you had to do. It is a recognition that, at least in my belief, there are very few thrills in life ever that are greater than being elected to Congress the first time you do it. After Gerry Ford had been defeated in 1976, but was still in the White House, he had a few of us down, and, before a crackling fire, he started reminiscing over his political career. He said, "It may be hard to believe in view of all of the thrills that came down the line, the greatest thrill of all in my entire

93

political life was the night I heard I had won, and I was on my way to the Congress of the United States."

You may have one moment of thrill ahead of you that rivals that, and that's that day next month when you walk onto the floor of the House and, your children and your spouses and your friends watching, you raise that right hand, and you're sworn in and become a member of the greatest deliberative body in the history of mankind.

Though I've shared your personal joy and gladness and the joy and gladness that because of your victory we retain the chance and the opportunity to continue the new beginning that we have started under the leadership of Ronald Reagan, the sadness and the sorrow that I mentioned is that there aren't more of you, that some of our colleagues have fallen by the wayside.

Monday of this week, I went to the graduation of the freshman class of two years ago. Fourteen of those fifty-two ran and lost on November 2nd. One by one, they went around and told just a little bit about their campaigns and what had happened to them and how big those turkeys were who had the audacity to run against them, but you can imagine, there was a great deal of nostalgia in the air, sorrow over the fourteen who weren't making it back. In fact, the first one said how happy he was to be with everybody, with those who had won and those—who did not win. He said, "I described it that way because I can't say that other word."

One of the others who had lost—not lost—one of the others who did not win, stood up to speak, and he happened to be the class comic. No matter how bad the situation, he always had people rolling in the aisles, and, when he stood up, even though he hadn't won, an anticipatory chuckle went through the whole group. And he said, "All you other people have quoted Shakespeare and Longfellow." He said, "I prefer to quote Teresa Brewer." He said, "It's my party, and I came here to cry"—then went on to say, "When I heard I'd lost, I did pretty well, and, then, when I had to make that concession speech to the hundreds of workers who had done so much for me, I did pretty well." He said, "I did extremely well when I went before the television cameras and the lights for the last time." He said, "I even did well when I drove home in the middle of the night, and my wife was beside me, and my kids were in the back seat." He said, "And then I got home; I went down in the basement

94

and hid where my kids and my wife couldn't see me and, then, I cried."

And he went on to say how proud he had been to have been here, to have been a member of the House of Representatives, and then he went on to say he was even prouder of something else, and that was the recurrent theme through the whole night of those who won and those who did not. And that was how proud they were to have been members of that freshman class of 1980.

You're going to have that same pride someday because that which gave them pride is what will give you pride. They felt they were members of a class that made a difference and that continued, started us, in a new direction. Thanks to your victories, we have the possibility that their efforts and sacrifices will not have been in vain, and we can continue this new direction on the road to growth, opportunity, and prosperity and freedom for all.

I know that your first two years won't be as easy as their first two years, and those years weren't very easy. Fifty-two of them came sweeping in. Only twenty-six of you came sweeping in, and we lost some votes. I wish we had been dealt a better hand on November 2nd in the form of more votes. Those of you who dabble in cards know that it isn't always the number of aces that you hold; it's how you play the cards that determines whether you win the game.

I wish we had been dealt better weapons, in terms of more votes, but the weapons we have aren't so bad. They are formidable, indeed. We have the issues; we have the ideas; we have the forward look. We have two-thirds of the American people telling the pollsters emphatically they don't want to go back to the old programs of the past. We have a leader in the White House of unmatched communicative ability, the ability to articulate the hopes and the dreams of the American people for a better tomorrow. And we have the talent and the winning spirit and the energy and the vitality that you bring to the effort, and we have an outstanding Republican team that you met this afternoon, and I know you were very, very impressed.

Together, we can continue to move America in a new direction with these weapons. Our situation is perhaps analogous to the situation that is described in this poem with which I will close:

95

This I beheld, or dreamed it in a dream:
There spread a cloud of dust along a plain;
And underneath the cloud, or in it, raged
A furious battle, and men yelled, and swords
Shocked upon swords and shields. A prince's banner
Wavered, then staggered backward, hemmed by foes.
A craven hung along the battle's edge
And thought, "Had I a sword of keener steel—
That blue blade that the king's son bears—but this
Blunt thing—!" He snapt and flung it from his hand,
And lowering, crept away and left the field.
Then came the king's son, wounded, sore bestead,
And weaponless, and saw the broken sword,
Hilt-buried in the dry and trodden sand,
And ran and snatched it, and with battle shout
Lifted afresh, he hewed his enemy down,
And saved a great cause that heroic day.

A New Beginning

Congressman Vander Jagt went to Trevose, Pennsylvania, on October 18, 1982, to speak at a fundraising dinner for Congressman Jim Coyne. Of all of the speeches in this collection, this is the most representative of the campaigner at his work, bringing Republicans to the mountain top for an inspired vision of a better future. After the conclusion of this speech when the band played "God Bless America," everyone was standing, and most had tears streaming down their cheeks.

Jim Coyne's introduction of Vander Jagt is typical, too, of those many others he has received from Republican candidates all over the country for the last eight years. Congressman Coyne said:

It's a great pleasure for me to have you all here tonight. Obviously, we've got fifteen days in the campaign, and, at this point in the campaign, there's nothing that you would rather do for all the people who work hard and put in the support, financial, their time, their wisdom, than to give them a real rousing, good, old-fashioned barn-burner of a speaker. That's why it's my privilege this evening to bring to you the finest orator that I know of in the United States Congress, in government, today.

But he's not only somebody who knows how to talk; this is a man who knows how to perform. When he became the leader of the National Republican Congressional Committee in 1975, and I don't have to tell you to think back to 1975 and ask yourself where was the Republican party in 1975, he picked this organization up, and today, over the past seven years, there is no success story that you can point to in politics that's anything like what Guy Vander Jagt has done for the National Republican Congressional Committee.

It's been unbelievable. We have fifty-two freshmen Republicans in Congress today who made the difference, who gave President Reagan the votes he needed when he needed them. We have fifty-two freshmen Republicans in Congress, bright, hard-working, all of them, I think, going to be reelected. And they are there for one reason: because the Republican party at the national level started working like a team, and it is a great honor for me to introduce all of you to the man who made all of this possible in the last seven years, the chairman of the National Republican Congressional Comittee, Mr. Guy Vander Jagt from Michigan!

T HANK YOU very much, and thank you, Jim for a most generous introduction. I appreciated those words not just because they were so exceedingly generous, but because of the very good friend and the very outstanding congressman from whom those generous words came. Thank you very, very much.

Congressman Jim and Gay Pendleton, our master of ceremonies, Bill Donnelly, representing Montgomery County, and Gary Fawks, chairman of Bucks County Republicans, the very lovely Holly, Elaine Zemke, and Jay Kirk who gave us that beautiful Presbyterian invocation, and friends of Jim Coyne all, it is a tremendous privilege and pleasure to be able to thank you all for all that you are doing to send back to the Congress of the United States one of its finest members—your congressman, Jim Coyne.

It's a great year for Republicans in Pennsylvania! One good turn deserves another, and that's what you are going to give Governor Dick Thornburgh on November 2nd. I know that you're going to send back to the the United States Senate John Heinz, with the kind of overwhelming victory margin that his outstanding record so richly deserves, but I also know that the people of the Eighth Congressional District of Pennsylvania are going to send back a dynamic new leader who has such a tremendous career ahead of him in the House of Representatives.

You're going to be so proud of him in the years to come and proud that you were here in the beginning of what I know will be a great career, and when you send Jim back to the House, you're going to be doing two wonderful favors for the House of Representatives at the same time: number one, you're going to be sending back to the House of Representatives a very, very fine person, and that's a favor for the House, but, number two, you're going to make sure that Peter Kostmayer doesn't get back to the House, and that's also a favor for the House.

When Jim came to town in January of 1980 with that tremendous Republican freshman class of fifty-two members, they literally turned Washington upside down. They started a revolution, and for the first time in fifty years, Congress voted to limit rather than to increase the government. Jim serves on the House Administration Committee, and he got to thinking that, if we're going to cut spending across America, maybe the place to begin is with the House itself. And so, in the House Administration Committee, he proposed the unthinkable—that the House spend ten percent less on itself than it had the year before. And thanks to Jim and the united, enthusiastic, energetic, won't-say-die spirit of the fifty-one other freshman Republicans, that Coyne proposal was adopted, and for the first time in fifty years, the House spent less rather than more on itself, a truly phenomenal achievement!

Jim brought to the House a tremendous wealth of experience in government as a supervisor educationally, in business. He has an undergraduate degree from Yale, and an MBA from Harvard. He's been on the faculty of the prestigious Wharton School of Finance and has been a highly successful president of a highly successful business. He—when you try to describe, or when I try to describe to you, the words that describe Jim's service in his first term, these words flock to my mind: honesty, integrity, conviction, dedication, compassion, caring, giving. I could go on and on, but let me try to summarize it for you with really just one phrase. Over the past couple of years, it has been my privilege to campaign for over two hundred Republican congressmen in each of our fifty states, literally from the snow-capped peaks of Alaska to the sandy beaches of Florida, from the California deserts to the craggy coastline of Maine, and I can tell you tonight that nowhere, no time, no place have I ever campaigned for a finer young congressman than your congressman—Jim Coyne.

And what a contrast between Jim and his opponent, wherever you look. Jim is a family man, and he and his lovely and beautiful and effervescent Holly have three young children. They live in a

99

home they own in the district among the people that they represent. His opponent is single, and he doesn't own anything in the Eighth Congressional District of Pennsylvania.

Jim's campaign is financed with hundreds and hundreds of contributions from the people of this Eighth Congressional District. Jim's opponent? Over forty percent of all the money that he has raised has come from labor unions and a variety of liberal organizations scattered all across America that probably never heard of Bucks or Montgomery County.

Jim, while he has been there for the last two years, has lobbied for the people. His opponent has lobbied for Japanese companies. While Jim was working, trying to launch an attack on Japanese trade violations, his opponent was lobbying for the Sony Corporation. While Jim was developing "Buy America" legislation to preserve our jobs, his opponent was lobbying the American people, urging them to buy from foreign countries. I wouldn't believe, I couldn't believe that, when I first heard it, and then I got a copy of the letter signed Peter Kostmayer, president. He says, "Sometimes U.S. distributors don't have the best prices. You'll receive information on how to buy money-saving bargains direct from overseas. Fine linen and crystal from Ireland, perfumes and teas from France, watches and cameras from Hong Kong, porcelain from Germany, bone china from England and more." The only thing he doesn't have on there is steel from the steel-dumping nation of Western Germany and imported cars from Japan. How any working American can possibly choose to send that kind of individual to the House of Representatives with all of the troubles that we have, utterly defies my imagination.

But infinitely superior as Jim is to his opponent, there's another reason even more important than that for sending Jim back to the House of Representatives. Jim and his freshman colleagues did start a revolution last year when for the first time in half a century they voted to limit instead of increase the size of government. And most of those budget cuts, those spending cuts, those tax cuts, passed the House by a vote of one or two, and now we are headed in a new direction, and on November 2nd, we are engaged in a great war, testing whether that new direction or any new direction so conceived and so dedicated can long endure. If we gain seats, we will have gained momentum to change the direction that we have been traveling If we lose seats, we will lose momentum, possibly never, ever, to regain it again, and that's why November 2nd is an election of destiny shaping America's future, not just for the next two years, but possibly for many decades to come.

The American Revolution was not decided in one great, nation-wide battle line, but a series of battlefields like Valley Forge and Bunker Hill. The outcome of this revolution is going to be decided in individual battlefields called individual congressional districts, and the Eighth District of Pennsylvania is one of the key battlefields in the nation. It boils down to just a couple of dozen districts, and the Eighth District of Pennsylvania is one of them. You're not just talking about electing an outstanding man. You're talking, really, about being part of history and destiny in one of the critical battlefields of that war. I don't think that there is any commitment that you could make that is more important than that.

Thursday night, last week, I was campaigning for congressional candidates in Denver; one of those candidates was Jack Swigert. Jack Swigert was an astronaut. One of the six U.S. flags on the moon was planted there by Jack Swigert. A little over a month ago, Jack Swigert was in the hospital, and his doctor called and said he wanted to meet him that night when the rounds were over because he had the reports of the medical tests. Jack Swigert called his campaign staff and said, "I want you in the hospital room so that we hear the news together." The news of the doctor was chilling. Jack Swigert has cancer of the bone marrow. Although he once pulled a miracle in space, bringing a spaceship that might have been spinning around in infinity forever back to earth, and though miracles on earth are also possible, it is also very possible, that in three or four months, Jack Swigert will be dead.

What would you do if you had three or four months to live? Would you put yourself into a grueling campaign for a seat that you probably will never serve in? Jack Swigert is running for an open seat in Colorado. It's one of those two dozen that will determine the destiny of this nation just like this one, and he explains it pretty much like I just did to you a few moments ago. Jack Swigert said, "We can't let this seat fall into enemy hands where they'll drag us back to the policies of the past. We've got to keep it in our column where it will pull us forward with a tomorrow of hope. If you will stay with me, I'll keep runnning, and we will win."

Ladies and gentlemen, that's commitment, and it's the kind of commitment that it takes to win revolutions.

When those fifty-six men signed the Declaration of Independence down there in Independence Hall, they pledged their lives, their fortunes, and their sacred honor, for making that Declaration stick. That wasn't some rhetorical wording. That turned out that one of every six who signed gave his life in the war that followed. Dozens had their fortunes wiped out, but, of course, not one of them lost his sacred honor.

Tonight I'm not asking anyone of you to risk your life, just some more time, making one more telephone call, knocking on one more door, sending out one more letter, talking to one more friend. I'm not asking you to risk your fortune. Maybe some more contributions when you've already given more than you really can afford. But I think all of us risk our sacred honor if we don't do everything we can to make sure that we continue on this new direction when it could be our last chance.

I hope you catch a sense of the excitement and exhilaration of being on a battlefield that might determine the future of this country. I remember the morning after the election, when we knew those new fifty-two Republican freshmen were coming to town, and the Senate was going to be Republican, and Reagan had swept in on a landslide. I received a call from Captain Red McDaniel of the U.S. Navy. Red had been a prisoner of war in Vietnam for seven years. He wrote a book called *Scars & Stripes* in which he set forth in excruciating detail the pain, torture, suffering, hopelessness, and despair of those seemingly never-ending seven years. He said, "Guy, I just want you to know that yesterday's election filled me with a greater sense of exhilaration than the day I walked out of the POW camp in Vietnam because," he said, "that was a release for me as an individual. Yesterday can be a release for America as a nation. It gives us a chance to head in a new direction." Thanks to the fifty-two Republican freshmen of which Jim Coyne is such an outstanding example, we did head in a new direction. Rather, tonight, than giving you the facts and statistics of that new direction, let me try to summarize it for you by quoting David Brinkley, on national television a few months ago. And it is so seldom that national television ever describes accurately anything we Republicans do in

Washington that when they finally get it right, we ought to repeat it again and again. David Brinkley said, "1981 transformed that art of politics in America. For fifty years," he said, "the art of politics was the art of addition. Congress would add this spending to that spending, would add this funding to that funding. And every two years the congressmen would run back home to their constituents and say, 'Look at everything I added. Look at what a good boy I am. Vote to send me back there for two more years so I can add some more.' In 1981," David Brinkley said, "for the first time in fifty years, congressmen finally figured out that, by golly, there really is a subtract button on the adding machine and," he continued, "under some not-so-gentle prodding by Ronald Reagan, the congressmen actually summoned the courage to hit the subtract button on the adding machine."

I ask you to ask yourselves tonight, if we who hit the subtract button on the adding machine were to lose rather than gain seats in November, how many decades do you think it would be before Congress ever again summoned the courage to hit the subtract button on the adding machine? This could be our only chance and your only chance in the Eighth District.

I believe the whole issue was put into clear focus for us the afternoon of July 27th, a year ago, when Tip O'Neill strode to the well of the House to speak to the House just moments before the vote on the president's historic tax-cut package. You'll remember six days before, Tip O'Neill was talking around Washington that finally he had Ronald Reagan beat, had him beat by thirty-five votes. Then the president went on national television; he asked the people to help him a little bit. When the vote was taken, we had won by a big margin, but just before it was taken, Tip O'Neill spoke to a House that was packed, and as Jim knows that doesn't happen very often in the House of Representatives. He spoke to a House that was hushed, and that happens even less often in the House of Representatives, but it was packed and hushed because we sensed that maybe an historic shift in direction was about to take place. And the speaker argued very earnestly, in essence, "America is great because of all the good things that government has done for people, and because America's greatness lies in government," he said, "we Democrats are so proud that every year we've been able to deliver more government than the year before. We cannot vote to cut resources and taxes for government programs," he pleaded, "because to do so is to cut America's greatness."

Republicans argued exactly the opposite. We said, "America isn't great because of what government did for people; America is great because of what in America a free people had the chance to do for themselves." That's what America is all about, and for the first time in half a century, the House voted to send America in that direction.

Now Tip O'Neill and Teddy Kennedy and Walter Mondale and Jimmy Carter are saying, "Yeah, but that program doesn't work. The economy is sluggish." And the economy is sluggish, but eighty percent of the individual income tax cuts specifically designed to stimulate a sagging economy didn't go into effect until eight weeks ago. Forty percent of it won't go into effect until July 1 next year, and I don't know of any medicine in the world that can cure a sick patient before you take the medicine out of the bottle and give it to the sick patient. And make no mistake about it, Jimmy Carter left us a very sick patient on our doorstep: interest rates, twenty-one and a half percent and going up, inflation, twelve-point-four percent and going up, the recession deepening, and unemployment increasing and a one trillion dollar national debt.

The interest just this year on that debt is 110 billion. Operationally, Ronald Reagan has a balanced budget, current income equals current outgo. It's a 110 billion dollar carrying charge on the national debt, largely run up in the last twenty-six consecutive years of Democrat control of the Congress, twenty-six years where the Democrats in Congress, including Jim's opponent, spent money like drunken sailors.

Some of you might remember that in my keynote address in Detroit, I used that phrase. Unfortunately, there were a couple of drunken sailors in a bar in San Diego who happened to hear me say that. You ought to see the letter that they sent to me. Drunken sailors think it's an insult to be compared to the Democrats in Congress. You know, you can't blame them because there is a mighty big difference; at least drunken sailors spend their own money, and you know whose money the Democrats were spending.

But I think the program is going to prevail, and it's going to prevail, I believe, for the same reasons you are going to prevail for

Jim on November 2nd, and I'd like to share those three reasons with you very briefly tonight.

The first reason is this: we have ourselves an incredible leader in the White House in Ronald Reagan. Even those who disagree with him find it so refreshing to at last have somebody there who knows where he wants to go, and how he wants to get there, and doesn't change with every new monthly public opinion poll.

Symbolic of the way in which Ronald Reagan has taken Washington, D.C., by storm is the fact that jelly beans have invaded every nook and cranny of that city. You find them in elegant restaurants, in offices, and, of course, in the White House itself, and it's really something to go to a leadership meeting with the president in the White House in the morning, to go into the Cabinet room, and there's that huge Cabinet table, and in the middle of that table is an enormous jar of jelly beans. It is so big, it is obviously ceremonial. You couldn't get them out unless you had a stepladder; you couldn't pass it unless you had a crane. But as soon as you are seated, a whole bunch of little jars of jelly beans emerge, and what a sight to behold: grown men at 7:30 in the morning, before breakfast, reaching into the jelly bean jar after their favorite flavors under the watchful, approving eyes of the president of the United States.

But the program is going to prevail for a reason far more fundamental than the personal qualities of any one man, no matter how great, and it is going to prevail because its founded on a premise that is widely supported by the vast majority of American people. And it is simply this: that in America, government must always be the servant and never the master of our people.

I don't think I need to tell this audience of how the regulations that came spewing out of Washington over the last couple of decades absolutely suppressed and suffocated and straitjacketed our ingenuity and our creativity and our enterprise. My own favorite illustration is that beloved agency OSHA which two years ago issued 198 pages of regulations on the use of ladders alone, including this wonderful gem on page 23: "When ascending or descending a ladder the user should always face the ladder." It really doesn't take a governmental agency to say that when you go up and down a ladder, don't do it backwards. It got so bad some people just kind of snapped under the frustration.

There was a plant down in Louisiana that wanted to expand

and had their lawyer fill out all the necessary forms and applications, including an abstract of title for the land on which they were going to build. The abstract went back to 1803. Now bear in mind that this was Louisiana, and that the abstract went back to the year 1803. Nevertheless, they got this letter back from the government: "We received today your letter enclosing application for your client and supported by abstract of title. We have observed, however, that you have not traced the title previous to 1803, and before final approval, it will be necessary that the title be traced previously to that year." That was too much for the lawyer. He just went bonkers, and he sent back this letter which I give you word for word. I couldn't embellish this if I tried. "Gentlemen: Your letter regarding the title received—I note that you wish the title to be claimed further back than I have done. I was unaware that any educated man failed to know that Louisiana was purchased from France in 1803. But here goes: the title of the land had been acquired by France by right of conquest from Spain; the land had come into possession of Spain in 1492; it was by right of discovery by an Italian sailor named Christopher Columbus. The good Queen Isabella took the precaution of securing the blessing of the Pope of Rome upon Columbus's voyage before she mortgaged her jewels to help him. Now, the Pope is the emissary of Jesus Christ, Son of God, and God created the world, therefore, I believe that it is safe to assume that God also created that part of the United States called Louisiana, and I hope to heck you are satisfied."

As the president put it in his magnificent inaugural address, "It is not my intention to abolish the government, but to make government work for us. Government should stand at our side helping us, not ride on our back dragging us down."

Finally, I think the program is going to prevail for the same reason you're going to prevail on Jim's behalf on November 2nd, because I believe that President Reagan has an unmatched ability to draw out of the American people the best and highest and finest that they have in them.

I saw an example of that on that afternoon of July 27th, a year ago, right after we had voted on the tax cut, and we had prevailed. I went up to a Democrat congressman who had voted for the tax cut, and I thanked him and said, "It took a lot of courage for you to do that, but we couldn't have passed it without your votes, and I want

106

you to know how much we appreciate your voting for it." He said, "Guy, you got that all wrong. It didn't take any courage." He said, "After I got them 778 telephone calls from my congressional district saying vote for the president's tax cut or else, it didn't take no courage at all to vote for the president's tax cut."

I went up to another Democrat congressman and I thanked him, and he said,"You know, I wasn't going to do it, not even after all the cards and letters and telegrams, but," he said, "those telephone calls—they were something else." He said, "They'd call; they'd say, 'Vote for the president's tax cut.'" He said, "I'd say to them 'How much money do you earn?' They'd say, '$15,000.'" He said, "I'd say to them, 'How many children do you have?' They'd say, 'Two.'" He said, "I'd say to them, 'Man, have I got a surprise for you. Under our tax cut, and I have the two tables here in front of me, you and your family will get $121 more in tax relief in the first two years than under the president's tax cut.'" He said, "Time after time there would be a pause, and then they'd say, 'I don't care. Support the president's tax cut, and get America working right again!' That," he said, "is unprecedented in my experience," and so is it in mine.

I saw an example of the president summoning this forth just three days before the assassination attempt on his life. I took into the oval office an elderly lady from the Netherlands, Lieske van Kessell, and a lady from my congressional district, Mandy Evans. It had all started during World War II when Mandy was ten. Her Jewish parents had been murdered by the Nazis. Her life was spared because the van Kessel family took her in, pretended she was their own little Dutch daughter at the risk of their own lives, of course, if it were discovered.

Nights, the young husband of that Dutch family would sneak out into the dark. He'd rescue shot down American flyers and hide them until he could ship them through the Dutch underground back to England so they could fly their planes again.

Well, Mandy Evans hadn't seen that Dutch mother, and she had really become a mother to her and who had saved her life, in thirty-five years. WGN radio in Chicago had a dream contest and Mandy won, except her dream wasn't for herself, it was for her Dutch mother, that Lieske van Kessel and she might have a month's tour of this America that Lieske van Kessel loved so much but had never seen.

They wrote to me because Washington was on the itinerary, and I arranged for the usual tours for them, and then I got to thinking, wouldn't it be nice if this nice Dutch lady could visit the president of the United States, whose nickname, after all, is "Dutch" Reagan. And whether that was it or not, my request was granted. We went in for what I thought would be a quick picture, a hello; we'd be on our way, but the president was so captivated by their stories of heroism and courage and remembrance and appreciation that he insisted that they sit down, and a half-hour conversation ensued, and I sat there totally spellbound as Mandy Evans and the president started speculating together on what is the greatest moment in a person's entire life.

Is it the moment the first child is born? The moment you pledge your love and your life to another until death do you part? The moment when the business, after years of struggle, finally turned a buck? "For you," she said, "Mr. President, I'll bet it's when you heard you'd won, you knew you were going to be president of the United States of America." She said, "For Lieske and me, this moment in the White House, with the president of the United States, comes awful close to being the greatest moment in our lives.

"But," she said, "in my case, there is another moment that far, far transcends even this. It's that afternoon in August of 1944, when those dirty and dusty and tired and exhausted but triumphant and grinning American G.I.s came marching down the cobblestone street of our little Dutch village, and I knew I was free and safe again."

That prompted the president to get reminiscing about his own war years when, as he put it, "I flew a desk." He said, "It wasn't as big or as nice as that one," pointing to the one in the oval office, "but there was a tremendous flow of paper work going over it, including," he said, "recommendations for medals of honor." He said, "I'd fish those out, and I'd hide them under the blotter where I could read them in my leisure and savor them and draw inspiration from them. The one I remember best," he said, "was about a B-17 that had been hit over Germany. It was trying to make its way back home, and some of you may remember that in the belly of a B-17 was a bulge. In that bulge, sat the machine-gunner. Well that had been hit, and the door was jammed, no way to get the door open, just a hole through which the machine-gunner could stick his arm and his wrist and his hand. It became clear that that plane was going to crash, so the pilot gave the order to bail out, and one by one the white parachutes opened. The last crewman to jump, just before he jumped, looked back over his shoulder. This is what he saw: the pilot slowly removing the parachute that he had so carefully strapped to his back, hooking it on the seat, and walking back to the midsection of the plane, and grasping the upstretched hand of the machine-gunner, and saying, 'Sergeant, it looks to me like you and I are going to have to fly this plane down together.' "

As he stood up to say goodbye, there were tears not just in the eyes of two ladies, but in the eyes of a congressman from Michigan as well, and in the eyes of the president as he hugged and kissed and embraced Lieske van Kessel goodbye. And, as we walked together out of the door of the oval office, Lieske said to me in her very broken English, "Congressman Vander Jagt, your president is a man with a very big heart, and you know," she said, "he's counting on the best from your American people, and I believe your people will give him the best that they have."

I think so too. I know you will give the best that you have to Jim Coyne so that then together, with renewed momentum, we can complete the task that has thus far been so nobly begun.

Together we can give this nation under God a new burst of freedom and opportunity and prosperity for all.

The Three Rs

Vander Jagt's standard design of advocacy is clearly revealed in "The Three Rs." Here he presents three, really four, reasons why he felt Republicans would win additional seats in the House in 1982. Even when other Republicans were painting a grim picture of party prospects, he remained optimistic. As it turned out, Republicans did not add to their number of seats in the House in '82, but it was not until October the 8th, when the monthly unemployment figure went over 10 percent, that the congressman's optimism, while perfectly logical and grounded in fact, was superseded by the reality of a lengthy recession and resultant unemployment.

He had used these reasons time and time again for almost two years, the full two-year election cycle through '81 and '82. They were expanded or condensed depending on the occasion, but they reappeared regularly when he represented the NRCC and his fellow Republicans.

In the speech presented here, Vander Jagt was speaking at the U.S. Chamber of Commerce Insider's Breakfast in Washington, D.C., on October 6, 1982. There were some two hundred and fifty business leaders in attendance, and it was the same day that he helped to welcome Republican candidates for House seats to Washington.

Small portions of the question-and-answer session after the speech were lost due to difficulties which the author had with the taping of proceedings. Changing tapes accounted for one of the breaks in the transcription.

T HANK YOU. Thank you very much for that generous welcome, and thank you, Hugh, for a most generous introduction. I count it a privilege and a pleasure to be with you at the U.S. Chamber of Commerce Insider's Breakfast and to have this chance and look out at such a sea of friends and allies who have done so much in such a significant way to bring about the revolution that has taken place in Washington, D.C., in the last two years. You did so much in the 1980 elections and, then, did so much in the trenches to bring about the significant changes in direction that have indeed taken place in these last two years.

This morning I'd like to share with you my predictions for what's going to happen in the 1982 congressional elections, and I do so against the backdrop of wildly fluctuating predictions as to what is going to happen. A little over a year and a half ago, even Democrats were conceding the possibility, at least, of Republicans capturing control of the House in 1982. And far more significant than their public pronouncements was the fact that Democrats were going out of their way to be nice to Republicans in the House in the anticipation of that eventuality. Now, in recent weeks, we have heard even White House spokesmen saying anything short of a thirty- or forty-seat loss for Republicans will be a moral victory. My own prediction to you this morning is exactly the same as it was a year and a half ago and exactly what I hope events will justify at the end, on election eve. My own prediction is that Republicans in 1982 will break history and add to our number in the House of Representatives. And I make that prediction fully cognizant of the fact that if we gain even one seat it will be the first time since 1934, the second time since 1870, that the party in power in the White House added to its numbers in any off-year congressional election. The only other time since 1870 was 1934. That was the year that Franklin Roosevelt was in the process of building a new majority coalition that governed for almost the next half-century, and we could be living in such historic moments today.

It is interesting to note that at about this stage of the election cycle back in 1934, the Democratic national chairman, Jim Farley, wrote a now famous "Dear Franklin" letter to the president of the United States in which he said, "It is my sad duty to point out to you that, in view of the fact that we have more unemployment today than we did when you were sworn in, that we Democrats will lose a minimum of forty seats in the November election." The Democratic speaker of the House was predicting that Democrats would lose a hundred and forty seats in the upcoming congressional election. Well, they didn't lose a hundred and forty. They didn't lose forty. They gained nine. And what happened? Was there a sudden bit of economic good news? Not on your life! The economic news that poured in was worse day after day after day.

What happened was, Franklin Roosevelt called the Democrats in Washington together. He said, "We're living in tough times. There's a lot of suffering and hardship, and there's, in tough times, a lot of disagreement among ourselves. We aren't heart or lock set on almost anything. As a matter of fact, I can only think of one thing on which we are all fully agreed, on which there is unanimity, and it is this: that that lousy Herbert Hoover and those terrible Republican policies left such a momentous economic mess on our doorstep that nobody, not even we, can clean it up in eighteen short months. And from this moment on, we're going out of here tonight, we're going on the attack, and we're going to remind people that their vote in November is either a vote, if it's for a Democratic candidate for Congress, to continue in the new direction that we have started, or, if it's a vote for a Republican candidate for Congress, it's a vote to go back to those policies that were so thoroughly discredited less than two years ago."

Well, they did, and they gained nine seats. And I think that possibly we Republicans have been a little remiss in allowing Jimmy Carter to slither off to political oblivion instead of reminding people that he is the inevitable culmination, the personification of twenty-six consecutive years of total Democratic control of the House and of the Senate, of the Congress, of the purse strings, with total control over the spending and taxing and deficit levels of this nation which brought about the economic problems with which we are wrestling today.

When I made my prediction a year and a half ago that we would break history and add to our number, I said there were three reasons for which I could make that prediction, and I called them the three Rs. And let's take a look today, a year and a half later, at how those three Rs still stack up.

The first R is Ronald Reagan. Ronald Reagan is truly an

112

incredible political leader whose approval rating remains very high. As a matter of fact, the overwhelming majority of American people continue to support the new directions that he has set for America. As a matter of fact, Ronald Reagan dominates the political landscape today as no political leader has dominated it since Franklin Delano Roosevelt in 1934.

The second R was redistricting. And it is true that we Republicans did not get the bonanza we had hoped we would get when redistricting started. But now that it is all over, there is still a basic demographic Republican tilt that gives us opportunities that we never had before. It's true we were out-gerrymandered by the Democrats, but nevertheless when you take four seats out of New York City as the census does, where we have never been competitive, when you add four seats to Florida, which the census does, where we are competitive, there is only so much that gerrymandering can do. Now that the dust has settled, there is a Republican demographic tilt, and we will benefit by opportunities that are presented to us that we never had before.

The final R is resources. We will outgun our Democrat opponents by a factor of about eight-to-one in terms of the assistance that we can bring to bear on their individual campaigns and the individual districts, not just in dollars, but in terms of expertise and knowledge and know-how and training and managers and all of the things that go into a successful, winning congressional campaign. And it is also very, very interesting to note where our dollars came from, especially with the Democrats trying to portray us as having these resources because we are the party of the "fat cats."

Last year, of all the money that we raised at the National Republican Congressional Committee, 81.4 percent of the total came in contributions under one hundred dollars. In contrast to that, 88.8 percent of all of the money that the Democrats raised in our counterpart committee came in contributions in excess of two hundred dollars. On the basis of the record and the facts, the Republican party has become the party of the little giver, the Democrat party, the party of the "fat cats," and where the money comes from is going to make a very, very significant difference.

But heading our list of superior resources are our candidates. We have, I believe, the finest stock of candidates and challengers that any party has been able to field in a long, long time. And I say that even as almost a proud father of that crop of candidates in 1980 that came flooding into here, and that many of you did so much to help get here. This year's crop in 1982 is even better than that crop. I still remember going to a reception over a year ago for our candidates that many of you attended. I walked into that reception, and the first four that I met—the first one was an all-American from Stanford; the next one was an orthopedic surgeon; the next one was a prisoner of war who returned to a hero's welcome in the congressional district where he is now running; and the next one was an astronaut who had been to the moon and back, and the candidates went on and on like that.

We have our leading candidates, almost a hundred of them, in town today. I'm going from here over to the White House where, for a day, the Cabinet, the president, and the congressional leaders will brief them and send them charging out of Washington for this home stretch.

Since those first three Rs that I gave a year and a half ago, I've added a fourth reason, and that is the total, complete absence of any Democrat alternative whatsoever. That first hit me like a sledgehammer the night after the president's State of the Union message this year. The networks made available to the Democrats a half hour in which to respond, and I relistened to that tape three or four times just to make sure that it's true, and it is true, that in that whole half hour, there was not one hint, not one suggestion, not one whisper, not one word of any Democratic alternative whatsoever. And we see that in the ensuing year in the performance and in the record.

You know, the only thing left in this town that is run by the Democrats is the House of Representatives. And the House of Representatives really only has two major constitutional responsibilities: that is to originate the appropriation bills and to originate revenue measures. Well, on appropriation bills, as we now are into the next fiscal year, the House has passed only three of thirteen appropriation bills. And on the revenue bills, they not only didn't look at the bills that came from the Senate, they totally washed their hands and said, after they had publicly met and caucused for days, "We," and they announced, "We cannot agree among ourselves on any alternative whatsoever." So on their only two major responsibilities, they blew it on both of them.

And so this country is indeed moving in a new direction. It is in the midst of a revolution. And I can cite to you all sorts of facts and statistics about how we have cut spending by $135 billion over three years, and, after all is said and done on taxes, we are left with a 500 billion dollar tax cut over the next five years, a tax cut that remains true to its original premise that the individual ought to be able to keep a little more of the extra dollar that his extra effort and investment earn for him, the first tax cut in half a century that was aimed not at the redistribution of existing wealth but at providing an incentive to people to create new wealth and therefore new jobs, and opportunity, and prosperity for our people.

But rather than give you facts and statistics, let me try to summarize the revolution that took place in these last two years by quoting David Brinkley on national television a few months ago. And it is so seldom that national televison describes accurately anything that goes on here in Washington that when they get it right, it bears repeating again and again and again.

But a few months ago, David Brinkley said, "1981 brought about a revolution in American politics. For fifty years," he said, "the art of politics in America was the art of addition. Congress would add this spending to that spending. Congress would add this funding to that funding. Congress would add this regulatory agency to that regulatory agency. In 1981, and then every two years," he pointed out, "congressmen would go back to their constituents and say, 'Look at what a good boy I've been. Look at everything I added. Vote to send me back to Washington for two more years so I can add for another two years.' But in 1981," he said, "for the first time in half a century, congressmen finally figured out that, by golly, there really is a subtract button on the adding machine, and for the first time in fifty years, under some not-so-gentle prodding by President Reagan," and he might have added some not-so-gentle lobbying by many associations, "Congress finally summoned the courage to hit the subtract button on the adding machine."

Now this morning I ask you to ask yourselves if we who voted to hit the subtract button on the adding machine for the first time in half a century were to lose rather than gain seats in November, how many decades do you think it would be before Congress ever again summoned the courage to hit the subtract button on the adding machine? That's why I believe the elections of November 2nd are

115

elections of destiny and can shape America not just for the next two years, but for the next two decades and beyond.

All of you here this morning are experienced enough in Washington to know that if we gain seats we will gain momentum in our efforts to achieve a momentous task of shifting the direction of a country as vast as the United States of America, and you know that if we lose seats, we will lose momentum far beyond the actual numbers involved, momentum that might never be regained. The 1982 elections should be considered, in our desire for a new and a different America, not just our last, best chance, but our only chance. If we can't do it now, I don't know when we will ever have the opportunity again.

Finally, I believe, the whole issue of these elections was set in sharp, clear, historical focus for us by none other than the Speaker of the House, Tip O'Neill, on that afternoon of July, a year ago, moments before the vote on the president's tax-cut plan. Tip O'Neill strode to the well of the House, and he spoke to a house that was packed. You all know that that doesn't happen very often in the House of Representatives. He spoke to a house that was hushed, and you know that happens even less often in the House of Representatives. But the House was packed and hushed because we sensed that possibly an historic shift in direction for this country might be about to take place. And the Speaker pleaded very earnestly that America is great because of all of the good things that government has done for people. "And because America's greatness lies in government," he said, "we Democrats are so proud that every year we have been able to add and deliver more government than the year before. We cannot vote to cut taxes and therefore resources for government programs," he pleaded, "because to do so is to cut at the heart of America's greatness."

The Republicans argued exactly the opposite. We said, "For heaven's sake, America isn't great because of what government did for Americans. America is great because of what, in America, a free people had the chance and the opportunity and the incentive and the freedom to do for themselves. That's what America is all about."

And for the first time in half a century, the House actually voted to move America in that direction. We voted, as President Reagan described it in his State of the Union message, we voted not to save free enterprise. We voted to "free" enterprise so that together we could save America, and whether we continue in that direction will, in large measure, be determined by whether we gain or lose momentum on November 2nd.

I think we will and can gain momentum because I believe that we must.

QUESTION: [The question was not loud enough to be heard and taped].

ANSWER: Everybody hear the question that the *Washington Post* recently editorialized that the balanced budget is not possible even for '85 and '86? What would I advise the president to do? Promise a balanced budget for the out-years?

The president, of course, has promised a balanced budget in that he has said that is what we are moving toward [break in the tape] and he is trying desperately to get those lines to come together. It's kind of like a run-away team going down the track; you don't just stop him dead in his tracks. It takes enough, a bit, of time; the president has also said, and he did what I would have advised him to do. He didn't have to ask for my advice on it, but to ask for a balanced-budget amendment as an effective tool in helping him bring about his goal to which he is obviously committed—which is a balanced budget.

The balance-the-budget amendment, in my own opinion, is an effective tool, but I do not believe it is indeed a panacea—in that I believe that Congress is so filled with ingenuity that, if we had a balanced-budget amendment, it could come up with a couple of dozen ways of getting around the requirements of a balanced budget. Just to cite one example, instead of making a grant, you guarantee a loan that doesn't show up at budget time. I think it's an effective tool; it's putting Congress's feet to the fire [break in the tape], that kind of thing.

The real way to balance the budget is to elect a Congress that has the courage to make the votes that are necessary to balance the budget, and there is no substitute for that. I do believe that the balanced-budget amendment is also an effective tool as a campaign device because we got a record vote on it, and there are a number of congressional incumbents who, under great pressure, went ahead to sponsor the balanced-budget amendment, and then when it came time to vote for it, voted against it. And that, of course, is the charge

117

that many of our challengers are making. These guys talk very conservative back home, but their votes are very liberal up there in Washington. Well, that's the proof of the pudding. There were those who sponsored the balanced-budget amendment who couldn't bring themselves to vote for it.

So I think the president is doing exactly the right thing, both in terms of his commitment to a balanced budget and his commitment to the balanced-budget amendment.

QUESTION: Today more people are employed than we've ever had employed in this country in our history. Friday brings the announcement of the new unemployment figures, unemployment D Day [not loud enough to be heard and taped]. I think many of us are concerned as to what these statistics actually show. How many, for example, today, compared to 1967, are, say, partners in a married couple where before, one person was employed, and then two were employed, and now only one is employed, and one is still able to earn an income for that family? How many of those statistics are people who are aliens or illegal immigrants who have somehow gotten hold of a social security card and somehow got on the unemployment rolls, and our tax money is going to support them, but they count as an unemployed person? How many people are in that category in those statistics on unemployment?

ANSWER: The question expressed concern about the fact that on October 8th, there may be the announcement that unemployment has reached ten percent in this country. The concern was expressed that, will there be any examination of that statistic as to the components that go to make it up and what it really means? And in the preface to the question, you yourself, sir, made a very good point of some things we need to remind ourselves that, even if unemployment should hit ten percent, for example, the fact of the matter is, that unlike 1934 when the total number of employed continued to drop between '32, '33, '34, and '35, in this case there are more people employed today than when Ronald Reagan was sworn into office. And there is a greater percentage of the working-age population employed today than at any time in our history. And so those statistics need to be examined very carefully, and that's exactly what our Republican challengers and candidates, hundred strong, will be learning about from David Stockman, from Ed Meese, from

118

President Reagan, and from all of the others in this day-long briefing session over at the White House.

It is also, I think, critical to make an additional point, and that is: who is responsible for the unemployment? Right now, at least as of September 15th, when the American people are asked the question, "Who is responsible for the recession and unemployment, Jimmy Carter and the Democrats, or Ronald Reagan and the Republicans?"—by forty-five to seventeen percent, the American people blamed Jimmy Carter and the Democrats for the recession and the unemployment, not Ronald Reagan and the Republicans. That's an amazing statistic, more than two and a half to one, and the most amazing part of it is that the spread is growing. More people blame Jimmy Carter and the Democrats for unemployment today than they did in the spring. So ten percent unemployment can be a weapon, a sword that we can catch the handle of and use rather than the other way around.

QUESTION: What is your solution to the social security problem, and when will Congress have the courage to face it?

ANSWER: What is my solution to the social security problem, and when will Congress have the courage to face it? Well, actually the Republicans on the Ways and Means Committee had the courage to face that question about six years ago. It was then that social security was running into red ink, and it was going to fall apart, and we had to come up with a solution. The Democratic solution, of course, was to give us the largest tax increase in history, with still more figured in on January one. That was to make us solvent to the year 2020. It didn't. We now face bankruptcy again this coming June.

At that time, over weeks and months, the Republicans unanimously, on the Ways and Means Committee, came up with an alternative solution. Our alternative solution contained a number of reforms such as federal workers coming under the system. Since they wind up getting the benefits, they ought to contribute to it. Most of them wind up getting the benefits, but we also contained, in our proposed solution, a phased-in, delayed retirement for full retirement benefits so that by the year 2010 or something, instead of retiring at sixty-two with full benefits, you'd have to wait until sixty-five. That didn't affect anybody who wasn't under—only people thirty and under would be affected by that, but just the mere mention of that set off such a brushfire of opposition all across this country that our proposed solution wasn't even looked at. It wasn't even examined. It wasn't even debated. It was just brushed aside by the majority on the Ways and Means Committee.

I think we could go back to the proposal we made then and find that there are a number of very, very worthy reforms contained in there that might still be the solution today. I am sure that the blue ribbon commission, Democrat and Republican, that is looking at the situation—they are to report on November the 15th, in time for the lame-duck session, and at least Senator Bob Dole believes that, who is after all chairman of the Finance Committee, believes that the lame-duck session might be the most propitious time for Congress to summon the courage at that particular time to do what needs to be done to reform our social security system.

The alternative to that is waiting until the next session of Congress with money running out in June, Congress under the gun with the clock ticking away, then have to do something in May. You know the kind of crazy actions that Congress takes in emergency situations like that. So I personally favor addressing the situation and solving it in the lame-duck session.

QUESTION: In these last weeks before the election, what is the best way that the business community can help in the election?

ANSWER: Oh, what a wonderful question. Did you all hear that? In these last weeks before the election, what is the best way that the business community can help in the election? The only way that could have been rephrased would have been: in these last weeks, in the homestretch with only twenty-nine days to go before the election, what is the best way the business community can do to help the election? The best thing the business community can do to help the election is to recognize that this is a historic election; it is not just another off-year election, and that the revolution that we had a chance to begin in '80, whether we can continue it or not, will in large measure be determined by the outcome of those November elections. I think, I sense, that some of the excitement, of the exhilaration, of being engaged in a historic turning is missing from people as they approach this election. It isn't for the opposition. They know that this could be their last-ditch stand and that, if they were to lose, that then we're on our way to really a new historic turning for America and not just a blip, not just an aberration. That's why labor, in the PAC figures that just came out two days ago, ninety-nine percent of what they're giving to their PACs goes to Democrat candidates. On the other hand, business and industry in their PAC figures that came out two days ago—fifty-five to forty-five.

Well I, serving on the Ways and Means Committee, seeing how the Congress is constantly doing it to business and industry, do understand the need for access; I understand all of that, but you don't win revolutions and you don't win wars by making your bets on a sort of fifty-fifty basis. We've got to understand, recognizing all of the importance of keeping wide contacts with all sorts of people, we've got to understand we are involved in a historic decision, and it takes a little better than a fifty-fifty hedging of bets in order to be successful in a revolution, and that what we're talking about is not just the next two years but the next two decades. So I guess business could be a little more energetic in getting the resources to the candidates to enable them to present to their district what, in their district, the issue is all about because, if they have the resources to frame the issue, then, indeed, Republicans will not just gain, there will be a landslide.

On September 15th, when the people were asked, is it better to stay with Reagan economic policies for two more years or go back to the Democrat policies of the past, by sixty-one to thirty-three the American people believe it's better to stay the course. Now, they aren't translating that into their vote making any difference as to which way we go on November 2nd. It's resources that frame the issue and show people how they have to vote to carry out what they themselves believe is better. You don't have to change anybody's mind. You just have to show them how they have to vote in order to stay the course.

To the Committee

On January 22, 1982, Vander Jagt spoke to the staff of the National Republican Congressional Committee. His aim was to inspire staff members to their greatest efforts in what he considered to be a most significant off-year election. He felt that the continuation of the new direction in American politics depended on Republican success in November of 1982.

The meeting was held in the large conference room on the fourth floor of the NRCC half of the Eisenhower Center in Washington, D.C. The room was packed. It was home territory and the proper time for regrouping to launch the year-long campaign to cement the gains made in 1980.

Several of the staff members, it is noted, are mentioned by name. These long-standing relationships lent to the occasion an air of informality which accounts for Vander Jagt's unusual show of in-house humor and his extraordinarily conversational style in the choice and arrangement of words.

T HANK YOU. Thank you, Nancy, for those generous words which are appreciated because they come from such an outstanding executive director. Thank you all for your welcome; I'm very privileged to be with you, to watch the monthly staff meeting series for election year 1982.

Some time ago, John Rhodes, then minority leader, said

publicly that the staff of NRCC is the best, most professional staff that has ever been assembled in American political history. I think he was right then; I know he is right now. And if imitation is the sincerest form of flattery, then you all ought to be very, very flattered indeed because Tony Coelho, my counterpart, when he became chairman of the Democratic National Campaign Committee, said that his goal was to emulate what the NRCC has done. And the NRCC has done that through its staff, so I am pleased to be here this morning to let you know that I'm proud of all of you, and I'm proud of each of you.

And I was very proud, together with my wife, Carol, to have you all in our home this Christmas season. I was delighted to discover that not only are you a very professional group, you are a very spirited group. You have the spirit of Christmas, the spirit of a new beginning, and a lot of "spirits" of the holidays. Very seriously, if you had half the fun being in our home as Carol and I did having you there, then it was one of the highlights of 1981.

As a committee, we have had a lot of highlights in 1981. There was the Senate-House Dinner. The all-time record until last year was a million dollars, and I had to stretch it a little bit to make that a million-dollar dinner. This year without any stretching we beat that by a factor of three and had a three-million-dollar Senate-House Dinner, and that symbolizes the tremendous, unbelievably tremendous, work of Wyatt Stewart and David Himes giving us the resources that we need to do our job. They are so good that they make it look easy, and I'd like you to know that there are some very difficult and very trying and very agonizing and very nerve-racking moments behind that easy facade.

The major reason for our fantastic financial success last year was the phenomenally successful fundraising letter signed by President Reagan in the new aura and the new freshness of his new inauguration.

Well, that letter was almost stopped before it got started. Some of you will recall that it was on the day early in the year when the vote was taken in the House to raise the debt ceiling, which we had to do to keep the government running, that Tip O'Neill had obtained a copy of this letter, and he had called a press conference. There at the press conference he was crying crocodile tears and bemoaning that fact that how, when he was helping the president round up

Democrat votes to raise the ceiling, how could the president himself be saying such nasty things about him, Tip O'Neill, and the Democrats in the House? Well, somewhat understandably from his point of view, Max Freidersorf panicked, and he said, "Oh, the president didn't know about that letter. It was an unauthorized letter. That was just that crazy group up at NRCC that was going off on their own," and shortly thereafter came the order to cease and desist the mailing of that letter. Had we done so we would have been millions of dollars poorer than we are today, and more important, we would be hundreds of thousands of contributors fewer than we have today.

Now, fortunately, only I can give an order to stop a letter, and the order came from the White House to Wyatt Stewart to stop sending the letter. And would you believe that Wyatt Stewart couldn't find me anywhere in Washington, D.C.? He couldn't find me the next day? Two weeks later, with me hiding out in hotel suites, Wyatt Stewart still couldn't find me. By the time he did find me, I then had two weeks of trying to just somehow miss connections with the White House. So with that time, we finally had the summit meeting at the White House, and sat down, and we agreed that we would indeed stop the letter as soon as the pipeline ran out in June some time. And that was agreeable, and tens of millions of letters continued to go out producing the most successful financial and educational letter that has ever gone to the mailboxes of the American voters. So there are some difficult moments behind the easy facade.

Other highlights, of course, of 1981 were, through Joe Gaylord and Liz Kochevar, the training of 165 candidates. That also was an all-time record in an off-year. And then, of course, our national advertising campaign with our Cecil B. DeMille, Steve Sandler, coming up with the theme, "Leadership that works for a change," and Steve's monster of a tax-biter that wound up on T-shirts that many of you wore. And then Chris Hurst who had an incumbent's program for members and their staffs, a dozen seminars right in this room, hundreds of telephone calls and visits to offices to make sure we are able to hang on to what we already have in the process of adding to our numbers.

It was an important year because 1982 will perhaps be the most important year in the history of the staff of the NRCC, and you, this year, will be in the eye of the political hurricane in this country. You will be right at the center of where the action is. A year ago this week, just up the street at the Madison wing of the Library of Congress at a gala dinner, an inaugural dinner, President Reagan was asked, "What in the world are you going to do for encores?" and he shot back, "We're going to elect a Republican House of Representatives in 1982." That was and that is the number one priority on their political agenda.

Now, I'd be less than honest if I didn't admit that once in a while their eye gets diverted from that goal, and they concentrate on other projects that they have. We had promised people that sold tickets to the Senate-House Dinner in excess of $50,000 that they could go in before the dinner and meet the president. Well, that happened to be when he was recuperating from the assassination attempt on his life, so it wasn't until early fall that I finally took the crew of super ticket salesmen into the Rose Garden for an appointment with the president. That happened to be right after President Reagan announced his second round of budget cuts, many of which were going to be extremely painful in my own unemployment-plagued state of Michigan. When the president emerged from the door, I ran to the door and whispered in his ear as we walked to the group about what the group was and the pitch I wanted him to make, and he was his usual charming and winning self, and then he said to the group, "Now, I have a favor to ask of you. I would like to ask all of you to help me make sure that Congressman Guy Vander Jagt votes for every one of the budget cuts that I have issued at the meeting." I said, "Mr. President, you've got it all wrong. You're supposed to be telling this group to work with me to make sure that we sell more tickets for the Senate-House Dinner in 1982 than we did in 1981." The president laughed and slapped my hand and said, "Guy, in politics, one hand washes the other hand."

If their diversion comes, it is only momentary, and in a dinner just before Christmas, a private dinner with Jim Baker, he told me he's in the process of totally restructuring his responsibilities so that in '82 he can concentrate totally and completely on politics. He said that he wanted me to know as far as the president is concerned and everybody else on down they are fully aware of the fact that the first

125

report card that the president receives from the American people will be the House results in November of 1982. So you really are in the eye of the hurricane and where the political action is going to be in 1981.

I wish that I could tell you how many hundreds of candidates across this country who made agonizingly difficult decisions to make the sacrifice to run, who are literally deciding to run: because of you, because of the resources that you can deliver to them, because of the candidate training, because of the campaign manager training, because of the counseling of the field representatives, because of the advertising that will be a banner under which all Republicans for all offices can run, and because of the development of the issues and themes for them and for the Republican incumbents here in town that can carry us to victory in 1982.

So a lot of people are looking to you, but I think in a way this whole universe is looking to you because upon the outcome of your efforts determines the direction that America is going to travel. For many, many years, I have been saying that America has to change direction, and we can't change direction by changing presidents. We can only do so by changing Congress because Congress sets the spending and taxing levels in this country. Now, a year ago we changed presidents, and last year we did change the direction that America is traveling, but unlike what everyone else thinks, I do not believe we changed America's direction because of a change in the presidency. I believe we changed, that we changed directions because Ronald Reagan was such a great president with such outstanding communication skills that he was able to persuade the Congress to vote the change in direction for the first time in half a century.

Now, that's kind of a tenuous foundation on which to build permanent change for much more than a year. And if we are to make sure that the new beginning is completed, we have to make sure that the House itself is changed, so that the principles that we all share, the program of Ronald Reagan, will be swimming downstream in the House of Representatives instead of upstream, so that lower taxes, lower spending, less regulation, more defense, and more opportunity and freedom for our people, that, for those principles, we won't be sailing into the wind in the House, but that we'll have the wind at our backs as we sail out of the stormy, troubled waters that forty years of misdirection in Congress have brought to this nation.

126

Back in January of 1976, speaking to the staff of the NRCC, I said, Now, if we really do our jobs, really do everything we're supposed to, and we elect a whole bunch of Republicans in November, it's going to be so phenomenal that America is going to wonder, how did they do it? And there is going to be a cover story in *Time* or *Newsweek* analyzing what you, the staff of NRCC, did. Well, that didn't happen in '76. Very few people knew we were around or what we were doing. It was the same thing in 1978. But in 1980, when we gained thirty-three seats, we didn't get a cover story in *Time* or *Newsweek;* we did achieve in America's political community the kind of respect and envy and awe and admiration that I hope enables everyone of you to walk tall in that political community because you're associated with this committee.

And if in '82 we can do the job of breaking the cycle of history and elect a Republican House, then belatedly my prediction may come true, and we may have a cover story in *Time* or *Newsweek.* If we do, I hope the person featured on the cover of that cover story is some unheralded, unnoticed, unsung member of this staff whose dedication to excellence and to that extra effort symbolizes the kind of excellence and extra effort we have to have as a team if we're going to do the historic job. If we do it, America will be analyzing this staff and what it did in '82 for many decades to come. And if we do it, you, yourself, will be talking about your role in it, and what you did this year probably for as long as you live, probably to the great boredom of your grandchildren.

I just do want you to know what an exciting place to be in this is for you, what exciting work to be engaged in, in one of the most exciting years in America's political history.

Go to it! Good luck! Give it all you've got!

Wake Up, America!

Recognition as the premier Republican congressional campaigner in the country accompanied the keynote address Vander Jagt delivered on July 16, 1980, at the Republican National Convention in Detroit, Michigan. For the first time, he was given extended national coverage on network television. He was probably seen and heard by a greater number of people in this one speech than in all his live speeches to that point as a congressional campaigner.

Surprisingly, this national TV coverage did not make the stories and poems he used in the keynote obsolete. It enhanced their value because on subsequent speaking occasions he was told by many people that they attended just to hear them over again. His only modification of these supporting materials has been to preface them with that thought. For example, it has become standard practice that he introduce the story of his father on the docks of Hoboken by recounting that the story in the keynote address precipitated an avalanche of letters from people all over the country who had similar stories to tell. The repetition is not only explained in this way; the story's effect is heightened.

The keynote was interrupted over forty times with applause, punctuating key ideas with appropriately positive reinforcement. It generated letters by the hundreds, some coming years after the speech had been delivered. This speech was printed in *Vital Speeches* on August 15, 1980.

THANK YOU. Wow, you sure know how to make a fellow feel like giving a speech. Thank you very, very much for that welcome, and thank you, Congressman Ed Bethune, for a marvelous introduction.

Last night I was here all dressed up in my brand new suit waiting to speak to you, and I waited and I waited and waited and around midnight when I peeked around the stage and looked at you, I decided you looked more like you wanted to go home and go to sleep than hear another speech. But I hope you're ready for one now.

And coming to the delivery room without delivering anything last night was not without its rewards. It is the great privilege and pleasure of the wives of scheduled speakers to be seated in the box with the next first lady of the United States of America, the beautiful and lovely and warm and wonderful Nancy Reagan. That was the privilege and pleasure of my own lovely wife, Carol, last night, and tonight she's here in an honored spot on the platform! So we get two rewards, and I only have to deliver one speech. And whether it's Monday or Tuesday or Wednesday, I think I have to be the luckiest guy in America to be able to have this opportunity to try to give expression to your hopes and dreams for America as we launch this campaign.

We, we want to make America great again, and we know that under the leadership of Ronald Reagan and a new Republican Congress, America can be great again. The American people know that, too. The only "malaise" is in the leadership in Washington, not in our people, and that's good because that's the source of America's greatness, and it always has been and always will be.

Years ago, the French were so intrigued about our greatness, they sent a writer over here to answer one question: what is it that makes America great? He studied and wrote a book and answered the question when he said, "I searched for America's greatness in her matchless Constitution, and it was not there. I searched for American's greatness in her halls of Congress, and it was not there. I searched for America's greatness in her rich and fertile fields and teeming industrial potential, and it was not there. It was not," he wrote, "until I went into the heartlands of America and into her churches that I discovered what it is that makes America great. America is great," he said, "because America is good and if America ever ceases to be good, America will cease to be great." And because the American people have never ceased being good, America can be great again.

But I'm a lucky guy for another reason tonight. Because, except for the waiting, I have about the easiest job in America. To appreciate just how easy my job is, think for just a moment of how hard is the job of my counterpart, Mo Udall, who has to keynote the Democratic National Convention. Poor old Mo has to try to make Jimmy Carter look good. Now that's not a hard job, that's an impossibility.

But it is my easy task and great privilege to speak to you tonight about a man whose leadership America so desperately needs: our great candidate, Ronald Reagan.

Ronald Reagan comes to this convention a winner, a winner over the finest field of presidential candidates that any party ever assembled, and we're proud of all of them. But Ronald Reagan's victory is a victory of the people and by the people and for the people. From the ranks of the people he comes, and for the people he speaks, oh, so eloquently.

When Ronald Reagan started the campaign, he did not have the support of the country clubs, the boardrooms, the media, the Washington establishment or the Republican establishment. The only thing Ronald Reagan had was the support and loyalty and love of the people. He had that and an unmatched ability to feel and to express the hopes of the people for themselves and for America, and so the people responded to Ronald Reagan; with their hearts and their minds and their votes they responded.

And so from all over America, we have come here to Detroit this week to select Ronald Reagan our standard-bearer. We will go forth from Detroit to elect Ronald Reagan our president. And just as Ronald Reagan has brought unprecedented unity to our Republican party, Ronald Reagan can bring America together for a new beginning.

It is our historic opportunity as a united party to be the chosen instrument by which and through which the American people reach out to change the direction we're traveling, to restore the American dream, to make America work again, to make America great again.

It is so fitting that we gather here in Detroit for Ronald Reagan to launch the crusade for a new beginning and a new greatness for America, here in Detroit where the stilled assembly lines, the closed factories, and the jobless workers proclaim the bankruptcy of Jimmy Carter and his policies. We feel the anguish of our people—that unemployed auto worker who has to try to explain to his little daughter why the long-promised birthday bicycle is not there because "daddy doesn't have a job anymore."

And the bad news is that things didn't have to get this way. The good news is that under Ronald Reagan, things won't stay this way. The tragic news is that all of this was deliberately brought about by the Carter administration. Really—on purpose—they increased interest rates; on purpose—they tightened credit; and on purpose—last fall the Carter Congress adopted the Carter budget of despair which their chairman said was deliberately designed to slow the economy down. "Slow the economy down" means "put people out of work." They projected it and they succeeded—889,000 added to the unemployment rolls in May alone. That's the biggest monthly jump in history, including the depths of the Great Depression.

The pathetic answer of Jimmy Carter to this heartache is more of the same. They reject our Republican call for a tax cut to stimulate the economy as irresponsible. I say it is the height of irresponsibility to deny a desperately needed, long-overdue tax stimulus to a sagging economy right now. I say that it is the height of irresponsibility and callousness to deliberately plunge one million more fathers into the heartache of saying, "Daddy doesn't have a job anymore."

Carter says that in this crisis people have to sacrifice and make do with less while government grows and grows—87 billion more next year alone. Republicans say, oh, no, no. It's the other way around. In this crisis, government ought to sacrifice and make do with less so that people can grow and work and produce again.

Our system is sound and great because it's founded where all greatness has to begin—upon a faith in God. That's the bedrock, and everything springs from that. And, that faith is enunciated at the very beginning in the opening words of the Declaration of Independence, "We hold these truths to be self-evident, that man is endowed by his Creator with certain unalienable rights." That's the source of our rights as Americans, not the government, but God. All, all the rest of it was set up to preserve and protect the rights that God gave us when he created us in his own image.

And, because our founding fathers believed that, they put our government under a Constitution to give limits to government and unlimited opportunity to people. They put a Bill of Rights in that Constitution not to guarantee what government must do for us, but to guarantee what government could never do to us, could never take away from us.

Democrats understood that. Woodrow Wilson said, "The history of liberty is the history of the limitation of government, not the increase of it." And, there are millions of good Democrats in America who agree with Woodrow Wilson and Ronald Reagan that the only limitation on liberty is too much increase of government. But the Washington establishment, big government Democrats, long separated from their own heritage and their own people, by making government ever bigger and stronger, are making people smaller and weaker. Like a great athlete who has neglected and abused and punished his own inner strength for too long, America has toppled from the top of the heap to the bottom of the heap in terms of increased productivity.

It is time that we concentrated again on the inner strength that made America great in the first place. It is time that we paid just as much attention to reward and incentive to the people who do work as we do with welfare for the people who do not work. That is the way to get America working again. And we need to carry that message to every hamlet, and like that first Paul Revere, make our message: wake up, America; wake up, Americans; this is your chance; this is your opportunity for a new beginning. Those early Americans responded to Paul Revere's message. They roused themselves from their slumber, rubbed their sleepy eyes, rolled up their sleeves, reached for their muskets, and they raced to the battlefield. And it was the longing for economic freedom that got 'em up out of bed. They felt a big government smothering their flourishing enterprises. Tom Jefferson put it this way in the Declaration. "He, the king, the government, has established multitudes of new offices, and sent hither swarms of officers to harass our people through too much regulation and to eat of our sustenance through too much taxation." Then, as now, they felt overregulated, overinterfered with, and overtaxed. And now as then, it's time for a new uprising, a new beginning, a new direction under new leadership.

But the hour is late, for by ever-increasing government the

Democrats have brought America to the point where one of every six Americans works for government, one of every three Americans is dependent upon the government. The lines have crossed, and now for the first time more Americans live from off a check from out of the government than work and pay taxes into it. One-third of all the land in America is owned by government. And in spite of the rhetoric, this Democrat Congress continues to spend money like drunken sailors. Last month out in San Diego a couple of drunken sailors overheard me make that statement. They almost strung me up from the nearest lamp-post. Drunken sailors think it's an insult to be compared to the Democratic Congress. You know, you really can't blame them because there's an awful big difference. At least drunken sailors spend their own money. You know whose money the Democratic Congress is spending.

In fact, they've been spending money they don't even have for so long that inflation is rampant, and if Carter's inflation of the first quarter continued unabated, by the time today's babies are finishing their education, the bill for a cheeseburger, a milkshake, and french fries at the Big Boy would come to $355. And if you think that's bad, by the time they're ready for their three-bedroom dream home in the suburbs the price would be over seven million dollars, and steak at the supermarket $1,093 a pound.

Obviously, we can't continue down this Carter pathway much longer; obviously it's time for a change, but it will be difficult because we are bearing the burden of the excesses of Democratic congresses past. And every penny that you pay in income tax this year together with two-thirds of the American people—all of it, all put together—will do absolutely nothing this year except pay this year's interest on our national debt, eighty percent of which has been piled up since the Democrats last seized exclusive control of the national cash register twenty-five years ago.

And Democrats can't break out of that spending and taxing cycle, because the Washington establishment, big Democrats, believe that America is great because of all the good things that government does for people. Republicans—all Republicans together—believe just exactly the opposite. We believe that America is great not because of what government does for people, but because of what in America a free people can do for themselves and for their country.

That's what America is all about, that's what Republicanism is all about, and that's what the November 4th election is all about, but we've got to change the direction we're traveling because now we're on a Titanic course. When that big ship sailed on its maiden voyage, it was considered the finest, the most modern, the safest ship ever built. But more amazing than the amazing fact that the unsinkable ship sank, is that in spite of hours and hours of repeated and received radio messages "that there is ice in your cruise lane; there is danger if you don't change direction," when the big ship did smack into the iceberg, it was traveling full speed, straight ahead. The bands were playing, the people dancing, and most of them sound asleep in the cabins below.

We need Paul Reveres to awaken people as to how we can change the direction America is traveling. Right now they don't know how, and they're sleeping through elections. Two out of three who could vote didn't vote in the last congressional elections. And they'll tell you that they didn't because it doesn't make any difference, that six times in twenty-five years they've changed presidents, and nothing changed in what came out of Washington. And there's an element of truth in that because not once in those twenty-five years did we ever change the Congress. And which person sits in the White House is no more important than which party and philosophy runs the Congress in setting the economic rudder of this nation. No president, no president ever spent a penny that Congress hadn't appropriated, or collected a tax not levied by the Congress, or promulgated a regulation not authorized by the Congress, and for twenty-five years in a row that Congress has been Democratic. If we want a change, there's only one way to get it, and that's to change the Congress from Democratic to Republican control.

You know, if we want the weight of government, if we want the weight of government, off our back, and the hands of government out of our pocketbook, we can't do that by putting the same team in charge that put government there in the first place. The only way to do it is to get ourselves a new team, and the only way to do that is vote Republican—for a change.

A new Republican Congress under the leadership of Ronald Reagan can brush aside forever President Carter's admonition that we must limit our dreams and we must hunker down and adjust to a

134

no-growth economic policy. It is true that Carter has made a nightmare of the American dream. People say, "Oh, but he's such a nice man. He has such good intentions and tries so hard." Well. Proverbs tells us that the road to hell is paved with good intentions.

Four years ago, four years ago, Carter ran for office running against high taxes, high inflation, and high unemployment. He's missed the ball on all three. Taxes—they've gone up under Carter in three years more than any three-year period in the history of the Republic. That's strike one. Inflation—Carter's doubled it, tripled it since he's been in office. That's strike two. Unemployment—we're adding to the rolls faster than ever in history, and that's strike three. Any baseball umpire will tell the batter, three strikes and you're out, and it's back to the dugout for you. On November, on November 4th, we'll have the chance to tell Jimmy Carter three strikes and you're out, and it's back to Plains, Georgia, for you.

. But I didn't come here tonight to tell you how bad Jimmy Carter is. You know that; the American people feel it. There's no need to dwell on it. I'm here tonight to tell you how good America can be again. The most exciting thing to hit Washington in many a moon is the enthusiasm of the Republican Freshman Class in Congress, personified by the wonderful Ed Bethune who introduced me. These guys and gals are brimming over with ideas and solutions; they're ready to act; they're ready to govern. There's only one thing they need, and that's reinforcements from the congressional elections this fall to swell their ranks and give them a majority.

With Ronald Reagan, they do not believe that the best is behind us; they believe that the best is yet to come, and they're ready to make it happen for America and our people. They believe about America and our future the way it was described in this poem that once summed up for me how I felt about coming home to America after a long visit to Europe.

'Tis great to see the old world and
wander up and down
Among historic palaces and
the cities of renown
And admire crumbly castles
and the statues of the kings,

But now I think I've had enough
of antiquated things,
So it's home again and home again—
America for me.

My heart is turning home again and
there I long to be,
In the land of youth and freedom
beyond the ocean bars
Where the air is full of sunlight and
that flag is full of stars.

Oh London, it's a man's town,
there's power in the air.
And Paris, it's a woman's town
with flowers in her hair.
And it's sweet to dream in Venice and
it's great to study in Rome,
But when it comes to living,
there is no place like home.

I know that Europe's wonderful,
yet something seems to lack,
The past is too much with her,
the people looking back,
But the glory of the present
is to set the future free.
We love our land for what she is and
what she is to be.
So it's home again and home again—
America for me.

I want a ship that's westward bound
to plow that rolling sea,
To the blessed land of room enough
beyond the ocean bars
Where the air is full of sunlight and
that flag is full of stars.

The reason, the reason that Ronald Reagan wants to revive the old fundamental values of America is not because of the glory of the past, but because of that glory that is yet to be, the dreams that are yet to come true.

Sixty-six years ago this month, my father stood on the docks of Hoboken. He stood there in clothes that were patched and tattered, but they were the very best that he had because he had just immigrated here from the Netherlands. No man has ever been poorer in material possessions or richer in dreams than that little fourteen-year-old Dutch lad standing there in wooden shoes on the docks of Hoboken.

He was dreamin' some mighty big dreams. He dreamed that if he really worked long and hard and saved, he might one day own his own transportation. He dreamed that if he really worked hard, he might one day own his own home. And into that home children would be born, and maybe those children could receive what no member of the Vander Jagt family had ever received back in the old country—a high school diploma. Wouldn't that be something! And maybe, just maybe, one of those children might go on to a university and receive a college degree. Can you imagine that?

Now his dreams stopped there. Maybe his children's children might go on beyond and be a doctor or a lawyer or something wonderful like that. But that would be too far to go all the way from the docks of Hoboken in just one generation. And if anybody had come up to him and told him that Harry Vander Jagt's son would one day serve in the Congress of the United States and stand here tonight delivering the keynote of a great convention of a great party, launching a great and historic campaign, he would have thought that man was plumb out of his mind. That was an utterly impossible dream, even in America!

But you know the rest of the story. His dreams, like the dreams of millions of immigrants, came true beyond their wildest expectations. And as they climbed the ladder of opportunity, building better lives for themselves, working for everything they got, but in America having the chance to keep what they had worked for, as they built better lives for themselves and their families in the process, they built a better America for all.

And the dreams, the dreams of our young people aren't very

much different today. They want a car, with gas plentiful enough and cheap enough that they can drive it. They want to own their own home. They want a good education for their kids. And they want America to be strong enough and secure enough and steady enough to maintain peace and freedom in the world so that tomorrow can be better for their kids even than America is for them today. That's the American dream!

And in order to maintain that, in order to maintain that, we have to grow and progress, and I think we have to adopt John Connally's suggestion and make sure that this year GOP stands not just for Grand Old Party, but get the message out that the heart and guts of our Republican platform spell GOP—Growth, Opportunity, and Progress for people.

We can have that in America again if we have faith in God and the blessed system that flows from it, faith in America and our future. We can, if we believe. As I look out at this arena, an arena that is named for an Alabama sharecropper who came here to Detroit with only the clothes on his back and a dream in his heart and made us all proud as he made his dream come true. As I look out at Joe Louis Arena, I see a wonderful audience of Republicans. And you have been a wonderful audience, and I thank you for it from the bottom of my heart. I love you all, but when I look into those television cameras, I see a different audience. They're an audience that I see not of Republicans or Democrats, of black or white, rich or poor, young or old, male or female. I see an audience of Americans, each one with their very own dream.

Those two words—American, Republican—have a great deal in common, especially this year. The most obvious thing they have in common are that the last four letters of each word are exactly the same. Republican ends in "I can." American ends in "I can." There are no two words that have better described our American spirit than "We can." Whenever duty said to Americans you must, Americans responded, "If we must, we can, and we will!"—and we did!

Today, no matter how big the stumbling blocks, we can make them even bigger stepping-stones into a brighter tomorrow. Let us heed the advice of Ralph Waldo Emerson when he wrote: "So nigh is grandeur to the dust. So near is God to man. When duty whispers low, thou must, Americans answer: we can." If we, if we Republicans can get that message into every hamlet, people will respond again and once more rouse themselves from their slumber, rub their sleepy eyes, roll up their sleeves and reach not for a musket, but for a ballot, and race not to the battlefield, but to the voting booth to change America, the direction we need to go.

Longfellow promised that would happen. I'm sure you all remember how he began that poem about Paul Revere: "Hey, listen, my children, and you shall hear of the midnight ride of Paul Revere." The important thing is the promise Longfellow made in the last four lines for today:

> Through all our history to the very last,
> In the hour of darkness and peril and need,
> The people will waken and listen to hear
> The hurrying hoofbeats of that steed
> And the midnight message of Paul Revere.

Our message for 1980 is: wake up, America! Wake up and under the leadership of Ronald Reagan and a Republican Congress, together, we can make a new beginning! We can have a new birth of freedom and opportunity! Together, we can build a greater, richer, freer America than ever before, an America where dreams can come true!

A Nation in Prayer

For more than thirty years, members of the House and members of the Senate have been meeting at weekly prayer breakfasts to discuss and to pray about problems facing them in their deliberations as legislators. When President Dwight Eisenhower first met with both groups in 1953, the "Presidential" Prayer Breakfast was initiated and became a standard annual event each February. The idea of the prayer breakfast has spread to all sorts of groups across the country and to countries around the world from Europe to West Africa to Latin America and the Philippines.

Prayer breakfasts were a natural speech situation for a graduate of Yale Divinity School. One sermon followed another as Vander Jagt was invited to speak at prayer breakfasts held by various associations, governors, and state and local groups all over the country. By the end of the 70s, his reputation as a speaker earned for him the pulpit at the Annual National Prayer Breakfast in Washington, D.C., on February 7, 1980. He was selected by his colleagues in the House and in the Senate. This is the "Superbowl" of prayer breakfasts. There were over three thousand of the country's leaders present.

Government officials, congressmen, and civic leaders responded to his presentation with a torrent of letters and phone calls of congratulations. Senator Mark Hatfield summed it up when he wrote in a handwritten letter, dated February 18, 1980:

Since the accolades on your presentation at the Prayer Breakfast continue to flood the conversation and evaluation of the event, I have

140

decided that I already have the perspective of time to declare your speech the "greatest."

This reaction was based on a comparison of Vander Jagt with other National Prayer Breakfast speakers like the Reverend Billy Graham and Bishop Fulton J. Sheen.

The speech's impact was increased by being printed in the July/August 1980 issue of the *Saturday Evening Post*.

P RESIDENT and Mrs. Carter and friends: Never before in the history of these prayer breakfasts has the need for and the desire for prayer been greater. I thank you, my friend, Jim Wright—I think—for this great honor. I say "I think" because I'm scared. I'm scared in a cosmic sense for our world; but I'm scared in a personal sense at preaching to so vast a congregation. And I thank you for the hundreds of prayers, which I have felt, that the words of my mouth and the meditations of our hearts might be acceptable in God's sight and that something good and great and powerful might happen to us this morning.

Thirty-two years ago, I stepped for the first time before a pulpit in a little white wooden-frame church in Tustin, Michigan. Incidentally, Mr. President, Tustin, Michigan, is even smaller than Plains, Georgia. And I did my very best to persuade that all-time record turnout of a congregation—eighteen people—that a seventeen-year-old young man could struggle through as their minister during his senior year in high school. I doubt if they've noted very much improvement since then, but I know that they would note a whale of an improvement in the size of the congregation. I'm sure that those elders wished they were here with me this morning to pass their collection plate before this vast group. But I got to thinking, as I was preparing, that if I had remained in the ministry and preached my whole life in the churches of Michigan, that a whole lifetime of preaching all put together would not have reached as vast a congregation as this morning alone in terms of the congregation's potential for good and potential for impacting the world and changing that world.

141

One year ago, Mr. President, in your very moving remarks to us, you pointed out that the three biggest news stories of 1978 had all been connected with religion: a tragic mass suicide in Guyana, the elevation of a Polish cardinal to Pope John Paul II, and the Camp David peace accords. And you shared with us that when it began, you, Begin, and Sadat agreed that prayer would be a part of your daily deliberations. And you did share with us that that was the only thing the three of you agreed upon for the first several days. But the three of you—a Moslem, a Jew, and a Southern Baptist—kept on praying and you kept on trying, and a triumph ensued. And we honor you, and we thank you, and we pray for you. You then said, Mr. President, a haunting sentence. You said, "I would guess that the big news story of 1979 will be the impact in the Persian Gulf in the Middle East of religious fervor because," you explained, "the great events that move men and nations are intimately connected with religion and the spirit." How prophetic! This morning, on the ninety-sixth day of our hostages' captivity in Tehran, we pray not only for our countrymen, but we pray also that somehow, some way, God will reach through the religions and lay on the heart of the Ayatollah Khomeini His age-old ancient plea, "Let my people go." So, I would pray that the big news story of 1980 would be the safe release of our hostages and a spiritual awakening here at home.

America has always turned to God in time of need, for we are a nation founded upon a faith in God. It's there at the bedrock, the Declaration of Independence: "We hold these truths to be self-evident, that men are endowed by their Creator with certain unalienable rights." That's the source of our rights as Americans; not the Constitution, not the Courts, not the Congress, but that all of them were put together to preserve and protect the rights that God gave us when he created us in his own image. Our Declaration is, first of all, a declaration of dependence on God. So when America loses its God, it loses the basis for its rights.

Based on that faith, we strode so rapidly into greatness as a nation that the French were intrigued. They sent a young French journalist over here by the name of Alexis de Tocqueville to answer the question, "What makes America great?" In pursuing the answer to that question, de Tocqueville wrote a book, *Democracy in America*, which still stands as a classic today. President Eisenhower quoted him in a speech: "He patiently and persistently sought the greatness and genius of America in our fields and in our forests, in our mines and in our commerce, in our Congress and in our Constitution, and he found them not. But he sought still further and then he said: 'Not until I went into the churches of America and heard her pulpits flame with righteousness did I understand the secret of her genius and power. America is great because America is good—and if America ever ceases to be good—America will cease to be great.'"

The miracle of America is based on prayer, for prayer begins where all miracles must begin, with the individual. Prayer can miraculously transform human life and we all need it, some more, and some less, but we all need it. How often do we resolve to be a better congressman, judge, executive, husband or wife or person. And God only knows how soon we slide back into our old routine ways. "For all," says the catechism, "have sinned and come short of the glory of God."

Through prayer our concern goes beyond ourselves to the other person and, oh, how much the world needs that now. As split as it may be, psychiatry is united on one principle, and that is that every person who ever lived, every person within the sound of my voice this morning, has a heart that hungers and craves notice, recognition, appreciation, admiration and, above all, love. Prayer enables us to look at the other person through God's eyes, the eyes of love, and discover that in him which is important and worthy.

When Willie Davis, that great hulk of a football player, heard that his beloved coach, Vince Lombardi, lay dying here in Washington, he hopped on a plane in Los Angeles, came here and went straight to Lombardi's bedside for just a few minutes and then right back down the stairs of Doctors' Hospital into the waiting cab, back to National and the very next plane for L.A. When he landed, the press was waiting and asked him, "Willie, you crazy guy. Why did you do that? You've just flown all the way across America twice just to stand for a couple of minutes in the presence of a man who probably didn't even know you were there." And Willie answered, "I just had to because," he explained, "whenever I was with that man, he always made me feel like I was important."

That gift enables the other person to say of you what the poet said:

I love you
Not only for what you are,
But for what I am
When I am with you.
I love you
For putting your hand
Into my heaped-up heart
And passing over
All the foolish, weak things
That you can't help
Dimly seeing there,
And for drawing out
Into the light
All the beautiful belongings
That no one else had looked
Quite far enough to find.

The impact of a person committed to Christ upon another person is never-ending, and there's no limit to what it can do. Nineteen congressmen learned this a few years ago as we were flying from Brussels to Strasbourg. We had left too early on that Sunday for church, and we were going to arrive too late for church. I confess to you that I didn't think that was the biggest tragedy that had ever happened to me in my life, but for one of our members it was. L.H. had a perfect attendance record of fifty-seven years. He scurried up and down the aisle of that plane, pleading with us to have an impromptu makeshift church service when we landed. We agreed and we called the director-general of the European Community and said the U.S. delegation was going to be unavoidably detained for about forty-five minutes. We assembled in the control room on the second floor of the Strasbourg Hotel, and we had our service. Lester, a Jew, read the Old Testament lesson; Henry, an erudite Episcopalian, the New; John gave a Bible-thumpin' sermon; and yet, he was so sincere that Gus, a Greek Orthodox, and Tony, a Roman Catholic, seemed right at home with his message of sin and salvation.

When it was over, L.H. stood up and he thanked us. And he said, "Now I would like to tell you why it was so important to me." He said, "When I was born, our family couldn't afford a baby-sitter,

144

and mother didn't want to miss church and Sunday school, so when I was just a few weeks old, she used to take me with her in her arms to church. And we never missed. And when I was about ten, she became ill, and it got harder and harder for her to go to church. And then one Sunday morning she called me to her, and she said, 'Son, I don't think I'm going to be able to make it this morning. But I hope you go ahead anyway.' She said, 'You know, we've had our perfect attendance record together for quite a while now, and I guess I won't be able to go on. So you carry on for both of us. And will you do me a favor? Will you keep that perfect attendance record for me, just as long as you possibly can?'" And he closed with this simple prayer: "Dear God, Jesus promised that where two or three were gathered together in His name there would He be also. And Jesus kept that promise this morning. We felt His presence and through Him grew close to You and to one another. Thank You, God. Amen." And L.H. was right. We had, we had, drawn closer to one another and to God because of a mother's request and the impact of a person across fifty years and four thousand miles.

Every one of us here experiences Christ in slightly different ways. But let me share with you how I know. When I finished college, I was convinced that you simply could not philosophically prove the existence of God. And so I plunged into my first year of study at Yale Divinity School in a way of being a scholar that I had never been before, and that I have never been since, searching for the precise historical Jesus.

About the end of that year I became fascinated that the Apostle Paul didn't bother with all that stuff. In fact, with all of his writings, he never mentions that empty tomb and doesn't dwell on the resurrection. And yet, no man was more positive and confident that Christ was alive. And then I ran across Paul's verse, "I live, yet not I; but Christ liveth in me." So that's where he has to be! Not just in history in far-off Palestine or at the end of a philosophical syllogism, or even at the right hand of God, the Father Almighty; but here—in my heart!

Though Christ a thousand times
In Bethlehem be born,
If He's not born in thee
The soul is still forlorn.

Paul didn't see an empty tomb and therefore conclude that Jesus was alive. Paul experienced the living, resurrected Christ and knew that death could not contain Him! And then the book by Albert Schweitzer, *The Quest for the Historical Jesus*, put it all together for me. No one had ever more thoroughly or extensively researched the subject, and on the last page he concluded that you can't really pin down with precision the historical Jesus. But he reached a far profounder conclusion than that. In the last paragraph he wrote, "He comes to us as One unknown, without a name, as of old by the lakeside, He came to those men who knew Him not. He speaks to us the same word, 'Follow thou me!' and sets us to the tasks which He has to fulfill for our time. He commands. And to those who obey Him, He will reveal Himself in the toils which they shall pass through in His fellowship, and, as an ineffable mystery, they shall learn in their own experience who He is."

Surely where two or three thousand are gathered together in His name, there will He be also. And He says to each of us this morning, as He said to them of old, "Follow thou me!" And to those who follow, they can sing "Hallelujah." For they know He is risen, and they know that His power can transform their lives, our nation, and the world.

Speeches from the 70s

Gerald R. Ford

Late on election day in November of 1976, the twenty-two-foot by eight foot mural depicting the life of President Gerald R. Ford was unveiled in the Kent County Airport in Grand Rapids, Michigan. The president and the first lady were present as well as those persons who were most responsible for it: Paul Collins, the artist who painted it, Mrs. Bobbie Butler, chairwoman of the Mural Committee, David Mehney, moderator of the event and finance chairman of the Mural Committee, and, of course, Congressman Guy Vander Jagt, who was credited by Collins with having gotten and sold the idea in the first place. Many friends of long standing, dignitaries, and interested citizens of central Michigan were in attendance.

It was an emotionally charged occasion which finally brought the president to tears. His feelings were contagious, and there were tears in the eyes of almost every person in the audience. The event was televised nationally, but it was too late in the day for its full impact to have been felt at the polls. It had been postponed from election eve, and, since the election was determined by only thousands of votes out of the many millions cast that day, the postponement may have had a key significance in four full years of American history.

After introducing Paul Collins, who responded briefly, Vander Jagt took slightly more than his allotted two minutes to campaign for the president of the United States.

I can't think of a better time to introduce the moment we've all been waiting for. I would at this time like to ask the usherettes to unveil the masterpiece.

It is now my privilege to introduce to you the subject and central figure in that mural, a mural that took one solid year of Paul Collins' life to reproduce and, I guess, a lifetime of understanding. I know that all of you over this weekend have realized as perhaps never before that this man has come a long, long way since you first sent him down to Washington twenty-eight years ago. But what he and Betty have demonstrated this weekend is, he never forgot from where he came.

And there are so many things that well up in my heart that I'd like to tell you about this man, and yet the advance men and the schedule of Air Force One indicate that I have two minutes. That's probably not only a blessing for you, but for me as well in that I have to then distill it down to just one thing about this man. It is something that I have been privileged over the last two years to watch while I saw him wrestling with decisions that affect the destiny of the nation and saw him receive the high and lowly into the White House as the president of the United States. Watching that, I got to thinking of the greatness that is America, and I heard the president last night at Grand Rapids Junior College talk about America's greatness.

People have always wondered about what it is that makes us great. 'Way back in the early 1800s, the French were wondering how this little nation was becoming so great so rapidly. And they sent a French journalist over here by the name of Alexis de Tocqueville to answer one question: "What is it that makes America great?" For six months he lived and traveled among us, and then he went back home and wrote a book, still a classic today, Alexis de Tocqueville's *Democracy in America.* You can get it on that bookstand over there; it is still being sold there.

But it is not until the last paragraph of the last page that de Tocqueville answers the question, "What is it that makes America great?" He wrote, "I searched for America's greatness in her matchless Constitution, and it was not there. I searched for America's greatness in her halls of Congress, and it was not there. I searched for America's greatness in her rich and fertile fields, and it was not there. I searched for America's greatness in her teeming industrial potential, and it was not there. It was not until I went into the heartlands of America and into her churches that I discovered what it is that makes America great. America is great because America is good, and if America ever ceases to be good, America will cease to be great."

Jerry Ford is a good man, and because he is a good man, he has been a great president of the United States.

I think God was looking after America two years ago to have a man like Jerry Ford waiting in the wings in our hour of most desperate need. We were rent asunder with growing chasms between young and old, black and white, rich and poor, hawk and dove, demonstrations and riots in our streets, and the American flag was pulled down, spit upon, burned and trampled upon, and Americans hung their heads in shame and disgrace. What we were yearning for then, whether we knew it or not, was a man with the qualities of goodness, decency, integrity, openness, forthrightness, and devotion, a man who was secure, unpretentious, simple but strong, and solid as a rock, a man who loved and was devoted to his family and to his country, a man of the people. And that is what was waiting for us when Jerry Ford became the thirty-eighth president of the United States.

Those qualities did not descend on him like a mantle when he was sworn in. Those were the qualities he acquired here in Grand Rapids, Michigan, growing up as a boy, and those are the qualities that are depicted by the genius that is Paul Collins as you see in the mural, a kaleidoscopic panorama of his life from the infant in the mother's arms to that two-story white frame house, and his old jalopy there parked in front, and the young boy with the dog, all dressed up getting ready for a Grand Rapids parade, or the hard work of a news carrier, or the grace and ability of an athlete, and the portrait of a young and lovely and hopeful bride as Betty and Jerry went off to Congress for the very first time. We began to better understand why Jerry Ford has cherished her so much and so consistently for so long, and the family of which he is so proud, all of it captured there on the canvas for those who pass through this airport.

When you look at that, you look at the making of a man, and, therefore, the making of a president, 1974, the making of a president that we so desperately needed.

151

When I look at that mural, words like this come to my mind: loyalty, fidelity, competition, hard work, love, faith, patriotism, qualities that I think America needs for another term.

But whether America receives those qualities for another term or not, win or lose, Jerry Ford has performed his historic mission for America. And throughout the third century, people will look back on the thirty-eighth president with affection, with love, and with gratitude for what he did for America in America's hour of desperate need. Because of what he is as a man, this nation will stride into the third century with a spring in our step, with a lilt in our voice, and with a sparkle in our eye as we learned on that glorious Fourth of July, 1976.

When I look at Jerry Ford or at that mural, I look at an unusual life. He said on national television last night that, "I came from the ranks of the people," and in a way that's true because he's one of us, but in a way, Mr. President, it isn't true because you're more than that. When I look at the president and that mural, I see a special mirror, a mirror that is held up to each of us of the best that is within us, a mirror that is held up to America of what ought to be and what can be.

Yes, Jerry Ford is a good man, and because he is a good man, he has been a great president. That goodness, acquired here in Grand Rapids, Michigan, has been captured in this mural for all of us to wonder at and marvel at and be inspired with in the years ahead.

Ladies and gentlemen, one of the great privileges of my life—as I present to you now—the good and great president of the United States, Gerald R. Ford.

Count Your Blessings

In 1975, Guy Vander Jagt began his own campaign to breathe new life into the Republican party. Since the 1930s, the party had remained, except for a brief time in the late 40s and again in the early 50s, the minority party of the Congress. After Watergate, the National Republican Congressional Committee was virtually defunct. There were only 25,000 Republicans contributing $900,000 to the committee in 1974, and both these numbers were going down. The word was being passed in Washington that the United States might lose the GOP and possibly the two-party system.

How does a Republican react to such a situation? What does a public speaker say to revive the corpse-like shell of a once well-organized and vibrant political party? Well, Vander Jagt started with the birthday of Abraham Lincoln, the party's founder, and proceeded to list American and Republican blessings, short though the list may have seemed at that time. As he recounts in this speech, "One fellow heard the title of tonight's talk, 'Count Your Blessings,' and said, 'Thank goodness, it will be a short speech!'" But he found enough blessings of sufficient scope to pump hope into the hearts of literally hundreds of thousands of people in well over a thousand audiences when he gave this speech from 1974 to 1982 everywhere from Seattle to Tampa, from Portland, Maine, to San Diego, California. Listeners applauded and became Republicans. Republicans applauded and became donors. By 1982, there were 1.7 million Republicans donating $37 million to the party, and these numbers were going up!

One of the most complete versions of this speech was his

Lincoln Day speech delivered in Wayne County, Wooster, Ohio, on March 18, 1976. The break in the speech just before the concluding story about Lincoln occurred when the chief justice of the Supreme Court of Ohio, the Honorable C. William O'Neill, came from the back of the room, down the aisle, to the lectern to correct the congressman; Vander Jagt had been referring to him as "O'Brian."

W ONDERFUL Republicans of Wayne County, it is a great honor for me to be here with you tonight.

I'm glad to be here to join you in saying a belated "Happy Birthday" to Abraham Lincoln, the founder of our party. The fact that Abe Lincoln's birthday party is in March on the day after St. Patrick's Day makes me wonder if an O'Brian didn't have something to say about the date of his birthday observance. But any man who has been chief justice, speaker of the House, and governor of a great state ought to have a little influence on the selection of a date.

I am very honored, Mr. Chief Justice, that you included on your list of five "musts" the annual game with my alma mater, the University of Michigan. I regret that you lose judicial impartiality on those days. I regret even more that Michigan has provided so much pleasure for the last few years.

But I, like you, Mr. Chief Justice, come to this microphone tonight with trepidation because I follow in the shoes, or try to fill the shoes, of Mary Regula. I know that many of you were secretly hoping that Ralph and I would be circling around up there so that Mary would be able to speak again. I know Mary wasn't hoping that, though. I think you'd have been a lot better off, Ralph. I think you could lose your seat to the gal sitting next to you.

You know, Ralph told me that the Republicans of Wayne County were great people. And I can tell in the brief time that I have been here that Ralph, as usual, is telling it like it is. And I think it altogether appropriate that great Republicans be represented in the House of Representatives by Ralph Regula because Ralph is a great United States congressman. He's an independent thinker, he listens to the issues, all the facts, and then he makes up his mind and has the courage and conviction of independent judgment. He also is there on the job working for you. Now, you might expect that a friend of Ralph's and a colleague would say nice things about him. But this is not just rhetoric. The record is there to match the rhetoric. I said "on the job." Ralph's percentage of attendance last year was 99.7 percent. That's far higher than any other congressman from Ohio in either party. Justice O'Brian said it's even better than Ivory Soap, by one-tenth of one percent.

Ralph, because he is the kind of person that he is, and because he has acquired the skills that he has in the Ohio legislature, serving there eight years, didn't take very long to earn from his colleagues in the House their admiration, their affection, their respect. And once again the record is there to match the rhetoric. He's only in his second term, and yet he is appointed to the powerful Appropriations Committee, an honor that usually comes, as my fellow legislators here know, only near the end of a very successful career, certainly not at the beginning. It takes enormous respect to get there as fast as Ralph did.

What am I trying to say? I'm trying to say that in a very short time, Ralph Regula has come a long, long way since you sent him down to Washington. But Ralph Regula never forgot from where he came or who sent him there. I know of no congressman who is more dedicated to the service of the people that he feels so privileged to represent.

What am I trying to say? What I'm trying to say is that Ralph is a great United States congressman, and I thank you for giving him to us. In fact, I thank you for giving him to us with a greater margin in '74 than he had in '72, and there were only four Republicans in America who had that distinction in the November election of '74. I just am very, very honored to be here, to be able to thank you for giving us Ralph, and to thank you, Ralph, for that introduction. Actually, I'd be money ahead if, after all those wonderful things you said about me, I just went back home now, basking in your glory, instead of talking and bringing it back down to earth.

If we just had one hundred more Ralph Regulas in the House of Representatives, America couldn't be in the sorry state that it is in now. Speaking of the sorry state that America is in brings me to the title of my Lincoln Day talk tonight. It's entitled "Count Your Blessings." Now, that might seem like a strange title—with America in a mess, facing overwhelming problems, our Republican party in the latest poll down to eighteen percent of the American people claiming it adheres to the Republican party, and here comes this Republican from Washington to tell you, "Let's count your blessings." One fellow heard the title of tonight's talk, "Count Your Blessings," and said, "Thank goodness, it will be a short speech!" Well, he had blessings he could count.

By the way, that eighteen percent of people who adhere to the Republican party, the worst part of that is that the pollster tells me that eleven of those eighteen percentage points are kind of wishy-washy about the whole thing.

You know, I think we have blessings to count tonight, as individuals, as Americans, and as Republicans. So often we get so much, we wind up being thankful for almost nothing, and we become so blessed that we lose sight of all the blessings, just kind of take them for granted.

You know, until it gets dark, you can't see the stars. Stars are always there. It's only when night comes and a layer of darkness envelops the earth that through the darkness we can see the stars that are always twinkling there. Only the oyster that gets wounded develops a pearl, and the pearls of American progress and the pearls of Republican progress have almost always been in response to challenge as we turned our stumbling blocks into stepping-stones toward a greater tomorrow for America.

And we have many blessings to count, and we should be ashamed for letting the glitter and the glamour go out of the things that should never lose their glitter and glamour, as individuals, and Americans, and Republicans.

I think of the couple celebrating their forty-fifth wedding anniversary. Lucky for the old guy, he didn't forget. When he came home that afternoon, he had some costume jewelry, a nice bunch of flowers, a box of candy. He burst into the house and shouted out, "No dishpan hands tonight, honey. We're going out on the town! We're gonna do it up big." And they did. They had a couple of cocktails, a nice thick steak, they danced a couple of numbers. They stayed out real late. They didn't get home until about a quarter to nine.

When they did get home, he went straight to bed. He was in his room snoring; she was in her room crying. Her crying woke him up. He came to the bedroom and said, "What's the matter, dear? Didn't you have a nice anniversary? Didn't you enjoy yourself?" She said, "Oh, I did, John. It was wonderful. I loved every minute of it. But I got to thinking, and to remembering; forty-five years ago, you kissed me goodnight, and you didn't do it tonight."

With that, the fellow made a quick move. Over went the footstool. He gave her a little peck on the cheek and went right back to bed. In seconds, he was in his room snoring, and she was in her room crying. (By the way, ladies, don't worry. I'm not getting into too hot water. I can back out of this without any damage being done.) But her crying woke him up a second time. He said, "What's the matter with you, anyway? Why in the world can't you go to sleep?"

She said, "Oh, John, I just got to thinking and remembering; forty-five years ago what a caveman you were. A Don Juan, Romeo, and Casanova all rolled up into one. You nibbled on the lobe of my ear. You bit me on the back of the neck."

He made another start. Over goes the footstool again. This time the telephone goes over, too. He gets to the corridor, he turns left. She said, "Oh, John, don't be mad, don't go away. I didn't mean anything." "Mad," he cried back over his shoulder, "I'm not mad. I'm just going to the bathroom to get my teeth. I'll be right back!"

We let the glitter and glamour go out of things that just never, ever lose their glitter and glamour. You know, no matter how little you have, you've always got something to be thankful for, like the lady who only had two teeth, but she said, "Thank the Lord, they hit." She probably had more gratitude for those two teeth because they hit than we do for our fine sets of teeth.

Or like the mommy who took her little six-year-old daughter out to see Santa Claus in Washington just before last Christmas. When the little girl was through telling Santa Claus all of the things she wanted for Christmas, Santa, I guess just to break the monotony, said, "And mommy, if you could have anything you wanted, what would you like Santa Claus to bring you this Christmas?" Mommy thought awhile and then she said, "You know, Santa, I guess I really don't want anything more. I just want to be able to keep what I already have for a little while longer."

And when you stop to think about it, that's not a bad prayer for most of us.

The other day upon a bus I saw a girl with golden hair.
She seemed so gay
I envied her and
wished that I were half as fair.
I watched her as she rose to leave. I saw her
hobble down the aisle.
She had one leg and wore a crutch, but on her
face—a smile.

O God, forgive me if I whine.
I have two legs, the world is mine.

Later on, I bought some sweets, and the lad who
sold them had such charm.
I thought I'd stop and talk awhile. If I were late,
would do no harm.
And as we talked he said, "Thank you, sir, you've
been so very kind.
It's nice to talk with folks like you because, you
see, I'm blind."

O God, forgive me when I whine.
I'm blessed indeed, the world is mine.

Later, walking down the street, I saw a boy with
eyes of blue.
He stood and watched the others play, it seemed he
knew not what to do.
I watched and then I said, "Why don't you join the
others, dear?"
He looked straight ahead without a word and then I
knew, he couldn't hear.

O God, forgive me when I whine.
I have two ears, the world is mine.
Two legs to carry me where I go.
Two eyes to see the sunset's glow.
Two ears to hear what I should know.
O God, forgive us when we whine.
We're blessed indeed, the world is mine.

What we do as individuals, I think, we also do as a nation. We forget the blessings that we have as a nation. We're blessed not just as individuals, but we are blessed as Americans, blessed as no citizens have ever been blessed before. This system of ours, the freedom and the incentive, has provided for more abundance and distributed that abundance more widely to a greater percentage of our people than any economic system in the history of the world.

In America tonight, two-thirds of the people who live below the so-called poverty line live lives of luxury compared to the better-than-average family in three-quarters of the nations of the world. If America were half as rich as it is, it would be the richest nation in the world. We have much to be thankful for and many blessings to count as Americans and many blessings to count as Republicans.

Oh, I despair over those Republicans who wring their hands in despair and gloom over the corruption Watergate investigations did reveal. You know, you can look at a glass of water and say that it is half-full or half-empty. It depends upon what you're looking for. There is a flip-side to the record. The investigations of that time revealed other things, too.

Take the investigation into the life of Gerald R. Ford in connection with his confirmation as vice-president. Did you know that at one time 183 FBI agents were working full-time, digging into every nook and cranny of that man's life? Our districts overlap in Michigan, and I now represent part of what he once represented, and, during that time, I was at a farmer's place outside of Grant, Michigan, and that farmer had been visited the day before by an FBI agent who wanted to know if it were really true that eight years before, he had given a sack of apples to then-Congressman Gerald R. Ford.

Gerald R. Ford had to release the name of every doctor who had ever treated him for anything, and had to tell that doctor, "Anything you learned about me when you treated me, share it with the rest of the country and everybody else." And he had to do the same thing for every doctor who had ever treated his wife and all of his children for anything.

After that most thorough investigation in the history of the world into the background of one man, there was revealed a spotless record of integrity and honesty and decency after twenty-five years in the rough-and-tumble of American politics.

We need to count as great blessings the careers of honesty of people like Gerald R. Ford, Ralph Regula, Senator Van Meter, and Justices O'Brian and Herbert, and all the other young men.

You know, we've got something else that we need to be thankful about, and that is people like you who make those careers of honesty possible, people like you who work and give and are involved in politics because you believe in good government and believe that good government needs good men, and good men need good support. And I think it's a great blessing: people like Republicans here in Wayne County who make these careers of honesty and decency possible.

But it is also a time to be blessed as Republicans because this year, 1976, is our year of great opportunity. As Ralph mentioned, across the way there is a revival going on, and 1976 is the year of our great Republican revival. Our opportunity is so wide because the record of the Democratic Congress is so bad. Senator Van Meter was talking about the chaos in the Ohio legislature. Well, I doubt if the chaos could surpass the chaos in the United States Congress.

You know, the *Washington Post* just loves the seventy-five new freshmen Democratic congressmen, loves them and protects them. The *Washington Post* reported that over half of the freshmen Democrats believe that the United States is a greater threat to peace than communist Russia. Can you imagine that? These men are writing our laws. These men believe the way to improve the CIA is to destroy it. So, many of our institutions they are wrenching and tearing, and, you know, American people today are saying, "Let's go that way," and the Democratic Congress is taking us that way.

There is a new wind blowing in this land. There is a longing for change. You know those same polls that show the Republicans and the Democrats losing party adherence, those very same polls show that the American people are becoming far more conservative. The American people by the millions are embracing the beliefs that we Republicans have stood for and voted for since the founding of our party by Abraham Lincoln over a century ago. Millions of Americans are becoming Republicans. They just don't know it yet! And it's our job between now and election time to let those Republicans know that they really are Republicans and make sure they cast that ballot the right way when they step into the voting booth in November.

You know, these are not just words. The Democratic governors

160

from California to Massachusetts are sensing this new mood, and they are calling for less government, no more big government, no more big spending. They're singing our Republican song. But Democratic congressmen just can't learn the words, and if they could, they just couldn't carry the tune. You see, they're kneejerk spenders. They just can't help it.

Forty-four years ago. Harry Hopkins told them, "Democrats, tax and tax, and spend and spend, and elect and elect." And, for almost half a century, they have lived by that ideal, and it has served them mighty well. You know nobody shoots the bartender when the drinks are on the house. And yet, the American people are beginning to realize, I think, that somebody has to pay for those drinks, and they're suddenly beginning to realize, "My goodness, it's me!" And yet, the Democratic Congress just can't change.

Do you know the three hardest things in the world to do? For a mountain climber to climb a mountain that is leaning toward him, for a man to kiss a woman who is leaning away from him, and for a Democratic congressman to vote no when there's an opportunity for more spending.

Last December 4th was a very interesting day. Eighty-two percent of the American people said that they wanted a reduction this year in federal spending. That's what 82 percent of the American people favor. President Ford proposed a $395 billion spending ceiling this year. That wasn't the 5 percent reduction that the American people wanted. That wasn't even holding the line on spending. That was just saying, "Hey, boys in the Congress, can we hold the growth in federal spending down to 8 percent?" And the Democrats couldn't even bring themselves to vote for that. And the Republicans voted for that spending ceiling by 97.8 percent of their membership. Don't you ever let anybody tell you there's no difference between a Republican and a Democrat!

And how in the world the Democrats can run against big government and big spending absolutely baffles me. Like Walt Disney running against Donald Duck. Or Edgar Bergen running against Charlie McCarthy. It's their creation. It's theirs. Remember that no president has ever spent a penny that wasn't appropriated by Congress. No president has ever hired a bureaucrat or promulgated a rule or regulation not authorized by the Congress, and that Congress has been controlled lock, stock, and barrel by the Democrats for forty out of the last forty-four years. If people want a change in this country, there's only one way to get it and that's to change the Congress from Democratic to Republican.

What have they done in those decades that they've been taking us in the wrong direction? Well, very briefly, today in America one out of every six Americans works for government; one out of every three Americans is dependent for his livelihood on a check from government; one-third of the land in America is owned by government. You know, the people will pay more on the interest on the national debt this year than it took to run the whole government, exclusive of defense, as recently as 1959. And that wasn't very long ago.

In fact, you can take every penny of income tax (I hate to mention this with the 15th of April coming up on us), but you can take every penny of that income tax that two-thirds of the American people will pay this year and it won't do anything—nothing—but pay the interest on our national debt, which is growing by another $75 billion this year.

In 1930, government took from the American people twelve percent of the gross national product. You all know what our gross national product is. That's the fruits of the labors of a free people, the totality of their efforts. But that's part of what the American Revolution was all about. In this bicentennial year, we'll hear a lot about individual liberty, and that was the important part and a vital part of our Revolution. But the passion that fueled the Revolution was the desire for economic liberty.

The colonists had had it up to here with too much government from England, too many regulations, too many taxes, and the English put on one too many, and it erupted in the Boston Tea Party, and the Revolution was on its way, and the American people were told something that no people had ever been told before: "You may keep what you earn. You can keep what you earn to enjoy and to use to produce more next year."

And that's why, in 1930, government was taking twelve percent of the gross national product, the same percent that it had taken back in 1830, a century before. Today, this year, government will take forty percent of the gross national product away from the people who earned it and produced it, and the president told us, in his State of the Union message, that if the trends go on as they are, by 1985, government will be taking away over half of the GNP from the people who produced it and earned it. That's getting serious, and it's getting dangerous, and that isn't just a lot of rhetoric. It's real.

You know, the Democrats don't mind that. We Republicans look upon taxation as a reluctant device to be used to finance something that is necessary. Democrats love it. They do because with taxes you can reallocate your wealth and you can redistribute your resources, and they believe in that, at least the Democrats who control the caucus that controls the House believe that. Those Democrats believe, and they argue it eloquently, that America is great because of what government does for people.

Republicans say that's nonsense. America isn't great because of what government does for people. America is great because of what our government permitted a free people to do for themselves. And because the Democrats believe that America's greatness lies in what government does, they always vote for more government, more spending, more taxing, more regulating. And Republicans vote for less. Don't ever let anyone tell you there's no difference between the two parties.

We Republicans believe in that economic liberty that was at the forefront of our Revolution, and we think it's time for a revival of that principle once again. And as the Paul Reveres raced through the countryside in 1776, awakening Americans to the danger that they were about to lose their newly won freedoms, it's time for Republicans to race through the countryside in 1976 and awaken Americans to the fact that they are in danger of losing those freedoms.

I guess, if we were completely honest about it, we can't say that it was only our economic system that produced all of this abundance. We had a lot of other blessings going for us, too, in America: a rich land, great resources, a wonderful people, and a lot of luck along the way, and a lot of blessings to be thankful for.

I think of Boeing when Boeing was developing the jet airplane. Many of you can remember that. They were having difficulty. They were having what Boeing described as "minor technical difficulty." The wings kept falling off the airplane—that was just a minor technical difficulty. They got so desperate they asked their employees for suggestions. One fellow wrote on his card: "If you want those wings to stay on the airplane, all you have to do is drill little holes in a straight line all across the wings, and that'll do it."

Now, it didn't make any sense, but they had tried everything else. They didn't have anything to lose. So they tried it, and it worked. The very next plane stayed up in the air. They called the employee in. They thought they had a genius on their hands. It turned out he was the janitor at Boeing. They said, "Where in the world did you learn all about aerodynamics?" "Me?" he said, "I can't even pronounce that word." They said, "How did you know about the little holes in the straight line all across each wing keeping the wing on the airplane?" He said, "Well, all I know is whenever you go to tear off a paper towel, the darn thing never comes off where the little holes are." Think about that the next time you look out the window at the jet you're riding on.

Luck. We've had luck. We've had great resources. We've had a great people, but that economic freedom, that incentive system, more than anything else, has produced our blessings of abundance. Where we are tonight, we don't all have problems. No, we have more energy per capita, more food per mouth, more clothes per body, more cars per driver, more homes per family, more wages per worker, more opportunities per dream than any people that ever lived.

What a story we have to tell to this nation, and what a lousy job we've done in telling that story. You know that six percent of the people in America believe that free enterprise has anything to do with our abundance or our greatness. If free enterprise dies, the epitaph on the tombstone will be "The Greatest Story Never Told."

We'd better get busy telling that story and what it means to the individual. You know that statement, "Build a better mousetrap, and the nation will beat a path to your door." That's only half true because it's only half a sentence. Build a better mousetrap and the nation will beat a path to your door—if, and only if, the nation knows that you've got a better mousetrap.

We Republicans have a better way: the American way. We've got to let the nation know about it between now and November. I think that we will have that Republican revival if, in the process of telling that story, we let the American people know that we Republicans care about them—each and every one of them. The highest and the lowest.

Ralph Regula cares about each and every constituent, every one of them that comes to his office and that he has an opportunity to serve. And we Republicans better care about every person, all of them.

What president out of all of the presidents we have ever had symbolizes more than anything else a caring for people, a loving of people? The man whom we honor tonight: Abraham Lincoln. And our party better care about people, too. You know, the Democrats care about people, but with other people's money. We care about all people. We also care about the hard-working, tax-paying, law-abiding citizen in this nation. And we care about the impoverished too. You know, there are only two sectors in any society: the productive and the nonproductive. We can only take so much from the productive to give to the nonproductive or the whole thing collapses, as New York City and England are experiencing today.

We better get concerned about killing that goose that has been laying the golden eggs for all of our people because if it collapses, the ones who suffer the most are the impoverished, the needy, the aged, and the poor. We Republicans care so much about those people that we don't want to bamboozle them, and we don't want to make them forever dependent upon us to the third generation of welfare.

Wouldn't Abraham Lincoln weep in anguish if he saw three generations of the same family on welfare? You know, you help people not with a handout, but with a helping hand. You do not help a man permanently by doing for him what he can do and should do for himself.

We care. We care, and we care in a responsible way, out of love for that person.

Just one illustration of the allegiance of Lincoln's caring for people. The story is told, and I loved the story you told of Lincoln's life, and I think it was Chief Justice O'Brian who mentioned the Gettysburg Address—my goodness, I kept you an Irishman, but I turned you into the wrong kind of Irishman—I think what bothered me is, when Ralph talked about your great, great American, he talked about scarlet in the office, and I figured an Irishman ought to have green.

One story and then I've got to close. The Michigan basketball team is on television at ten o'clock, so I can't talk too long.

After Lincoln delivered that Gettysburg Address, he returned to

165

Washington, and he was walking up and down the Avenue. You know in those days the president didn't have a whole retinue. He was walking along alone on Pennsylvania Avenue when a little boy came up to him. He said, "Mister, mister, would you do me a favor?" Lincoln said, "Well, what is it?" The little boy said, "Can you draw up a will?" Lincoln's mind reached across the miles and the years to that walk-up law office in Springfield, Illinois, and he said, "You know, I think I probably can still draw up a will. Why?"

The little boy said, "My brother, who was a soldier, is over in Doctors' Hospital at 16th and K, and he's dying, and he knows he's dying, and he asked me if I could come out and catch somebody who could help him draw up a will for the few possessions he has."

Lincoln said, "Son, take me to your brother." He went into that hospital room, and he drafted and executed the will. And Lincoln was about to go when the soldier said, "Say, did you happen to see the speech that the president gave over at Gettysburg the other day? What did you think of it?"

Lincoln said, "Oh, it was all right, I guess." "All right, you guess?" the soldier replied. "I think it was the greatest speech I ever heard. I feel that my sacrifice means something. I understand it better having read that speech. My one regret is that before I died I couldn't have met just once a man who could say words like that."

Lincoln stuck out that long, narrow hand and said, "Soldier, my name is Abe Lincoln."

Lincoln cared about people. He loved people. We Republicans need to care about all of our people. We need to be grateful for all of the blessings that all of our people have and instead of tearing down, build upon those blessings because they're important. We need a positive, affirmative attitude. We need the attitude expressed in this closing poem:

I saw them tearing a building down,
A gang of men in a dusty town.
With a yo heave ho and a lusty yell
They swung a beam and the side wall fell.

I asked the foreman if those men were as skilled
As the men he'd hire, if he were to build.
He laughed and said, "Oh, no indeed.
Common labor is all I need."

166

"For those men can wreck in a day or two
What builders had taken years to do."
I asked myself as I went my way,
Which kind of role am I to play?

Am I the builder who builds with care,
Measuring life by the rule and square.
Or am I the wrecker who walks the town,
Content with the role of tearing down?

We Republicans are builders. And America needs builders as never before. Help us build to a great victory in November 1976.

The United Nations

It seems inevitable that the young man who spent a summer during his college years and a year during his graduate education in Europe would become in Congress a member of the House Foreign Affairs Committee (now called the House International Relations Committee). It was just as inevitable that the young man who spoke in favor of communication among nations in "The Price of the Best" and "Bonn Report" would welcome as a congressman with these kinds of responsibilities a chance to analyze the benefits and the costs of the United Nations.

Here he undertakes an assessment of the work of the UN at the Annual UN Day Dinner of the United Nations Association of Tulsa of November 10, 1973. Notice that he brings a balanced judgment to his task, laying out failures and accomplishments, realities and ideals, problems and promises, pros and cons in arriving at his final conclusion. Like the relationship between the hand and the fingers, he said, the UN is an international grouping which subsumes individual national entities and, so, results in a complex mixture of purposes and functions. His design in this instance followed a highly sophisticated synthesis of contradictions that led to resolution in the Kissinger statement which he had heard a few weeks prior to this occasion and had half-paraphrased, half-memorized for his audience, an audience which numbered well over five hundred people.

T HANK YOU very much. Thank you, Dr. Strong, Mayor LaFortune, Mr. President, distinguished head table guests, and friends of the United Nations. It is a great pleasure and a very real privilege for me to be here for the United Nations Association of Tulsa to help commemorate the twenty-eighth anniversary of the UN.

I am here really for two reasons. One, the invitation of Dr. Strong was really extended through my legislative aide, Jon Hawley, whom Dr. Strong indicated I stole from the University of Tulsa a few years ago, and in those few years, I think Jon has become the outstanding legislative aide on Capitol Hill. So an invitation from Jon isn't an invitation; it's sort of a command performance. I have to do it.

Jon has said so many nice things so often about the University of Tulsa and about the city of Tulsa that I thought it would be kind of fun to come on out here and see for myself. It has been a pleasant discovery to find in the warmth of your welcome, your hospitality, your friendship that, as usual, Jon is telling it like it is. In my own case, he's even telling it like it is when he talks about the wonderful weather of Tulsa.

I am also here because I believe very much in the importance of the UN, and I would like to congratulate all of you who have worked on this project, and on UN Day, to congratulate the mayor for all of these efforts that have gone into underscoring the importance of the United Nations. I think on this twenty-eighth anniversary maybe the UN needs it more than it ever needed it before because our American public has replaced the apathy and indifference which they shower in large doses upon the United Nations with a growing hostility, and, at least on the surface, it seems that public support is diminishing, and criticism is increasing. And I think we do not serve well the cause of the UN if we just turn a totally deaf ear to those criticisms because the UN does, like all institutions, have in it imperfections, inequities, frustrations, and failures.

Certainly it is a bit ironic that the Maldive Islands with a population of less than 100,000 has one vote in the General Assembly, and the United States of America with 220 million people has one vote in the General Assembly, or that the 800 million people in the People's Republic of China, one-fourth of the world's population, is represented by one vote in the General Assembly, and less than 100,000 people on the Islands have that same one vote. It is, I think, a bit ironic that the United States with far less than one percent of the voting strength in the General Assembly, pays twenty-five percent of the bill for the programs that are passed, and the African bloc nations, for example, with something like thirty-five percent of the voting strength, pay only three percent of the bill. And that is not the wisest way to work out programs that are practical, efficient, and economical.

Increasingly, the United Nations has been a forum for harangues against the United States and our policies. Very often those harangues are short on reflection but very, very long in terms of demagogic, cliché phrases that really go over big back in the home country. People are saying that it is a debating society that just passes its proclamations because the world will go merrily on in its own way anyway, no matter what the UN says or does, and they are pointing to an increasing list of instances where that is the case. The U.S. Congress votes to order the purchase of chrome from Rhodesia in violation of the UN sanctions. North and South Vietnamese go on killing each other as the peacekeeping force stands helplessly by. South Africa continues to rule Southwest Africa with an iron fist in spite of the proclamation of independence for that region by the United Nations. And Russia obliterates freedom for the Czechoslovakians and the Hungarians as though the words about the rights of self-determination of people in the UN charter did not exist.

So there have been failures; there have been frustrations; there are inequities; and there are imperfections. Measured in terms of what we want the UN to be, measured in terms of our ultimate goal, I think perhaps there is cause for despair, but measured in terms of how far we have come since that day twenty-eight years ago, I think there is genuine cause for hope and for optimism and for justifiable pride.

The UN has accomplished a lot. For one thing, you know, just the fact that we're still meeting together as nations and talking together is no mean achievement. Henry Ford, of my own state of Michigan, once said, "Getting together is a beginning; working together is real success." And if that be the case, we have real success in the United Nations because, although the political failings and the confrontation tactics get the headlines and use up our impressions and our consciousness, over ninety percent of the UN s resources are devoted to nonpolitical endeavors in the social and economic and technical and scientific areas. And in these areas, the UN has made remarkable progress indeed. You see, the UN from the beginning recognized that peace is more than just the absence of hostilities, and recognized that it had to build the kind of world where peace could be a reality. It has done great work with all of the nations working together.

The UN health programs have reached the point where we are in sight of wiping malaria off the face of this earth. The UN development program surveys have turned up mineral deposits valued in excess of thirteen billion dollars: copper in Mexico and Panama and Malaysia, limestone in Togo, iron ore in Chile, and coal in Pakistan, and on and on the list goes.

And the UN has helped the transition for one billion people, one third of mankind, from colonialism to independence, and made that transition a peaceful one, and has aided and protected sixty new and struggling nations in their struggle for independence and for economic progress.

And the UN serves a tremendously essential function. If we didn't have the UN, we'd have to have another international organization to take its place in terms of the public service of bookkeeping, information gathering, regulations, and standards-setting on a worldwide scale.

And the UN has proved to be the absolutely essential mechanism through which the United States can formulate worldwide programs to meet worldwide problems. Let's just take one example: the environment. You know in America each year we not only have a UN Day, we have an Earth Day. On Earth Day, we don't just think about America's pollution problems, we think about the earth's environment, and that's why we call it "Earth Day" because we recognize that all of mankind's destiny is tied into the environment of this earth. That was so vividly illustrated for the whole world and, I think in unforgettable fashion, five days before the first Earth Day. If you will recall, that was when Apollo VIII developed trouble up there in space, and, for four days, millions of people watched the TV with their hearts in their mouths, wondering if our astronauts were ever going to get back to earth. And as you stepped into taxicabs or people came out of meetings, the question on everyone's lips was the same: How are they doing? Have they heard anything? How are they doing?

And when those three astronauts finally splashed down in the Pacific, their precious life-supply systems of air and water and power were running precariously low. The meager supplies they had left were rapidly being depleted, and they had only hours more to live, and time was running out for Lovell, Haise, and Swigert, no matter how great their cool and cunning and courage, and no matter how great the computerized technology behind them.

Well, the plight of the spaceship *Odyssey*, I think, dramatized the plight of man on this earth because in a very real way the planet earth is like a space capsule hurtling through the vastness of the universe with only meager supplies of air and water, and those precious life-supply systems for this earth are running precariously low. And, with the meager supplies that we have left, time is running out for man on this earth unless we do something to halt the rapid pace of the degradation and the destruction of our environment.

Now, if the United States had tackled this world environmental problem all on our own, we would have been an imperialist, a nation that had it made imposing our newly discovered environmental concerns on nations that had not. Wasn't it so much better that through the United Nations, through the Stockholm conference last year, the UN was able to develop worldwide concerns and worldwide programs to meet this worldwide problem?

The same thing is even more true in terms of the world concern with overpopulation. How much better to have the world working on this through the UN than having a "have" nation imposing the rate of economic growth and expansion on a "have not" nation.

And so there are a few examples of tangible success stories that the UN can point to, but even in that peacekeeping field, the UN has some remarkable successes to talk about. For twenty-five years now, United Nations peacekeeping forces, sometimes only a dozen men, sometimes several thousands, have been keeping the peace or restoring it when it has been broken all over the world in such perennial trouble spots as Kashmir and Cyprus. A decade ago, a substantial UN force went into the Congo and prevented that country from collapsing into a bloody civil war or total domination by an outside power.

And right now, at this very minute, in the uneasy and tenuous truce in the Middle East, the UN was the perfect mechanism. If the U.S. and the USSR had dictated a cease-fire, it would have been two superpowers imposing it. How much better that through the Security Council, by a vote of fourteen to zero, the UN was the mechanism for that cease-fire. And right at this moment there are peacekeeping troops of the UN from Austria, Sweden, and Finland who are providing that viable alternative to U.S. and USSR troops there confronting one another with all of the perils and risks that are carried with it, and for the first time in over a decade, under UN auspices, the Israelis and the Egyptians are talking together right now. This peacekeeping has not always been easy. In fact, it's been very difficult. It's been a little bit like the referee who is trying to pull two huge football players from each other's throats to prevent a whole holocaust from breaking out all over the field.

This year my wife Carol and I went to Panmunjom at the thirty-eighth parallel in Korea. We saw the odds in hate and hostility that are against UN peacekeeping forces. As Carol and I drove into the checkpoint at Panmunjom, the North Korean soldiers came running down the steps in order to spit all over our car to show their contempt and their hostility toward any representatives of the free world. And at Panmunjom itself, it is kind of a twilight zone, a neutral zone where armed armies have their guns loaded and trained on one another, peering at one another across that no man's land. And once in a while the hate erupts, and the guns fire. One hundred and fifty-four men were killed in border skirmishes in 1971 alone, and many of them were UN peacekeeping forces. And yet, through that unheralded, that unnoticed, that activity of the UN there, somehow, someway, a tenuous peace has been maintained there since the fighting in Korea stopped.

And so I think we can point amazingly to [break in the tape]. Who can put a price tag on what the UN has meant to the world in these last twenty-eight years? What returns we have on our paltry investment! And yes, I say, "paltry." Do you know that New York City spends more money to dispose of its garbage than the United States contributes to the UN to help that agency dispose of world problems? We can be proud of the returns that we and the world have received from our investment in the United Nations.

And the need for the United Nations has become even clearer

with two events that have occurred since its founding twenty-eight years ago: the perfection of the hydrogen bomb—it is easy to see how that shows the need for the UN. Professor Hans Therring said in an interview a few years ago that the H-bomb should be renamed the "end-of-the-world-bomb" because a single large one encased in cobalt can put an end to every living thing on this planet. Either we learn how to live and work together or none of us may be living at all.

Well, how does the trip to the moon underscore the need for the United Nations? The bomb, we're reacting and motivated by fear of what will happen to us if we don't. I think that trip to the moon gives us a more positive motivation because we never really saw the earth, did we, till we saw it from the moon.

No one who ever heard the Christmas Eve broadcast of 1968 and Apollo VIII will ever forget. Frank Borman described the drabness, the grayness, the dreariness of the universe except for the incredible beauty of that globe, that earth down below. And then Frank Borman said, "And now Apollo VIII has a Christmas Eve message for you." And then the voice of Astronaut Bill Anders, "In the beginning God created the heavens and the earth . . ." And that biblical account of creation in Genesis was concluded with the voice of Frank Borman coming back on, "And God looked down on the earth that he had created and, behold, God saw that it was good." Then Frank Borman said, "Goodnight. Goodbye. Merry Christmas. God bless all of you, all of you, on the good earth below." And then Frank Borman disappeared behind the backside of the moon.

And I think God did bless us that night by giving us a vision of the oneness of this earth and the oneness of the people who live here so that the nations that inhabit the earth, be they capitalists or communists, liberal or conservative, right or left, black, brown, red, yellow, or white, poor or rich, little or big, share one human species with a common destiny and with common hopes and aspirations and longings and dreams.

And it's that ideal, the ideal of the brotherhood of man, that the UN placed before mankind twenty-eight years ago. You know what an ideal is? An ideal is "an intense conviction of what ought to be" which we hold before ourselves so that we work together to try to attain it. "An intense conviction of what ought to be," and that's the ideal that the UN put before the nations of the world twenty-eight

174

years ago, and we've tried to work together to make progress toward that goal. And the going hasn't been as easy as we thought it was going to be. We haven't made as much progress as we would have liked to have made, but progress we have made. And that goal glitters all the more captivatingly as we are wiser and sadder than we were then, but it glitters more captivatingly because of the progress that we have made and because the H-bomb gives us a vivid glimpse of our common destruction if we fail, and the trip to the moon gives us a common hope that maybe, just maybe, we can succeed.

If you viewed the UN back then as a panacea, as a magic wand that would whisk our ideal into the real, then, of course, your hopes have been dashed on the realities of vetoes and quarrels and bickerings and failures and frustrations. But if back then, the UN held before the world an intense conviction of what ought to be that we could work together to try to attain, then your hopes have indeed been justified. We need the UN as we work for that goal and as we work for that ideal.

You know, I think that all of our ideals and hopes have to go through a sort of a collision process with reality. That's how we mature and toughen and deepen into a meaningful faith. Otherwise the ideal is just sort of a pollyannic optimism, kind of a wishful thinking or an irrelevant fantasy.

Peter Marshall, the great chaplain of the United States Senate, said that what man needs are the bifocals of faith, the bifocals with which to see the problems of today, but the ability to see above the rim to the promise of tomorrow. And he who looks at the UN today and sees only the promise of tomorrow and ignores the problems of self-righteous propagandizing, the selfishness, and the pettiness, does not really serve well the cause of the UN. But he who sees only those problems of today and ignores the promise of tomorrow does not serve well the cause of truth and the longing of all mankind.

Two of my friends in the Congress, Senator Gale McGee and Congressman Ed Derwinski, went down to the UN a few years ago to be a part of the permanent U.S. delegation to the UN, an honor which is bestowed upon four congressmen every year. Now Ed Derwinski is an outspoken conservative and a long-time critic of the United Nations. He made great political capital by taking on the UN, and he got standing ovations by kind of making the UN his private whipping boy. Senator Gale McGee, outstanding liberal internationalist, was a longtime champion of the UN. He made great political capital and got standing ovations by equating the UN with everything that is good and perfect in this world.

Now, as you might imagine, it was kind of interesting to see these two total opposites going down there and being thrown into the same actuality, the same reality. And what happened to them perhaps is not what you might have thought would happen to them. Congressman Derwinski did not suddenly see that his criticisms had been unjustified. Quite the contrary. He became more convinced than ever that he was right and that there was an awful lot that was awfully wrong down there at the UN. Congressman Derwinski saw something else too, and it's changed his life. He saw that ideal of the brotherhood of man, and he saw people of all races and creeds and colors working together, imperfectly, suffering setback after setback, but, inch by inch, trying to move this world closer to that ideal.

And Senator McGee? He didn't say to Ed Derwinski, "You see, Ed, you've been wrong all the time. That flyspecking criticism that you do, you see, well, you just missed the boat." And Senator McGee didn't refrain from doing that just because he's an awfully nice man and would never be the kind who would say, "I told you so." No, Senator McGee, confronted the pettiness and the frustrations and the problems and the propagandizing, and he became very frustrated, and he wound up saying, "You know, Ed Derwinski, you were right. Your criticisms were justified; there is an awful lot that is awfully wrong down there at the UN." And if that in the end weakened Senator McGee's faith in the UN, maybe it did for a few days when those realities first began impinging on his idealism, but you wouldn't know it today because he is more convinced than ever, more maturely convinced, of the need, the absolute essentiality of the United Nations and all that it stands for.

And they walked away, both of them constructive critics and eloquent champions of the UN and the world's need for the UN. That's the kind of process of strengthening and pouring steel into our ideals that we go through in every arena. And it's necessary.

I remember that when I went to Europe for the first time, twenty-one years ago, I was a student. I went on board the S.S. *Waterman*. There were 1,200 students on board that ship, a very memorable eleven-day crossing. But, on that trip, we had to fill out a questionnaire. Most of us had never been to Europe before, and one of the questions on that many-paged questionnaire was, "Do you believe that Europe can be united?" That was 1952, and we hadn't even really started toward the united Europe as we know it today. Ninety-four percent of the American students said, "Of course Europe can be united. Why, we united the United States of America."

Then they landed in Europe, and they spent a summer there, and they saw what the average Franchman thought of the average German, and what the average German thought of the average Frenchman, and they faced some of the barriers and difficulties of language and everything else. And, when that same group of 1,200 students came back on the same boat and filled out the same questionnaire, six percent believed that Europe could ever unite itself again. See what happened there? Ideals had come into contact with reality and, with the first brush with reality, they threw up their hands and said, "Oh no, it can't be done."

You know, we have a maturing process in a lot of areas. And just as a little parenthesis, I remember on the same questionnaire, the boys, the American boys, were asked to rate the women of fifteen different countries in terms of their beauty. You know where American women placed going over? Fifteenth, last. When they answered that same question coming home, when they'd been around a little bit, do you know where American women placed? Number one on that whole list! I don't think that's got much to do with the UN or ideals, but I remember that when I was on that ship, I believed in the brotherhood of man. In fact, I knew I was going to have to give a lot of speeches when I got back home so all the way going over on the ship, I started trying to put into speech form some of the experiences I knew were going to happen to me that would illustrate the brotherhood of man. Then I ran into some of those realities that had changed that poll around, and I began to wonder: you know, brotherhood of man means that everybody, everywhere, is exactly the same and, brother, I'm going to discard that ideal because we aren't.

And that type of questioning and wondering came to a climax for me near the end of the summer. I had met a university student named Wolfgang, and he took me with him to a place called the Schnitzelbank in Heidelberg. We went into the Schnitzelbank and all of the tables were filled except one off in the corner of the room. There was a very powerful looking middle-aged German man and his wife and two empty chairs. And we went over and were very welcome to join them. But this German at the table had taken in a few beers too many and that, coupled with the fact that I was with a German, made him think that I was a German. And he started to rant and rave about those bloody Americans. And the longer and the louder he talked, the more frightened I became about what was going to happen to me when he found out what I was. After a while he woke up to the fact that I was not German. He said, "By the way, young fella, what nationality are you?" Well, I was so scared by then I didn't dare tell him the truth, so I blurted out, "English." He said, "English, eh? Well, that's bad too. But it isn't quite as bad as being a bloody American." He said, on second thought, it wasn't bad at all because he was anxious to question an Englishman about the beautiful spots that every Englishman knows and loves very well.

I knew when I was in water over my head so I said, "I thought you asked me 'what language do you speak.' That's why I blurted out 'English.' I am an American." His reaction was not as violent as I had feared. In fact, we stayed around awhile, but as he prepared to leave, he leaned over the table and he said, "I just want you to remember this, young fella, there is more than an ocean out there separating Germany and America, and there's more than an ocean of difference between the old world and the new."

Well, I'll never forget how disillusioned and sad I felt as he stalked out of the Schnitzelbank in Heidelberg. I said to my new-found friend across the table, "Wolfgang, it seems to me that man is right. There is a lot of difference between you and me and how we think, how we approach a problem." He gave me an answer that I will always treasure. He said, "Yes, that's right. It seems that way at first glance, doesn't it? But," he said, "isn't that because of a coat of prejudice, a coat of misunderstanding, a coat of differing cultures? A coat of mud builds itself around our personalities, but whenever you scrape away the mud, and get down to the kernel, there people everywhere are the same. They have the same salty tears when they cry, the same red blood when they bleed, the same hopes and dreams and loves and longings and aspirations."

And he said, "It's your job not to throw up your hands in despair when you see a little mud in the street, but to scrape for all that you are worth, getting down to the kernel because the things which unite us, because we're human beings created by the same God, are far more basic than those things which separate us because we were born in different countries."

That's the kind of ideal that the United Nations put before the world twenty-eight years ago.

And I would like to close my remarks to you tonight by sharing with you a toast that I heard several weeks ago in New York City. It was my privilege to co-host with five other congressmen and Henry Kissinger, the largest and most glittering diplomatic dinner ever given in the history of New York City. It was a way that the new secretary of state had of showing how important he felt the UN was. Two days after he was confirmed as secretary of state, as the first official act of his office, he delivered an address to the United Nations. And then about ten days or two weeks after that, he hosted this dinner where either the foreign minister or the permanent representative of 128 countries of this world went to the Metropolitan Museum of Art for the diplomatic dinner. And what a spectacle it was with the costumes and colors and the creeds as they came together to have the dinner hosted by Kissinger.

And at that dinner, Dr. Kissinger gave a toast, and I think that his words, I think maybe that's the third reason I am with you tonight, I think these words are so important and so beautiful, far more than anything I may have said, these words convey what the UN is all about. Because it was a toast, they were never recorded anywhere so I think they will be new to you. But he said [that] all of us assembled here tonight present a glorious mix of tongues, creeds, and races. Here, tonight, are the leaders of an institution designed to serve all peoples of the world, not any special people or culture or national purpose. Here are leaders of the Congress of the United States who remind us that, from the days of Warren Austin and Arthur Vandenberg, all Americans, no matter what their political party, have supported the United Nations.

And honoring us here tonight by their presence are the artists, the academics, and the journalists who are the guarantors of our diversity and the trustees of our common destiny.

This assemblage here tonight symbolizes the world as it is. And even more, this assemblage symbolizes the world as it can be, because here in the United Nations, here at these tables tonight, we have come together, across the boundaries of our differences because of a common goal, a hope for peace and a better life for all mankind.

Ralph Waldo Emerson once quoted a legend of unknown antiquity, "The gods in the beginning divided man into men so that he could better help himself, just as the hand was divided into

179

fingers to better serve its end." That is a wisdom that neither nations nor men have yet understood or practiced. Across the centuries, we have emphasized our political and philosophical differences rather than our common destiny; we have been more given to conflict than to cooperation. Of all the species on this planet, man alone has inflicted most of his suffering upon himself. In an age of possible nuclear cataclysm, the vision of a world community is absolutely essential.

So let us make our ideals worthy of a big challenge, and let us remember that great works are never accomplished without deep commitment. Where there is oppression, let us sow justice. Where there is hunger, let us seek abundance. Where there is inhumanity, let us have compassion. Where there is ill will, let us strive for good faith.

And let us remember the difference between truth and self-righteousness. Let us remember that no nation or group of nations can demand to have their problems alone understood. Let us make sure that we never make the best the enemy of the good. And let us always remember that the ideal can only be realized in stages defined by the attainable. Let us remember, finally, that we will be judged not by our proclamations but by our deeds.

I pledge to you tonight, members of the world community, that the United States is ready to begin a journey toward a true world community. We will keep our sights raised even when our tread must be measured. We will not make excessive promises, but we will keep every promise that we do make. We know that peace will come when all, the small as well as the large, have a stake in its shaping And we know that peace will endure when all the weak as well as the strong have a stake in its lasting.

Hope has been likened to a road in the country. In the beginning, it is not there; as it is traveled more and more, it comes into existence. Let us then, tonight, seek to change our practices but not our ideals. And let us, in our daily labors, begin to travel the road of our hopes so that the unfamiliar will become natural and that our vision will become our reality.

Ladies and gentlemen, I ask you to join me in a toast to the United Nations—the treasury of man's noblest aspirations!

Thank you.

Will American Free Enterprise Survive?

This speech to two hundred managers in the Dow Chemical Company was delivered in Midland, Michigan, on September 25, 1973. Vander Jagt's interest and work in foreign affairs had brought him regularly into questions of foreign trade, taxation, and U.S. economic policy, an emphasis revealed strongly here as he attempted to move these businessmen into the political arena. This idea became one of his three or four chief themes throughout the Ford and Carter years: business people speaking for free enterprise and involved in government are essential to a free economy. He made the point time and time again that the federal government had gradually worked its way into the individual citizen's life to the point where private initiative was being lost in the face of public regulations and control.

Data illustrating the growth of government agencies, the growth of governmental regulations, and the growth of consumer protection served to background this presentation. A statement he made before the Committee on Ways and Means in June of 1973, *Foreign Economic Policy Consideration in Trade and Tax Matters,* was also included in his preparation for this speech.

Notice the conversational quality of his choice and arrangement of words. It strains grammatical punctuation, but, nevertheless, it has been preserved as what was said, rather than having been edited for written publication. His allusion to his novel introduction was a reference to the fact that his appearance at this gathering was kept a secret in order to surprise the audience. He was presented as a mystery guest.

T HANK YOU very much. It's nice to be with you. I think you will agree that that's probably the most novel way that you have ever been introduced to a congressman. I must say it's probably the most unique opportunity that I've ever had to be a part of a "think" session of top management of one of the top corporations of the United States, but I think probably both of us would agree that the growing crisis in relations between government and business kind of warrants as novel and unique an approach as either of us can devise in coping with the challenge and crisis that has arisen because we're all aware of how government reaches in and either directly or indirectly impacts upon almost every waking moment of our life.

From the time we get in the car in the morning, the cost of that car, of purchase, and operation, is determined by government standards. If we mail a letter, the price of the letter is set by the government. When you get to the office and try to cope with the decision of whether you borrow money to expand the plant or not, important in that decision is the cost of money and interest that is determined by the monetary policies of the Federal Reserve. The raw materials that you use to produce a product can well be determined by health or environmental standards or requirements that the government has set. The price that you pay the people who produce the product, the wage, is in a very real way determined by the federal government with federal minimum wage and the upward push that has on all other wages and certainly the withholding for social security, health, and other government-imposed fringe benefits. Then, the way you ship it, and when you ship it, and the container and the label, are all impacted by the truth in packaging and labeling legislation. And even when you go home at night, look on the TV, your television program is very much influenced by the regulations of the Federal Communications Commission. And then, if you get totally fed up, and you say, "To heck with it, I'm going fishing tomorrow and get away from all of this doggone regulation," even then there's the government waiting for you, telling when you can fish, where you can fish, what size fish you can catch, and wherever we go, we find government regulation impacting on us.

No one needs to tell you the great impact that the mushrooming in the last couple of years of a myriad of government agencies and boards, what impact that has directly on the operation of Dow. The

National Highway Traffic Safety Administration and its regulation impact on everything you sell to the automobile industry, the tire industry, and related industries. The Hazardous Materials Control Board, its regulations impact on the containers you can use for shipping, the labeling, and just how you can ship. And the Occupational, Safety, and Health Act and its regulations impact upon you and in, maybe, minutiae, and yet it demonstrates how far-reaching is the arm of government. They tell you exactly how high the wall has to be between the commodes in the bathrooms in your plant, how many square feet you have to have in your cafeteria. They've just issued a ruling that you cannot use ice to cool the drinking water. So government is reaching into the bathrooms, and even into that fabled cooling fountain, the drinking fountain in the office of the plant.

I think it is fair to say, and I think everyone would agree, that the decisions that are being made today in Washington—decisions on trade, decisions on spending because that will determine the decision on taxes and inflation, decisions related to the economy in general—that these decisions will probably more directly affect your profit and loss statement at the end of the year than any decisions that you can make in your corporate board rooms in research or in product management. It shouldn't be that way, but it is that way.

And those decisions will have a decisive impact. So, if governmental decisions have as much to do with your profit and loss statement as corporate decisions, then certainly it behooves the corporation and the top people in that corporation to involve themselves in having an impact on what those governmental decisions are going to be. You need to do that not only for the health and prosperity of your company, but I think you need to do it for the health and prosperity of the American people because, more and more, these decisions are being made without any reference to the scientific or rational or factual foundation. They are made without reference really to the goal they're supposed to serve, and, more and more, these regulations are being made in an atmosphere of complete and total hostility to business and to the free enterprise system.

The words "profit motive" are words that are sort of outmoded in discussions in Washington. "The free enterprise system" is sort of a Neanderthal phrase that very few with-it politicians want to talk about out in public. And, we need only look at just a very few statistics to see how the giant of the federal government has muscled its way into our free market economy and dominates it in a very real and overpowering way. This year we will pay interest on the national debt of $24 billion. That's more than it took to run the whole government in 1955, exclusive of defense. You can take every penny of income tax that is paid by two-thirds of the American people, and it doesn't do anything but pay the interest on the national debt. Between 1955 and '75, the amount we spend on what we call human resources will grow from $14 billion in '55 to $134 billion by 1975. And, three-fourths of that $120 billion increase is in the areas of guaranteed income like social security, unemployment compensation—the withholding tax area.

One-third of the land in America today is owned by the federal government and one out of every three Americans is dependent upon a check from the federal government for his income. But, even worse than just those few little statistics, and since you've been promised no speeches, I won't rattle more statistics at you, even worse than those—and there are many more I could give—is the climate of hostility, the dedication of anger against business, that prevails in the atmosphere and the climate in Washington today. And, I think the great paradox of our time is how business tolerates, and sometimes even participates in, its own destruction.

For example, much of the hostility and criticism emanates from colleges and universities, colleges that are supported by tax dollars generated largely by U.S. business, or by donations from capital funds that supposedly are controlled and owned by U.S. business. And what is the attitude toward business on the campuses today? In a recent nationwide college poll, the college students said that William Kunstler is the lawyer in America that they admire most. And William Kunstler said recently to a group of college students, "You must learn how to take to the streets, to revolt, to shoot guns. You must learn to do all of the things that property owners fear the most."

Steward Alsop, writing in a monthly Yale magazine, said, "Yale, like every major college in America today, is graduating scores and scores of bright young men who are practitioners of the politics of despair. These bright young men," he said, "despise the American economic system." In a recent poll of twelve major

184

representative colleges in America, almost half of the students interviewed said that they favored the total nationalization of all basic U.S. industries. And Ralph Nader, idolized by millions and millions of American people, was recently described this way in a profile on him in *Fortune* magazine, and, I think, it's an accurate description of Ralph Nader; it said the passion that runs in him—and he is a passionate man—is aimed at smashing utterly what is the target of his hate, which is corporate power. Nader thinks and says quite bluntly that the majority of top corporation executives in America today belong in prison—for defiling the consumer, for shoddy merchandise, for poisoning the food supply with chemical additives, and willfully manufacturing unsafe products that maim and kill the buyer. And he makes it clear, says *Fortune* magazine, that he is not talking about fly-by-night corporations, but the top management of America's blue chip companies.

Now that's really incredible, isn't it? It's unbelievable! It doesn't make sense to me that in the name of consumerism, there are those who would wring the neck of the goose that has been laying the golden eggs for the consumer. It really doesn't make sense that in the name of consumerism, there are those who would destroy the business system that has made a king and queen of the American consumer, because, really, if we stop to think about it, American business has made an incredible and unbelievable achievement. From the time you wake up to the buzz of the electric alarm, step into a hot shower, flick on the color TV to see the *Today* program, put the bread into the pop-up toaster, reach into the refrigerator for some milk, leave the home that you own and get into the automobile to drive to work, you are experiencing a luxury—any one of which would set a man apart as wealthy and powerful in three-quarters of the nations of this world, let alone all of them. And we don't even think of them as luxuries, but just necessities for our everyday living.

This system of ours has produced more abundance and distributed that abundance more widely to more millions of people than any system in the history of the world. So that two-thirds of the people in America today who live below that so-called poverty line, live lives of luxury compared to the rich in three-quarters of the nations of the world. It's been a phenomenal achievement. And we have a story to tell the nation, but we haven't done a very good job of telling that story. And I think in a way it's a little bit understandable.

185

I think in a way it's a little understandable that American business doesn't have a greater impact on political decisions because we have concentrated on this very, very difficult task for all these years.

The challenge of American business: how do you make a product a little more economically here? How do you shave the cost a little bit there? How do you make a better product? How do you come up with new technology that will solve a new crisis and deliver more comfort and leisure and convenience to the American people? That success story of American business is personified by Dow, with its emphasis on individual initiative and effort. And what a tremendous and dramatic story that has been, and we've been so busy doing the kind of thing that's important, we said, "Well, let somebody else worry about the political decisions. Let George do it!" And believe you me, George has done it. Into Washington have moved the Ralph Naders, the consumers, the environmentalists, the labor unions, and all of the rest. And they really can't do anything else except impact on political decisions. They don't have any achievements to their credit. That's all they do, but boy, they do that very, very well. And they've moved into the vacuum that you have left for them because you've been doing more important things.

And it probably has been a lot more important in the past when government was small. Yet we've seen how in the last decade or so it isn't so small anymore, but it is a giant that dominates every aspect of our personal lives and of our corporate lives. And so now we need to move into the arena and bring some balance to the decisions that are there, and we need to do so for one other reason than just the success of our company—the company that we work for and that we live for. That is, as we have seen, I think, from the quotations I've given you, that the system itself is under attack. There are people who think the system is no good, in spite of all the contrary evidence. And, I think that we, just as American citizens, for the benefit of our children and our children's children, have an obligation to see that this tremendous story that we have to tell the nation is told, and that its achievements and miracles are taken into account because it is the system and its survival that are indeed at stake.

If you'll pardon just a very homely illustration, but with all of the exporters, and the importers, and the smugglers, and the pirates, I got to thinking about the sea this morning. Pat and Mike were on a ship, and they were going across the Atlantic Ocean. And in the middle of the night, they awakened, and a terrible storm had come up, and they ran up on deck. And they saw that everyone was running around trying to fasten down the masts, and hold back the water, and Pat said to Mike, "My goodness, we'd better pitch in and lend a hand. It looks to me as though this ship may go down." And Mike, very shortsightedly, said to Pat, "Ah, I don't think so. Let the ship go—it isn't our ship." That was kind of shortsighted of Mike, because life, his destiny, depended on the welfare of that ship.

And I think that sometimes businessmen are tempted to say, "Well, all of this flurry of regulations is unreasonable coming down on me. I'm just busy enough just trying to figure out if I can fit in with them, how I can just get along. Now that's all I've got time to worry about." And yet we are all on this ship of state together. And I think it is imperative on all of us to be concerned whether that ship is dashed on the rocks or whether it charts a safe and secure and meaningful course. Just before the Supreme Court Justice Powell went on the Supreme Court, he prepared a memorandum for the United States Chamber of Commerce, in which he very graphically documented how the American business system is under attack. And then he came to his conclusion, and because I think it is so pertinent to your deliberations in the next hours, with your permission, I would like to read to you his conclusion:

> What specifically should be done? The first essential, a prerequisite to any effective action, is for businessmen to confront this problem as a primary responsibility of corporate management. The overriding first need is for businessmen to recognize that the ultimate issue may be survival, survival of what we call the free enterprise system and all that that means for the prosperity of America. The day is long past when the chief executive officer of a major corporation discharges his responsibility by maintaining a satisfactory growth of profits without due regard to the corporation's public and social responsibilities. If our system is to survive, top management must be equally concerned with protecting and preserving the system itself.

I think that system can be preserved and protected. I think there's a latent reservoir of good will and understanding in the hearts of the American people. And they will respond to the story that business has to tell, but it is something that must be done, and it hasn't really been done in these past decades. It was Edmund Burke who once said that the only thing that you need for the wrong to triumph is for good men to do nothing. Dante said that the hottest place in Hades would be reserved for those who remain indifferent, or apathetic, or neutral when there was a great moral challenge and crisis confronting their society.

One of the reasons that the political decisions have had such a bad impact and have been so bad in so many ways is that an enthusiastic minority always has a bigger club than an indifferent majority. And in the past, basically, American business has been indifferent to the story that Washington needs to be told, and a story that must be gotten across.

Will free enterprise survive in America? I'd like to close by answering that question with a story. I apologize for the story, because it's a homely one, and I have really tried to overcome my ministerial days that were in my past, and not be a preacher. I've tried very hard to sort of tell it like it is, and what the climate in Washington is, and what I think the challenge is. And now since I've come all this way, I ask you to indulge me for a minute and a half as I answer the question "Will free enterprise survive in America?" Because I believe this answer so deeply, that's why I wanted to be with you, and why I am with you this morning.

I can answer the question "Will free enterprise survive in America?" by sharing with you a legend that they tell about a southern German town. And this was a little town, but it had in it a man who had a reputation for being so wise that he always answered questions correctly. He never ever gave a wrong answer. There was a young smartaleck in that town who resented all the homage and honor that was heaped upon that wise old man, so he devised a plot to trip him up and make him give a wrong answer. And he ran off to a nearby forest and he captured a hummingbird so tiny that you could completely encompass the bird in the palms of your hands. Then he grabbed his cronies around him and he told them what he was going to do. He said, "I'm going to take this to the wise old man; tell him I have a bird, and I'm going to ask him if the bird is dead or alive. If he says the bird is dead, I'll open my hand, the bird will fly away—he'll be wrong. If he says the bird is alive, I'll just squeeze those hands together; then I'll show him the dead bird—and he'll be wrong. He can't give a correct answer to that."

So they went through the town, gathering as many of the townspeople as they could so they'd have as many witnesses as possible the day the wise old man gave a wrong answer. He knocked on the door of the cottage. The wise old man answered it, and said, "What may I do to serve you, my son?" And the young smartaleck said, "Old, wise, and honored sir," with mock reverence, "I hold here in my hands a little bird. And I wonder if you can tell us, is this bird dead or alive? The wise old man started to answer, then he paused, and a smile and a look of profound wisdom came over his face as he said, "The answer to that question, young man, is in your hands."

Will American free enterprise survive in America? The answer to that question, I believe, is in your hands—the hands of top management, of top U.S. corporations. If you care enough, if you want to badly enough, that free enterprise that has served us so well will continue to serve us in the future. Thank you.

Earth Day

"Earth Day" was delivered on April 22, 1970, at the Calder Plaza in Grand Rapids, Michigan. Vander Jagt spoke to an outdoor audience of four hundred. In just a few minutes, he related two of his key interests, space exploration and the environment.

F IVE DAYS ago the heart-in-mouth apprehension of millions of praying, listening, and watching people gave way to heart-wrenched relief as the space ship *Odyssey* made it safely back to earth. By the time the three astronauts splashed down, their precious life-sustaining systems of water, oxygen, and power were running precariously low. What meager supplies of water and oxygen remained were being rapidly depleted. Time was running out for Lovell, Haise, and Swigert, and they had only hours more to live no matter how great their cool, courage, and cunning, and no matter how great the computerized technology behind them.

The plight of the three astronauts in the space ship *Odyssey* dramatizes the plight of man on this earth. In a sense, the planet Earth is a space ship hurtling through the vastness of the universe. There are only limited supplies of oxygen and water to sustain life. Our already meager supplies are being rapidly depleted. Time is running out for man unless we reverse the galloping pace of the degradation of our environment.

This realization may be part of the sudden and overwhelming interest and concern for the environment, and the interest is overwhelming. As we observe Earth Day here in Grand Rapids, we join tens of millions of Americans all across this land in the greatest demonstration anywhere, anytime for anything. And the interest is sudden. Just a little over a year ago when the highly regarded Brookings Institute unleashed its vast resources and learned experts to draw up an agenda of priority concerns for the new incoming administration, the environment was not mentioned anywhere in the voluminous report. The environment has catapulted from relative obscurity to instant overnight stardom. Voices that have been crying alone in the wilderness for years have suddenly been swallowed up in a swelling chorus of housewives, students, politicians, and just plain citizens.

Hopefully, our interest in doing something about our environment is motivated not only by a fear of what will happen to us if we don't, but by an affirmative appreciation for the good Earth. Didn't it really begin on Christmas Eve of 1968? That night was the night all of us vicariously left the earth and went to the moon and peered down through the grayness and drabness of the universe on this beautiful Earth below.

As our attention was riveted upon the moon, we heard "Apollo VIII has a message for you. In the beginning, God created..." And then the biblical account of creation concluded by Frank Borman's voice, "And God looked down upon the earth and God saw that it was good." And Colonel Borman said, "Good night. Goodbye. Merry Christmas. God bless all of you. God bless all of you on the good Earth." And with that Frank Borman disappeared behind the back side of the moon.

And God did bless us that night by giving us a vision of how beautiful, how precious, how fragile, and how good is this earth on which we live. And so the stimulus for our war on pollution is not just fear of what will happen to us if we continue to contaminate our atmosphere, but also a new reverence for life, a new feeling for the goodness of our Earth.

Let no one underestimate the enormity of our task. During the 60s, trillions of tons, gallons, yards, and miles of pollutants were added to our environment. Garbage was dumped on our land; pollutants poured into our waters; sewage gushed into our lakes; rich topsoil laden with persistent pesticides spewed into our harbors; dark, dirty gases belched into our air, and concrete and steel sprawled forward into our ever-retreating landscape. Before the onslaught of noise, smog, sprawl, sewage, garbage, debris, and pollution, our efforts were feeble and inadequate, fragmented and overlapping, indecisive and retreating. Our air became smoggier, our water dirtier, and our environment uglier. And the wastes that an ever-exploding population of ever-increasing affluence must disgorge pile higher and higher. The enemy to a beautiful America grows more formidable with each passing moment.

The price tag for cleaning up is costly. It involves not just more money, but in some cases a reordering of values, a redirection of our goals. An old Spanish proverb tells us, "You can have anything you want if you want it badly enough." Do we want that clean environment badly enough?

There's been a lot of eloquent oratory and rhetoric about conquering pollution. A lot of rhetoric about pure air and fresh water. Who's against that? But so often, as in so many things, there's a yawning gulf between our words and our actions, between what we say we want and what we're really willing to pay for. In so many ways, we resemble Bill. Bill was so shy and bashful that whenever he was in the presence of his girl friend he could never manage to express the beautiful sentiments that rummaged around in his heart. So even though he only lived a few blocks away, and even though he saw her every day in high school, he took to writing her notes. One intercepted note read as follows:

> Dearest Sal,
>   I'd climb the highest mountain over the steepest rocks; I'd walk through the longest, hottest desert. I'd swim through the widest, roughest ocean just to stand for one tiny fraction of a second before the lovely beauty of thy countenance.
>
>   All my love, Bill

At the bottom was this P.S.: "I'll be over to see you tonight if it isn't raining outside."

Poor Bill never realized that the P.S. gave an empty, hollow ring to all of the flowery rhetoric of the letter, and so often we citizens don't realize that our actions, or inaction, gives an empty, hollow ring to all of our flowery rhetoric about a clean environment.

Our rhetoric sounds empty and hollow when we spend more on research to prevent possible pollution of Mars than we do on research to prevent actual pollution of Lake Michigan. Our rhetoric sounds empty and hollow when we permit the United States Navy to dump tons of raw sewage each year into the San Francisco Bay. Our rhetoric sounds empty and hollow when we spend more for chrome than for air exhaust systems on our automobiles. Our rhetoric sounds empty and hollow when we decry an exploding population and then grant tax incentives and rewards for people to have additional children.

The real question is not whether we want a clean environment (everyone wants that), but whether we are willing to pay the price of achieving that clean environment; not whether we can find some villain somewhere, some scapegoat, somebody else to foot the bill, but whether we, each of us, individually and personally, are willing to pay the price.

It may mean higher taxes to pay for a new sewage treatment plant. It may mean getting along with shirts that are not quite "whiter than white" because the polluting phosphates have been removed from detergents. It may mean settling for slower, smaller cars that belch less pollution into the air. It may mean the tedium of doing homework on difficult environmental problems instead of screaming for nonexistent quick cures. It may mean less viewing with alarm and more patience in trying to make the system work. It may mean becoming involved in the hard and often unappreciated job of citizen action for environmental quality, making legislators legislate and administrators administer for a cleaner environment. It may mean sitting through long and tedious planning and zoning meetings. It may mean less littering, more knowledge, quickened concern, and deepened knowledge of the environment for all of us.

It really means that then this Earth Day can go down in history as the launching of the proper shift in perspectives and priorities by the American people. At the beginning of the decade of the 60s, President John F. Kennedy set a goal for this nation of putting a man on the moon by the end of the decade. And this nation committed its heart, mind, and will to achieving that fantastic goal. Having reached the moon, it is indeed appropriate in the dawn of this new decade that Americans set a new goal, a goal directed not at the heaven above but at the Earth below whose poignantly precious beauty we rediscovered through our voyage in outer space.

Let that goal be: by the end of this decade America will be beautiful again. By 1980, America's waters everywhere will be pure;

193

America's air everywhere will be fresh; America's land everywhere will be abundant. Let us resolve, again, here and now, that "we will pay any price, bear any burden, overcome any obstacle, make any sacrifice" to reach that goal. Let's resolve that when in 1980 we sing "America the Beautiful," it will indeed be a beautiful America of which we sing.

Frank Borman

February 19, 1970, found Vander Jagt paying tribute to Colonel Frank Borman when the astronaut was awarded an honorary degree at Hope College in a midyear convocation before the whole student body. This speech of tribute clearly represents the classic form of the speech of advocacy which Vander Jagt used so regularly and so well later as a spokesman for Republican candidates who were campaigning for seats in the House of Representatives.

Notice how he introduced his presentation by modestly poking fun at himself. In the process of lending humor to the situation in this way, however, he was also revealing his credentials as a member of the House Committee on Science and Astronautics. Notice, too, how his sequencing of reasons for honoring Borman built from what was common knowledge about him to what was little known, from what the young congressman considered of least importance to what he believed was most significant among Borman's many achievements.

M R. CHAIRMAN, platform guests, chaplain, dean, members of the Board of Trustees, members of the faculty and administration, students, and ladies and gentlemen: it is a humbling honor and a personally satisfying thrill to return to my alma mater to present to you, Mr. Chairman, and to all those assembled here, a courageous astronaut, a great American, a dedicated Christian, an inspirational leader, and a good friend—Colonel Frank Borman of the United States Air Force.

195

The opportunity for me brings the circle of fate around full-cycle. To explain that, I must make a confession here in this college with its Calvinistic tradition which holds that confession is good for the soul. When I was a senior in high school, five other students and I hovered between two grades. On the last day of classes, the six of us were to participate in a panel discussion. The quality of our participation would determine whether we were awarded the higher grade or the lower grade. I got the lower grade and was fortunate indeed that I didn't plummet all the way down to an F or below because I refused to participate in that panel discussion. The topic the teacher assigned was so utterly unrealistic, so fantastically impossible that it was not a topic worthy of wasting the valuable and precious time of high school seniors in even bothering to talk about. The topic that the teacher assigned was: "Will man ever reach the moon?"

With that background of vision, it was almost inevitable that Congress in its infinite wisdom, yes, that's right, Congress did, it plucked me out of fifty-seven freshmen congressmen who arrived on the scene that year and plopped me in the Space Committee, the committee charged with the responsibility of getting Frank Borman and his colleagues to the moon and back. In the many hours we worked together, Frank, I decided I'd never rock your confidence by telling you that story until after you were safely back here on earth.

While I and so many others were using the phrase, "reaching for the moon" to describe fanciful, wishful thinking, Frank Borman was dreaming the impossible dream and, step by step, persistently and patiently, he was in fact reaching for the moon. As long as there is a recorded history, the name Frank Borman will live as the first man to take an open-mouthed world, live and in color, all the way to the moon. He will be remembered as the man who reached higher into the sky and deeper into the hearts of his people than any man of his age.

As fantastic as was Colonel Borman's Apollo VIII flight to the moon during Christmas 1968, that was not his greatest contribution. Two weeks ago. Frank's boss, Dr. Tom Payne, said that even greater contributions were made by Frank Borman to the space program as an inspirational leader, a planner, and an engineer.

Let's face it; any one of several astronauts could have piloted Apollo VIII. I doubt if anyone but Frank Borman could have saved the space program from possible abandonment and certainly future delay three years ago. Because of the magnificent precision and near perfection of the astronauts' performance (like great athletes, they make the hard plays look so easy) it is easy to overlook the extreme danger and hazardous risks surrounding each step of the way. Shortly after I went on the Space Committee, one spark, somewhere along the five and a half miles of wiring inside the space capsule and a malfunction of just one of the 10,000 moving parts, caused a flash fire in the capsule still on the launching pad, and we snuffed out three of the most beloved and admired of our astronauts. Panic and self-doubt and confusion swept the country and the Congress. The warning signals were up, and a final decision on whether to proceed with the space program was held in abeyance until our committee completed a painstaking month long inquiry into what went wrong and all the things that could go wrong in the future. Colonel Frank Borman, as the astronaut member of the Apollo review board, worked with us hundreds of hours. It was Frank Borman's quiet courage as much as anything that prompted us to take down the warning signals and flash the go sign for the moon.

Frank Borman's courage was a courage based on knowledge. He had an encyclopedic knowledge of the facts and theories of space. He began acquiring that knowledge as a student at the U.S. Military Academy from which he graduated in 1950. He acquired a master's degree from the California Institute of Technology in 1957. In between, he had racked up more than 4,000 flying hours as part of fighter squadrons in the U.S. and the Philippines. He returned to West Point as a professor in aerodynamics and fluid mechanics, then on to the Experimental Test Pilots School from which he graduated number one in his class. Borman's courage was first of all based on knowledge—a profound and complete knowledge.

Frank Borman's courage was a courage based on performance, performance that came as a result of a total dedication of body, mind, and heart to the personal sacrifice, discipline, hard work, and effort necessary to achieve. Colonel Borman was the command pilot of Gemini VII whose fourteen days in space give Frank the record for the space flight of longest duration. The rendezvous with Gemini VI was the first space rendezvous of two separate space vehicles. Colonel Borman holds the record for most miles traveled in outer space and for the greatest thrust out of the earth's gravitational pull

197

Frank holds another record which isn't often listed, a record that required courage of a different sort. After his return to earth, he addressed a joint session of Congress. A proud and happy nation poured out its gratitude through the applause of its elected representatives. In that speech recounting the achievements of Apollo VIII, Colonel Borman said one of his greatest personal achievements was when he, Episcopalian Frank Borman, persuaded Roman Catholic Bill Anders to read from the King James Version of the Old Testament.

Then looking down at the nine black-robed Supreme Court justices in the front row, with a gentle twitting of the folly of their decision on prayer in public schools, Frank Borman said, "Oops, in the presence of the Supreme Court, perhaps I shouldn't have mentioned the Bible at all." The approving applause and laughter that erupted from Congress set an all-time record for intensity, duration, and for greatest thrust out of the somberness and stuffiness of the hallowed halls of those chambers.

Colonel Borman's courage was a courage based on love of country and a conviction that serving that country was worth the risks involved. Colonel Borman's friend Roger Chaffee expressed this well in a response to an inquiry from a nine-year-old boy in Grand Rapids, Chaffee's hometown, about what he had to do to become an astronaut. Shortly before he was killed in that Cape Canaveral fire on the launching pad, Chaffee responded with these words, "To be an astronaut you must love your country. You must love your country so much that, as corny as it sounds, you feel the chills go up and down your spine each time you see the American flag or hear the 'Star-Spangled Banner.' You must love your country so much that you are willing to live for America and, if necessary, die for America." Colonel Frank Borman loved his country that much, and his courage was rooted in it.

And finally Colonel Borman's courage was a courage anchored in hope—a hope based upon a belief in God. No one who ever heard it will ever forget the Christmas Eve telecast. As our attention was riveted upon the moon, we heard Frank Borman say, "Apollo VIII has a message for you." Then Anders' voice, "In the beginning, God created ... " And then the biblical account of creation concluded by Frank Borman's voice, "And God looked down upon the earth and God saw that it was good." And Colonel Borman said, "Good night.

Goodbye. Merry Christmas. God bless all of you on the good Earth." And with that Frank Borman disappeared behind the moon.

And God did bless all of us that night. He gave us a new vision of how very beautiful, how precious, how fragile, and how good is the Earth which God has created.

Colonel Frank Borman has become an inspirational leader to all people everywhere but especially to young people. This is exemplified by the sophomore class's selection of Frank Borman as its class hero. As America, and especially its young people, turns its attention from the moon above to the earth below, Colonel Frank Borman is a fitting hero indeed. In facing our problems and challenges, young Americans, like the courageous astronaut, are dreaming the impossible dream of abundance, brotherhood, equality, and peace for all people. We are reaching for the moon here on earth. As we reach for the moon in social objectives, Frank Borman reminds us that an essential ingredient is courage based on knowledge painstakingly acquired, performance resulting from dedication of body, mind, and heart to the rigors of discipline, sacrifice, and effort, a love of country so deep that personal egoism recedes, and a courage anchored in hope because of a deep and abiding faith in God.

And that, Mr. Chairman, is why it is a humbling honor to present a courageous astronaut, a great American, a dedicated Christian, and an inspirational leader for the purpose of receiving an honorary degree: Colonel Frank Borman of the United States Air Force.

Speeches from His Early Years

Excerpt from
"Beyond a Reasonable Doubt"

While no transcriptions of his forensic speaking during the period from 1960 to 1964 exist, much later, in August of 1973, Vander Jagt had an experience which he describes in an unpublished essay, "Beyond a Reasonable Doubt." This essay gives insight into the kinds of questions that intrigued him as a lawyer and the kinds of reflective thinking and rhetorical treatment of evidence he brought to bear on them.

His friend and colleague, Harold Sawyer, had been defending a client whose trial was drawing to a close. Sawyer had chosen to defend him on the basis of his belief that there was a reasonable doubt about his guilt, and, when he searched for materials to include in his closing argument, he found very little in the literature which would clarify his legal position for the jury. He shared the problem with Vander Jagt, who developed a number of illustrations which would support the stance Sawyer was taking. He gave them to Sawyer while they were dining with their wives the evening before Sawyer's summation was to be given. After what seemed to be just a casual glance at them, Sawyer used them completely and expertly in his final argument the following morning to win the case.

O UR RESPECT for the persuasiveness of the state's case was intensified by the knowledge that the prosecutor had made this case a personal *cause célèbre*. For one thing he had a perfect record to maintain. He had never lost a homicide case in twelve years as Kent County prosecutor. Beyond that, over the past twenty-five or twenty-six years, four successive Kent County prosecutors had failed to obtain convictions in only four murder charges they had brought to trial. Harold Sawyer had been the successful defense counsel in all four of those murder trials—the only four he had ever defended! Each time the defense had been different: self-defense for the boy who had stabbed to death a blind man and had allegedly run from the scene with the deceased's wallet in his pocket; dismissal for the woman who had charcoal-broiled her child, after its alleged death by deliberate suffocation, so thoroughly that no cause of death could be determined, and, therefore, there was no *corpus delicti;* temporary insanity for the husband who had used a .44 Magnum to kill his wife with one bullet and permanently paralyze from the waist down her parmour with another bullet the night he discovered them making love in a friend's cottage; the black alcoholic indigent who was charged on the basis of a drunken braggadocio admission that it was he who had perpetrated the arson that resulted in the highly publicized death of four black cult members; and now a classic reasonable-doubt case.

But the question was how to give those jurors who believed Rog [Sawyer's client] to be innocent the ammunition they would need in the jury room to persuade those jurors who believed him to be guilty that even if they *believed* in his guilt they could, in fact under the law they *had* to, vote "not guilty" unless they believed in guilt beyond a reasonable doubt.

How can we get them to consideration of whether the proofs established guilt beyond a reasonable doubt rather than an argument between "He did it" and "No, he didn't do it," was a question Sawyer posed to me one Sunday afternoon. The trial had recessed for the weekend. My congressional session had recessed for the month of August. We were relaxing at our homes on the Pine River near Luther.

The challenge he presented intrigued me. "Believing beyond a reasonable doubt and to a moral certainty," was a phrase rich in content but made empty by being so oft-repeated that it had become almost ritualistic. Breathing life into worn out phrases that had lost their original zing and zip was a familiar challenge. As a Yale Divinity School graduate and sometimes guest minister and interim pastor, I had long wrestled with how to pump new twentieth-century meaning and relevance into phrases that had been repeated so many millions of times through the centuries that their original impact had become blunted on the modern ear. Phrases like "Forgiveness of Sin," "Salvation by Grace," or "Believe in the Lord Jesus Christ" might point to experiences as real and valid now as when they were formulated some fifteen centuries ago, but what the phrases themselves evoke to many a modern mind was far different from the original experiences they were formulated to describe. Centuries ago the king of England cried out to the architect showing him Westminster Abbey for the first time, "Amusing, awful, and artificial!"—and the architect, who was proud of his creation, was overjoyed at the royal compliment! In those days "amusing" meant "amazing," "awful" meant "awesome," and "artificial" meant "artistic."

To a far lesser but to a very important extent it seemed to me that belief "beyond a reasonable doubt and to a moral certainty" was a phrase that had lost by constant repetition the overwhelming impact it had to have had when its awesome demand was heard for the first time. How to clothe the bones of that old phrase with living, dynamic flesh and blood so that the full force of its original impact would be felt again was the challenge.

As we discussed it, it became clear that we had to convince the jurors who believed Rog did it that they *had* to vote "not guilty" even if they believed he was guilty, unless they believed he did it beyond a reasonable doubt. We had to sell the concept that "not guilty" was in no way a verdict of innocent. That's why the law doesn't give jurors a choice between guilty or innocent—instead it's a choice between guilty or not guilty. And not guilty is just what it says, no more, no less. "Not guilty" is not innocent; it's *"not necessarily"* guilty.

We thought of illustrating this with the story of the young boy who had been taunted by the smartaleck of the neighborhood with the question of whether the young boy's sister was ugly or beautiful. Now she was most decidedly not beautiful. She was, in fact, most plain. The young boy was too honest to call her beautiful, but he loved her too much to call her ugly. "Come now," the smartaleck demanded, "what is your verdict? Is she ugly or beautiful?"

"My verdict," the young brother answered evenly, "is that my sister is *not* ugly."

And his verdict was indeed an accurate one. It's true she wasn't beautiful, but she wasn't ugly either—at least not to someone who loved her.

There were those on the jury, we felt, who could never proclaim our client innocent and might hold out to the end against a verdict which proclaimed him to be that which they felt to be false. But a "not guilty" verdict did not say that. A "not guilty" verdict merely said guilt had *not* been established beyond a reasonable doubt, and so, therefore, "not guilty" no more proclaimed the defendant's innocence than "not ugly" had proclaimed the sister's beauty.

Just why the law had imposed such a severe test on the prosecution had to be made clear. The jury had to be made to *feel* just why our judicial system is built on the belief that it is better that one hundred guilty men go free than that one innocent man be punished, and that, therefore, is why it imposes such an awesome burden on the state. Sawyer had had the associates at his firm of Warner, Norcross & Judd (probably the most highly regarded law firm in all of Michigan and certainly outside of Detroit) search the legal literature for clues as to how this had been done in the past. Much to our surprise the legal literature contained no such clues. My own search of the thirty or so volumes of popularized legal contests revealed no such hints.

As we talked about it we hit upon comparing it to a mild version of Russian roulette. The jury would be asked to imagine twelve pistols on the prosecutor's table. The evidence had established that eleven were totally void of any bullets but that one was probably loaded for Russian roulette—five empty chambers and one loaded. The judge tells you to pick up one of the twelve pistols. Then he orders you to aim it at the defendant's heart and pull the trigger, but only if you are convinced beyond a reasonable doubt that the chamber is empty and the gun will not fire. Now you have every reason to believe that you are safe. The odds are certainly on your side. The odds are eleven to one that the pistol you hold has no bullet whatever in it. But even if perchance you hold the loaded one, there is only one chance in six that the chamber is loaded. But you wouldn't fire, would you? Of course not! You would slowly drop your arm and say to the judge, "No, I can't pull the trigger. I believe, I believe with all my heart that the pistol is not loaded. But I do not know that to be a fact beyond a moral certainty. Therefore, I cannot, I will not pull the trigger."

It is that same degree of moral certainty that the law imposes upon a juror before he can pull the trigger that takes a man's life with the verdict of "guilty." Rather than have him pull the trigger on an innocent man, the law asks—no, the law demands!—that he drop his arm and say *not* guilty even when he thinks the defendant is guilty.

We had anticipated that, since there is no capital punishment in Michigan, some might feel the analogy too severe, and we prepared to show that a verdict that took a father from four already motherless children, telling them that their mother was dead because their father had beaten her to death with a hammer, was a result so horrendous that death by a single shot might well appear as an attractive alternative.

Finally we decided that we should illustrate the classic definition of reasonable doubt that it might better be grasped by the jurors. The law placed upon the prosecutor the burden of proving his theory of the case beyond a reasonable doubt. As long as there were facts believed by the jury to be true, totally inconsistent with the prosecutor's theory, he had not met that burden. As long as there was *any* other explanation of what happened that remained possible, the prosecutor had not met that burden. We believed it to be like putting a jigsaw puzzle together. As long as there were some pieces that, no matter how hard you shoved or pushed, just didn't fit, then the theory had not been proved beyond a reasonable doubt.

One Lone Voice

Long before the actor who played the role of George Gipp in the movie *Knute Rockne: All-American* became president of the United States, the young campaigner Guy Vander Jagt was using the story of the "Gipper" in his own campaign speeches for election to the Michigan State Senate. It became the goose-pimple conclusion to his first televised campaign speech which was aired on WWTV, Channel 9, Cadillac, Michigan, in the fall of 1964.

Notice here how he repeats his theme, representation, through religious and patriotic examples from the past. This is one of the very few speeches in which he used a Teleprompter. A part of Dick Young's introduction of him is included here to set the scene.

Dick Young: A few weeks ago, I was very pleasantly reacquainted with one of my former students by the name of Guy Vander Jagt. I was very happy to learn that Guy had decided to project his talents and abilities in the direction of better government for Michigan by entering the campaign for state senate. I believe that Guy Vander Jagt is by far the best qualified man in the race for the senate and for any position in government over the last few years that I have known or had the privilege to know. At this time, I would like to introduce to you my former student and, in my opinion, your opportunity to put good government in Lansing, proudly, Guy Vander Jagt.

Guy Vander Jagt: Thank you very much, Dick. You know, talking into these familiar cameras once again reminds me of what a tremendous privilege and pleasure it was to have the opportunity of being invited into your homes night after night to present the top news stories of the day for one year and to give you my views and comments on the issues as they developed.

But of all the news stories that I ever reported to you, the story that I want to report about tonight is by far the most important to the people of this area. It's the story of reapportionment, redistricting in Michigan. The story moved into the final stages just a few weeks ago with a decision written by Chief Justice Earl Warren of the United States Supreme Court in which he said that the senate districts in states had to be as nearly equal in population as was practicable. In the wake of that decision, the Michigan Supreme Court adopted the so-called Austin Kleiner Plan No. 2. Now what that plan means to the state of Michigan I think I can best illustrate by zeroing in on the senate district for which I am a candidate; incidentally, the senate district where the WWTV tower stands smack dab in the center.

This new senate district begins up at the county of Leelanau, comes all the way down, takes in Benzie and Manistee with the exception of the city of Manistee, and then comes over and takes in Wexford, Osceola, includes Newaygo, cuts across, taking in Mecosta, Isabella, up to Clare, Roscommon, Crawford, across to Kalkaska, three townships out of Antrim, Grand Traverse County, and then back to Leelanau.

Now this district is a district that contains more than 11,000 square miles. And there is one lone voice to be speaking for it in Lansing under this new plan which has been adopted. This district contains ten major cities, and there will be one lone voice speaking for it in Lansing. This district is 150 miles from tip to tip, and there will be one lone voice speaking for it in Lansing. This district contains two great state universities and a college, and there will be one lone voice speaking for it in Lansing. This district contains acres and acres of the most beautiful forests and streams and lakes in the entire world, and there will be one lone voice speaking for it in Lansing. This district contains areas which formerly were represented by five state senators, and now there will be one state senator speaking for the entire district.

You see what happened is that previously the Detroit area had seven state senators. Under the new plan, they are given thirteen—that's almost double. But the total was not increased, and so what was added to the Detroit area had to be subtracted from outstate Michigan. In fact, we are in a situation where, roughly speaking, we have one and a half senators to speak for the entire northern half of the Lower Peninsula.

I think it is a time of crisis for our area, and I am particularly pleased to be able to offer myself as a candidate in this critical time. And it has been a thrilling time campaigning through this area. I've been so thankful for your support. The friendliness, the encouragement, the help which I have found throughout these fifteen counties have been beyond my fondest expectations. In fact, I think I uncovered a secret weapon in the campaign, and that was the support of people in all walks of life. And I pledge and promise here and now that I will try to be worthy of the support that you have so generously showered upon me.

I think that perhaps one of the reasons for that support is that you remember. You remember when I sat in your living rooms night after night, and you want the same kinds of things said on your behalf in Lansing now. I think you remember when I, with a camera television crew, went into every county in this new district and studied and reported on your history, your problems, and your opportunities. I think that you know that I know this area and its people far better than either of the other two announced candidates can claim to know the area and its people. I think you remember that I have preached in your churches. I have spoken in your schools. I have dedicated your auditoriums and delivered your commencement addresses.

Now if I am elected, I promise to make the first item on my agenda the restoration of the representation which we have lost. There are a number of things that we can do. There are two constitutional amendments which have already been introduced. There is a rehearing before the United States Supreme Court. Or we can appeal the decision of the Michigan Supreme Court which goes far beyond the requirements even of the U.S. Supreme Court decision. But the important thing is that we believe we can win; that we know we can prevail because our cause is just; that we're on the side of good law and true Americanism.

I would like to take you back to the year 1787. The scene is the

State House in Philadelphia. That cast of characters includes George Washington, Alexander Hamilton, James Madison, John Adams, Benjamin Franklin. It's the first Con-Con. The federal delegates are there to decide upon a U.S. Constitution, but they are about to break up in failure and to go home and announce that they can't agree on anything because there is one issue that divides them, and that is the issue of representation. The large states maintain that representation in Congress should be on the basis of population: one man, one vote. Where have we heard that before? The small states say, "Oh, no, because one large state with a heavy concentration of population could then dominate the entire Union." And it is in that impasse that Benjamin Franklin, eighty years old, stands to speak: "Gentlemen," he says, "I have lived a long time, and in that time I have learned that God governs in the affairs of men. If a sparrow cannot fall to the ground without His notice, is it possible that a nation can rise without His help? I make the motion that we begin our deliberations with prayer, seeking His supreme guidance." Two days after the motion was carried, the delegates agreed on a compromise—a compromise that was so simple that they were astounded they hadn't discovered it weeks before. It was this: they'd have two houses in Congress. One house, the House of Representatives, would be based on population. The other, the United States Senate, would have equal representation for each state based on geography, providing a system of checks and balances in a government of the people and by the people.

So ingrained did this become into the fabric of our American system of government that even Chief Justice Earl Warren was singing a far different song in 1948. Then Warren said:

> It is my conviction that the rural and agricultural counties of outstate California contribute far more to the welfare of this state than their total population bears to the total percentage. That is why I have never favored limiting their representation in the state senate to a strictly population basis. It is the reason that the Founding Fathers gave equal representation to each state in the U.S. Senate, regardless of population.

So we have tradition and the law on our side, and we can prevail because ours is not a government of the courts and by the courts. It's a government of the people and by the people.

Thomas Jefferson said that the ultimate power in our

government is in the people. Dwight Eisenhower said there is nothing the American people can't do when they get their dander up. And, believe me, we, in this area, ought to have our dander up over our loss of representation.

In other words, we stand in a great tradition, and there is a tremendous amount of inspiration in tradition. Let me give one illustration from football. It's George Gipp—that some of you may know the story—perhaps the greatest football player in the history of Notre Dame. It was the last season, the last game against Northwestern, and Gipp was in the hospital, but he slipped out of the hospital on the day of the game, and he sat on the bench huddled in blankets as a cold, raw wind swept across Lake Michigan over the Evanston Stadium. It was the last quarter, Notre Dame was behind, and a chant went up from the crowd, "We want Gipp! We want Gipp!" That chant, the score, and the pleas of his beloved player at his elbow, made Knute Rockne send Gipp onto the field. A few minutes later, Gipp and the Notre Dame team walked off with another of those fabled Fighting Irish come-from-behind victories. But the cold and the strain were too much for Gipp—he returned to the hospital, and, two weeks later, Knute Rockne was summoned by the doctors and told that Gipp would not live through the night. In a hushed hospital room, George Gipp acknowledged to his coach that he knew the end was near, that he would never see another football game. And then he said, "Rock, will you do a favor for me?"

Rock said of couse he would, "but what is it?"

He said, "Some day, Rock, when a Notre Dame team has its back to the wall, when the odds are against us, and it doesn't look like we've got a chance, will you ask the team to go out and win one for the Gipper?"

Rockne swallowed the lump in his throat and left the hospital and waited until the time was right. Eight years later, 1928, Notre Dame was playing Army: Notre Dame, thrice beaten; Army undefeated, unscored upon, No. 1 in the nation. At the end of the half, the score stood Army 6, Notre Dame 0. The sportswriters settled back in their chairs awaiting the massacre that they knew was to follow. And the only question was how many points will Army roll up. But in a quiet dressing room Knute Rockne knew that the time had come. He told the team the story of George Gipp and the dying boy's request for a favor. Then in a quiet voice, Rockne said, "Okay, men, this is it. Go on out and win this one for the Gipper."

A charged up Notre Dame team surged onto the playing field and wrote one of the greatest upsets in the annals of intercollegiate football history. The final score: Notre Dame 13, Army 6.

Well, it's only a football game, but it illustrates what inspiration there is in tradition and in the memory of those who have contributed to our cause. And what a memory and what an inspiration we Americans have: the George Washingtons, the Benjamin Franklins, the Thomas Jeffersons, the Abraham Lincolns, and the tradition of government of the people and by the people, and a system of government that has checks and balances.

Sometimes I think America could be analogized to the prodigal son in the Bible. You recall that he went into a distant land, and he strayed far from the traditions of his father. He squandered his fortune and was among the swine looking for food. And, then, the Bible says of the prodigal son, "When he came to himself, he said, 'I will arise and return to my father.'"

Our former patriots are awaiting for America to return to itself, its true self, waiting for Americans to say, "We will arise and return to the traditions of our founding fathers—the traditions which made this country great, the traditions which, with your support, will keep America and Michigan great."

Thank You...For What?

It was in the fall of 1957 that Vander Jagt undertook pulpit responsibilities in the Cadillac Congregational Church. After four months, the congregation had tripled, and pressure was on to keep the young preacher there on a permanent basis. But he had applied to the Georgetown University Law School earlier and had been accepted for the term beginning in January of 1958. He intended to keep that date because he had already decided to enter politics.

The sermon included here was given on December 1, 1957, a week after he had preached a Thanksgiving sermon entitled, "Thank You." In this earlier presentation, he invited the members of his congregation to question his thesis that Americans should be thankful every minute of every day. Someone among his listeners asked him to explain how he could be thankful in the face of evil as it is evidenced every minute of every day. In this sermon, "Thank You...For What?" he offers his answer. Here, again, his optimism in the face of strong cynicism surfaces and foreshadows his undaunted optimism much later as a Republican congressional campaigner.

That this sermon was indeed effective is attested to in a most unusual way. A member of his audience that Sunday morning in December of 1957 wrote to him over twenty years later from Bonanza, Oregon, that she and her husband were so impressed by the sermon that they had kept a written copy of it which they had requested at the time and which he had had typed for them. She enclosed a copy in her letter and asked him if his philosophy had changed. He replied:

214

What a lovely thing you did—taking the time to send me a sermon I had preached more than twenty years ago. It was my only copy, and I had long since forgotten it.

I hope that sermon may have been some help to people when I preached it then, but I'm certain it was far more help to me now. You asked if my philosophy of life had changed. No, if anything, time and experience have deepened it. But, in the hectic pell-mell routine of important responsibilities, I go for long stretches without thinking as much about it as I should. Moments of refreshment of faith and rekindling of inspiration are most necessary. Reading that sermon that I had thought about so many hundreds of hours provided that refreshment and inspiration. It had been so long that it was like reading it for the first time, and, yet in another way, it was like finding an old and familiar friend. At any rate, thank you for sending the sermon. It did wonders for me, and I'm glad to have it.

I SUPPOSE as we grow older we learn to be careful about the invita tions we make. Somebody might just take you up on one. When you're traveling and meet an old friend and you say, "You folks must come to Cadillac and visit us some time," you had better really want that carload that drives up for a long weekend because they might take you up on it.

I should have learned this back in the summer of 1952. I was on a train going from Paris to Rotterdam, and in my compartment there was a young Indonesian student. His name was Danny Yap. Somehow or other I got to telling him about Thanksgiving. I was so carried away by my description of turkey and cranberries and pumpkin pie, and there in the middle of France in the middle of the summer, America and Thanksgiving seemed so remote, that I concluded by saying, "Danny, if you ever get to America at Thanksgiving time, you'll have to have a real Thanksgiving dinner in Cadillac, Michigan." I heard no more of him and had forgotten all about Danny Yap. And, then in the middle of November, I received a post card which read:

Dear Guy,
        I'm coming for Thanksgiving.
                                Signed
                                Danny Yap

215

Well, last week I extended an invitation to anyone who had any questions about anything I had said and would like to suggest topics that you would like me to deal with, to let me know. Little did I think that I would be "assigned" the subject that we tackle this morning. It's about the last subject I would have selected! I was most reluctant to grapple with it. In fact, I must have consumed gallons of coffee this past week at the Northwood and the Snow White, seizing any excuse to run away from the topic I was so reluctant to turn my mind to.

But that Thanksgiving that Danny Yap was with us was one of the finest ever. And this subject has turned out to be, for me at least, one of the most profitable of any that I have dealt with thus far, and I hope that some of you may find it helpful too.

If I may be allowed to put the suggestion into my own terminology and to say it in my own words, it would run something like this. You preached a Thanksgiving sermon in which you said that God had created the world and everything in it. And He found it to be very good! And He gave it to us, and we should be thankful for everything every minute of every day. Well, when I look at the world, I sometimes find it not very good. On the contrary, I find it to be very bad indeed. I see war, famine, floods, suffering, pain, and death. You tell the man whose body is racked with pain to be thankful. I think his response might well be: "Thank you? *For what?*"

You see, that raises the age-old problem of evil and the suffering that evil causes in our lives. If God is all-good and all-powerful and all-loving, then how did evil get here? The question goes back to the early centuries of Christianity. One of the early church's theologians, Marcion, examined the world, and this is the way he described it, "The world is filled with flies, fleas, and fevers!" And Marcion concluded that the God of love that he had come to know through Jesus Christ could not possibly be the same God who had created the mess that he saw when he looked around. And so, Marcion concluded, there must be two Gods. He was called a heretic and expelled from the church. But that didn't answer the question he had raised, and the question is still with us.

Harry Emerson Fosdick's father once said that he'd want to go to heaven if for no other reason than to get God off in a corner and ask Him some questions. Surely, that somewhat irreverent mood has been shared by most. How we'd like to ask, "What about this?" or

216

"How do you explain that?" And high priority would be given to the problem of evil.

In dealing with the problem this morning, let us turn to the Bible, for a problem so profound as evil requires a book as profound as the Bible to deal with it. Perhaps some of you recently saw the cartoon which showed a man going into a book store to purchase a Bible. The clerk said, "I'm sorry, sir, we're all out of Bibles right now . . . but we have something just as good." I doubt that. I doubt that very much, especially in relation to suffering. For whatever has happened to you as you take it to the Bible, you can't read very far before you discover "your problem." Carrying on a dialogue with the Bible, you soon find it figuratively shaking its head and saying, "Yes, I know. I've been there too. I know how you feel." For the Bible is a record of men and their fears and problems and questions and doubt and even rebellion with God—and their faith!

And this morning we'd sort of like to arrange our thinking around that advice of Christ's when He said, "Be of good cheer for I have overcome the world!" Now the advice to "be cheerful" is sound enough when the sun is shining and the sky is blue. Of course, we prefer the man with a cheery smile and a hearty hello to the fellow who comes always with a recitation of the world's woes and his own ailments. But at other times, the advice "be cheerful" is almost an affront to our sensitivity. Show the man to me who knows the emptiness and loneliness that wells up within when someone he loves has died, the man who knows the agony of a body racked by pain, or the even greater agony of a mental or emotional illness, the man who has had the financial rug pulled out from under him and life seems to tumble in on him, or the man facing a personal, family crisis, and tell him "cheer up," and we can almost feel the resentment.

And yet, it was just for such situations that Christ intended His advice. And to make certain that we could not mistake His intended application, He prefaced his statement with these words, "In this world ye shall have tribulations, BUT be of good cheer . . ." As if anticipating the very objections which we have raised, "Yes, I know. It's true. In this world ye shall have troubles," but as some translators put it, "Have courage, take heart, for I have overcome the world and, lo, I am with you always." And how well He knew that there would be troubles in this world. He was a man of sorrows and

217

acquainted with grief, and He recognized the inevitability of suffering. It's something no one ever escapes. Someone has said the only two things certain in this life are death and taxes. We might add to that a third—suffering. For it comes into every life. If not sooner, then later, but come it will. We can be sure of that. Sometime we must face our own private Gardens of Gethsemane where we learn in the depths of our own being the meaning of Christ's prayer, "O God, if it be possible, let this cup pass from me." Have you never cried out from deep within, "O God, let this cup pass from me?" But if the cup does not pass from you, and you are forced to drink it to the last bitter drop, what then? How then can we be of good cheer?

Perhaps it would be helpful to make clear that good cheer is not exactly the meaning of the original Greek word. Some translators use the word courage as more nearly approximating the original meaning. "In this world ye shall have tribulations but have courage, take heart . . . "

Let me examine this text in the light of this morning's Scripture lesson. It began with Paul's affirmation that "all things work together for good to them that love God." Personally, I prefer the Revised Version's rendering of that passage: "In everything, God works for good with those who love Him." This wasn't just theory with Paul. He had known tribulations aplenty. He had been publicly whipped a number of times. Once he was nearly stoned to death. He suffered an illness that was a source of excruciating pain. He had failed to do the one thing he wanted most to achieve . . . convert his own people to Christianity. He had been shipwrecked, imprisoned, and was awaiting almost certain execution, and there in his cell he wrote, "In everything, God works for good with those who love Him."

The thought was not new with Paul. We find it back in the first book of the Bible, Genesis. Joseph had trouble aplenty. Because of his dreams and coat of many colors, he was thrown into a pit. Then his brothers sold him into slavery. He was just lifting himself up by his own bootstraps when he was thrown into prison because he resisted the advances of his boss's wife. The man who promised to help him when he was freed forgot all about Joseph when the chance came. Through all of this, Joseph remained of good cheer and faced his troubles with courage. Somehow he worked his way up to what amounted to the position of prime minister of Egypt. Joseph's

218

foresight in storing the abundance during the seven years of plenty prevented a great calamity during the seven years of famine. People came from far away to buy grain and food from Joseph's brimming storehouses. One day from a distant land, Joseph's brothers came to Egypt's prime minister to buy food, and in a dramatic recognition scene, they realize that the prime minister is their brother, Joseph. Of course, they cower in fear as they recall the suffering they caused him. But in the fiftieth chapter of Genesis we find Joseph speaking these very remarkable words: "Don't be afraid, as for evil, God meant it for good." God intended the evil to be used for good. That's the kind of God we're dealing with, a God great enough and good enough to take the evil and to use it for His own purposes.

A Chinese proverb says, "When a man throws a sword at you, you can either catch it by the blade, and it will cut you, or you can catch it by the handle and use it." Paul would have understood that. In everything, God can work for good with those who love Him. As for evil, good can come from it.

For one thing, God can use sorrow to teach us to know joy. Somehow life never reaches its depths until it suffers. The Arabs say, "All sunshine makes a desert," and the life that never knows hardship will be like a desert indeed. Edwin Markham has said it beautifully:

The heart that never knows mighty sorrow
Can never know mighty joy. Sorrow comes
To stretch out spaces in the heart for joy.

This is not poetry, not mere words. It has been demonstrated again and again in the fiber of life. Take the example of Ludwig van Beethoven. He had written great and beautiful symphonies, and then in the year 1801, he began to recognize the signs of growing deafness. By 1802, he was almost completely deaf. To be deaf is bad enough for anyone, but can you imagine what it means to a musician? His whole life was music and to be stone deaf, never to hear again the notes of a song? Longing to have his hearing back just for one day, Beethoven wrote in his *Heiligenstadt Testament:*

Oh, God—grant me at least one day of pure joy—It is so long since real joy echoed in my heart—Oh, when—Oh, when, Oh, God—should I feel it again? Never? No—Oh, that would be too hard.

219

That was Beethoven's way of praying, "Let this cup pass from me." But it did not pass. He drank it to the last bitter drop. But in a way that Beethoven could never have anticipated, he found joy again—in the drinking of that cup. For in the awful silence of his deafness, Beethoven began to hear music that no man had ever heard before. A spiritual radiance came into his music that surpassed anything he had ever written. And to the period of his total deafness belongs his greatest masterpieces—the Ninth Symphony, *Missa Solemnis*, the last string quartets. And those of you who know the Ninth Symphony know that the fourth and final movement bursts forth in a majestic happiness that for sheer joy has never been matched in all of man's music. As for evil, God meant it for good. In everything—even deafness—God works for good with those who love Him.

God can also use suffering to reveal Himself more completely and perfectly. We speak of the stars coming out, and we get to thinking that the stars begin to shine when the sun goes down. That's not the case, you know. The stars are always shining. They're up there shining right now. But we can't see them. It is only when a layer of darkness envelops our earth that through the darkness, we can see the stars twinkling in the sky above. Sometimes it is only when darkness surrounds us that through our suffering, we can see the love of God.

To illustrate, let me tell you about the man I consider to be the greatest living minister in America today, Harry Emerson Fosdick, pastor emeritus of Riverside Church in New York City. As a youth, Fosdick was a brilliant all-around college student. He graduated and entered Union Theological Seminary in New York City. He got straight As. And then at the end of his first year, life tumbled in on him. He cracked up. He suffered a complete and total nervous breakdown. Few thought he would ever lead a completely normal life again, let alone ever again step into a pulpit. But somehow Fosdick slowly and painfully fought his way back. Last year, he published his moving autobiography, *The Living of These Days*, in which he looked back across the eighty-odd years of his life and almost sixty years in the Christian ministry.

And do you know what he says was the turning point in his life, the time when he really came to know God? It was back there in his illness. Up until then, he said, he had heard of God with the hearing of his ear, but in that suffering he came to know Him face to face.

Fosdick had fantastic success in helping the sick minds and hearts that came to him throughout his more than a half century as a minister. He credits his ability to help and heal to the understanding and insight into others' problems that he gained through his own illness. In everything, even a nervous breakdown, God works for good with those who love Him.

Can we then thank God for evil? No, I don't believe so. At least I can't. Thank God for deafness? No, but thank God that out of deafness can come a Ninth Symphony. Thank God for a nervous breakdown? Never! But thank God that He is a God so great that He can use even a nervous breakdown to produce a more effective minister of Christ's, a minister more capable of healing the suffering souls that come to him for help.

That, you see, is what Paul meant when he said, "We are more than conquerors through Him who loved us." Not just that we shall succeed in pushing the cup from our lips, but that out of the drinking of the cup, a deeper good shall come. Paul had learned this the hard way. The New Testament speaks of Paul's "thorn in the flesh." It's never described further. There have been all kinds of speculation as to what it was. Some have said it was some form of epilepsy. Others speculated that it might have been some other kind of illness. But all that we know for certain is that it was a source of excruciating pain and handicapped his first missionary efforts. Three times he asked God to remove his affliction. Two times the only answer to his prayer was silence. The third time, God answered in this way: "My grace is sufficient unto thee, and my power shall be made perfect in your weakness." What was God saying? He was saying, "No, Paul, I'm not going to take away the cup. You must drink it. I'll not remove your affliction. but I'll do something better. I'll give you the power to face up to it, to overcome it, and to use it." You can be "more than a conqueror" over your thorn in the flesh.

And this brings us closer to the heart of the problem of evil. With all due respect, I say that it is an immature mind that seeks, fundamentally and primarily, for a theory to explain evil. That's the search of a man who knows evil as a theory. And then one day suffering knocks on our door, and evil is a painful, overwhelming reality in our own life. It is then that we seek not primarily for a theory to explain evil, but we seek somewhere and somehow to find the resources and strength to face it, to endure it, to overcome it, and, if possible, to use it. And that is the power which Christ makes available. Jesus never said, "I have explained the world." He did say, "I have overcome the world, and, lo, I am with you always. No matter what happens, be of good cheer for I have overcome the world, and, lo, I am with you always."

This is His promise: that He will be with us no matter what happens. As Paul put it, "For I am persuaded that neither life nor death, nor things present, nor things to come, nor any living creature shall be able to separate us from the love of God which is in Jesus Christ."

There are many ways with which man's mind has tried to deal with the problem of evil. On the one extreme, Christian Science says that evil is not really there. We just think that it is. Evil and pain and suffering, says this view, are just an "illusion of the mortal mind." Not our Christian gospel. There's no attempt to evade it, to hide from it, to pretend that it isn't there. At the heart of the gospel there is a cross. It walks straight to the very heart of the enemy territory, and there it stakes its claim. Where does our gospel begin anyway? It began on a hill, and on that hill there is a cross, and on that cross is a man, writhing in pain and crying out, "My God, my God, why hast Thou forsaken me?"

And on that black Friday afternoon, evil never seemed more conquering, suffering never more final. The disciples were overcome with despair and hopelessness and defeat. Their hopes smashed, their dreams shattered, they had given up. Peter spoke for them all when he said, "I go a fishing." Of course! What else was there for him to do?

But we know that that was not the end. That Friday was followed by Easter Sunday morning. And whatever else you think about that event, this much we *cannot* deny. He could not be stopped by a cross. Death could not down Him. He could not be enclosed in an empty tomb. But He burst the bonds of death and unleashed on this earth the most powerful force it has ever seen. He turned the despair of the disciples into confidence and hope and so filled their hearts that they went out to turn the world upside down, to turn B.C. into A.D., to transform for once and for all the cross as a symbol of shame and tragedy into a symbol of victory.

Yes, the cross has become the symbol, the reminder that Christ has once and for all overcome the world and that His love shall have

222

the last word and that nothing can overcome that love and keep it from us. To the enigma of suffering the enigma of the cross says to man that God's power is available to endure it, to overcome it.

George Matheson was a promising young doctor. In the hospital where he was an intern, the older doctors were already talking of his skill, of his possibilities, of the lives his talented surgeon's hands would be able to save. Then one day George Matheson felt a little pain in the back of his head. He went to an older doctor, a friend of his, and asked him if he could give him anything for his headache. The doctor examined him casually. Suddenly the casualness turned to concern. Other doctors were summoned for consultation.

It was the awful duty of the older doctor to take George Matheson to his office and give him the heartbreaking news that not only would he never be a skilled surgeon, he would never be any kind of doctor at all. For Matheson was afflicted with a rare but incurable disease that left its victims completely blind. The bottom dropped out of George Matheson's life. Everything he had worked for, dreamed about, was suddenly snatched away.

In despair, he went reeling back to the one thing he had left in this world, the love of the beautiful girl he was engaged to marry. Longing for her comfort and understanding, he sobbed out the pitiful news. She told him very quietly, but very firmly, that she had become engaged to a promising young physician—not to a blind man. And she walked out of his life forever.

Matheson plunged down into the abyss of despair and darkness. His whole life had tumbled in. But through the terrible darkness that overwhelmed him, he began to see the stars of God's love and goodness. And he found that the cross of Christ followed him even into that awful tragedy, and from his despair came these unforgettable words:

O Love that wilt not let me go,
I rest my weary soul in Thee;
I give Thee back the life I owe,
That in Thine ocean depths, its flow
May richer, fuller be.

223

O Joy that seekest me through pain,
I cannot close my heart to Thee;
I trace the rainbow through the rain,
And, no, the promise is not vain
That morn shall tearless be.

Nothing, no, nothing can separate us from the love which overcame the world on the cross at Calvary!

Yes, "in everything, God works for good with those who love Him," and, through that love, we may be more than conquerors, assured that "neither life nor death, nor things present, nor things to come, nor any living creature shall be able to separate us from the love of God through Christ our Lord."

"Yes, in this world, ye shall have tribulations, but have courage, take heart, for I have overcome the world, and, lo, I shall be with you always!"

John Marshall

One of the most common speeches given in our society is the speech of tribute. Often considered synonymous with a speech of introduction, these have become the political campaigner's stock in trade. When Vander Jagt campaigned for fourteen Republican candidates for Congress in one week in October, 1982, he gave as many speeches of tribute, highlighting the individual virtues of each and every candidate.

It has already been noted that the format for this type of speech is advocacy. The central idea sentence always supports the candidate, i.e., our candidate should receive our support, or our tribute, or our good will, or our vote, for good reasons which, in turn, constitute the main ideas of the presentation. Evidence is slotted under the appropriate main ideas. If the candidate has served the country well in the armed services, for example, specific reference to the demonstration of that service supports the main idea that the candidate is a patriot and, as such, should be given tribute or honor. Vander Jagt's early skills with advocacy fitted him perfectly for this kind of speaking, and, so, his student speech of tribute for John Marshall emerged as naturally suited to these skills. It was also excellent practice for what was to come for him later in his political career.

This project, it should be noted, began as a joint venture with Bruce van Voorst, a friend and fellow student who went on to become foreign affairs editor for *Newsweek*. Van Voorst was to write the speech and Vander Jagt was to deliver it, but, as it turned out, Van Voorst had very little to do with the speech in its final form.

Despite this fact, Vander Jagt shared with Van Voorst the money which the speech was to have earned for both of them. Ever since that time, although aides and assistants have researched subjects and suggested materials, his speeches have been distinctly his; their development, design, and delivery are uniquely his own.

"John Marshall" reached a wide reading audience by virtue of its publication in the *Detroit Times*. It has also been published, along with his two other student speeches which follow, in *Winning Hope College Orations, 1941-1966* by William Schrier, "Editor, compiler, coach."

HAVE YOU ever delivered a package? Have you ever driven your car along the highway? Or, perhaps, have you ever received a notice from your draft board to report for your physical? If you have, your life has been touched by just one of the many functions of a federal government in a modern society, functions that were never envisioned by the founding fathers when they first drew up our Constitution, a Constitution that occupies five printed pages in the *World Almanac* and can be read in half an hour. And, yet, within the framework of that Constitution has developed and grown a government of infinite variety and machinery. This evolutionary feat was made possible through the doctrine of implied power.

It seems strange at first glance that the man who was to impart this concept to the Constitution, John Marshall, was a man with only two months of legal training, who made more law than he ever read about, who was not so much a profound scholar as a zestful, exuberant athlete, proud of the fact that he could outbox, outrun, outwrestle every man in his regiment. And yet when you stop to think about it, this was the source of his greatness. This made possible the fresh originality of his genius, the brilliant logic of his intellect. Because of it he was able to cut through the periphery and get to the heart of the matter, to the spirit of the law, unrestrained and unrestricted by tradition and precedent.

Certainly John Marshall was getting to the heart of the matter when he maintained that the door ought to be left open for a government to change in order to keep pace with changing times. One of the phenomena of history is that a Constitution which served a tiny nation in the days of the stagecoach and log cabin is still serving that nation of world leadership in the days of jet-propelled plane and the skyscraper. It is implied power that made it possible for America to capture the spirit of Lowell's lines: "We shall not make their creed our jailer. New occasions teach new duties. They must forever onward sweep and upward who would keep abreast of truth, nor attempt the future's portal with the past's blood-rusted key."

Thanks to John Marshall, our Constitution is not an archaic antique, but rather a living, a dynamic document. Marshall infused with immortality the Constitution he had loved so well.

There's another concept that goes right along with this: that one that's reflected in the congressman's cry, "You can't do this to me! It's unconstitutional!" The authority of the court to declare an act unconstitutional was not specifically designated anywhere in that document, but Marshall deduced that it was *implied* there, and with that foothold, went on to establish the Supreme Court as one of the most respected and loved institutions of our land, transforming it from the weak, insignificant body that it was when he entered the bench.

It is this power to protect the constitutional rights of the citizen against even the right of law itself which makes the Supreme Court the bulwark of our liberty.

Don't you begin to see the genius of this man Marshall? On the one hand, through implied power, he made possible a dynamic government of change. On the other hand, through judicial review, he established the Supreme Court as the watchdog over those constitutional concepts which can never be changed, man's inalienable rights.

And then, finally, just as George Washington was the father of our country and Thomas Jefferson the father of the Declaration of Independence, so John Marshall was the father of our nation. He became a passionate believer in a strong federal government through his experience in the cold, cruel winters at Valley Forge. "I entered the army a Virginian," he said. "I left it an American." The stage was set for a dramatic struggle in a cold, windy afternoon in March, when the chief justice of the United States, John Marshall, a genius, dedicated to a supreme United States, administered the oath of office to the new president, Thomas Jefferson, a genius, dedicated

227

to the antithesis of that concept. Jefferson swept into office with a wave of anti-federalism. John Marshall, alone of the Federalists, remained in a position of authority and influence. And, yet, from that vantage point on the bench, he managed to guide the destiny of thirteen proud, but petty, quarreling states into the destiny of one nation, one United States of America.

It was in the historic *McCulloch* versus *Maryland* case that Marshall quenched once and for all the proponents of state sovereignty. In a statement for union that has never been surpassed for simplicity and yet eloquence, Marshall concluded, "This government, then, is a government of the people, and this government of the people is the supreme law of the land!" Upon that foundation, which Marshall provided, our country prospered and became great. Because of the foundation we are able to sing with the poet, "Sail on, O ship of state! Sail on, O union, strong and great!"

Because of that foundation, our country became strong and great. It was that foundation which Marshall provided that was all-important. It reminds me of a trip I took to New York with an engineering friend a couple of years ago. I stood before the Empire State Building for the first time, marveling at how far that building extends up into the sky and clouds. And I remarked to my friend that I didn't see how it was possible that it could withstand the storms from the Atlantic that sweep in and beat against it. My friend answered me, "You see, Guy, if the foundation is *deep* enough, and strong enough, there's no limit, absolutely no limit, to how high you can build." And today, ladies and gentlemen, the blast furnaces of Pittsburgh, the endless assembly lines here in Detroit, the waving wheat fields of the Midwest, and the skyline of New York are a living testimony to the fact that the foundation which Marshall provided was deep enough, and strong enough, for a great *United* States of America!

Bonn Report

This speech was delivered in one form or another over a thousand times, over a hundred times during Vander Jagt's senior year at Hope College. The stipends he received on many of these occasions paid for his college education.

Despite the general acclaim it received, the speech did not always fire the heart of each of his listeners. When he returned from Bonn later in his career, in the summer of 1956, he spoke at the New York Rotary Club, which was, in his mind, the Carnegie Hall of public speaking:

> I knew that Mr. J.C. Penney was going to be in the audience, and I also had had in mind at that time a project that would enable me to produce television programs about Rotary Foundation Fellowship experiences around the world to be shipped back to American audiences. I needed financing, and I thought in my devious mind: J.C. Penney would be just the man to finance it, and here is my chance to really impress him with a speech so that he will be receptive and responsive to the pitch that I will then make to him.
>
> I had spoken for about two minutes when J.C. Penney fell sound asleep. I threw into my speech a number of shouts, a number of loud clapping of hands, even jumped up and down a few times, improvised in my speech to find occasion for that, trying everything that I could to awaken Mr. J.C. Penney so that he would be duly impressed by my words.
>
> Unfortunately my clapping, my jumping, and my shouting were to no avail, and Mr. J.C. Penney had a beautiful snooze until the applause at the end of the speech awakened him. I decided that I would not make my pitch to Mr. J.C. Penney for the funding for my program.

J.C. Penney had the living speaker at hand and still slept soundly. The reader of these speeches has even less available, only print, and this fact represents one of the great barriers in writing about speaking. There is no possible way in print of catching the complete flavor and impact of the spoken word, the voice, the movement and physique, the power of the living speaker. There is no way to capture completely the speaker's living personality. When readers respond to a written message which depicts one spoken earlier and elsewhere, they are always one step removed from the flush of freshness immediately associated with the act of communication itself, and this act of communication is one step removed from the source of the speaker's message, the experience which gave rise to the speaker's need to communicate in the first place. As if these difficulties were not enough, capturing the spirit of Vander Jagt's speaking is further complicated by the fact that there is a rhythm to his delivery which is almost lyrical. This melody or music is muted by the printed page.

He speaks neither from a set manuscript nor from notes, it has already been said, and he has not done so since his college days. His speeches are always written, if at all, after the event. One airline passenger sitting beside him on a flight to Washington, D.C., asked him what it was he was writing so feverishly. When she found out it was a speech, she asked him when he would be giving it. He replied, "I've already given it. I want to remember exactly what it was I said." Needless to say, a conversation ensued where he was hard put to convince her he had replied honestly to her question. Perhaps, the best way to experience his speeches is to speak them, to read them aloud. Reading "Bonn Report" aloud certainly brings the reader closer to the source, making the experience much more pleasurable and real.

"Bonn Report" is a perfect example of Vander Jagt's incomparable use of the goose-pimple conclusion. The groundwork for the conclusion is laid in the introduction. It is not hard to re-create the young speaker's surprise and delight at being assigned a German sister. With this as background, who cannot picture a youthful, loving Lizi running on a railroad platform to catch the last glimpse of her brother, now a good friend, as he began his return journey to the United States?

A PARADOXICAL phenomenon is war! Although we know it means devastation and death, still, when we surround it with brass music, Hollywood extravaganzas, and parades, war sometimes takes on an attractive glitter. Of course I never exactly relished the thought of war. But I must confess that at times—when I thought of the world's tenseness, Russia's stubbornness, the UN's weakness—beginning World War III struck me as a welcome relief for ending the nagging uncertainty of this frustrating "cold war."

That's how I felt before going to Europe this summer. The city of Holland sent me to Bonn, Germany, as their community ambassador with the Experiment in International Living. Each year this organization sends five hundred Americans abroad to live with foreign families; a foreign "brother" awaits the American boys and a "sister" the girls. In any case the experiment motto, "Expect the Unexpected," proved appropriate. As we got off the train in Bonn, ten Germans ran up, eagerly asking, "What's your name?" When two feminine counterparts found each other, they kissed while the boys shook hands. I noticed a very charming, attractive, blonde German Fraulein in the group. My eyes paused for only a moment's admiration because I was busy trying to locate my brother. Soon the idea began to creep into my mind. "Is it possible that she and I..." And then I thought, "No, that would be too good to be true." But by this time she had walked over to me.

"Hello," she said.

I said, "Hello."

"Is your name Guy?"

"Yes, my name is Guy!"

Then she blurted out, "There's been a terrible mistake. Somehow they got mixed up in the main office and—well, I'm going to be your sister and you're going to be my brother for the summer."

It was all I could do to keep from jumping up and down with joy. I did manage to mutter, "Yes, that's a shame, isn't it?" And what a feeling to walk away with Elizabeth at my side and to look back over my shoulder and see the other fellows turning green with envy.

It was while getting to know "Lizi" that I learned three lessons about war: its physical destruction, its corruption of the human personality, and its utter futility as a means of solving problems. After I got to know Elizabeth, she would describe the horrors of war.

As she talked, I did a little mental arithmetic and remarked, "But Lizi, you were so young when these things happened. How can you remember?"

I'll never forget the expression on her face as she answered, "These things were so horrible—how can I *ever* forget them?"

I remember saying, "Elizabeth, all of these things were so terrible. It must be terrifying to think of them all happening over again." With that, the color drained out of her face, she clenched her fists until you could see the whites of her knuckles as she said fervently, "No, that cannot be. We could not stand it again. I am afraid that would be the end!"

I will never forget my first train ride through Cologne. From the train window one sees nothing but block after block of ruins. And it is commonplace to see men with both legs amputated above the knees on platforms with roller skates on the bottom pushing themselves along. The realization that the streets of Holland, or Alma, would look like that in the event of another war sent the chills down my spine.

The second lesson of war, the corruption of the human personality, I learned from Lizi's older brother, Karl. During a hike, we stopped to rest in a field. Karl explained that this field had been the scene of a great battle in the late war. In the painful silence that followed, I could not help thinking that if Karl and I had been born five years sooner, there was the possibility that he and I would have been in that field trying to kill each other instead of enjoying each other's friendship. When you've come to know and love someone, even the possibility that you'd be over there thinking of him as a "dirty Kraut" instead of as a friend and a brother, makes you sad at what war forces the individual to think and do.

Everywhere I saw remnants of the casualty of love. On board ship I talked to a young Dutch student coming to Harvard on a Fulbright scholarship. For an hour he discussed his dream of a united Europe. Then he concluded: "But I have this confession to make. I see the need for forgiving and forgetting. Yet when I travel across Germany, when the German customs officers get on board that train, I see that green uniform and I think of Rotterdam. I remember all the things that happened there—to my mother and my sisters. And when I do, I tighten up and I get sick inside. I hate that green uniform and the man who is in it." Clearly we see the by-products of war clinging to the human personality long after the war is over.

And then, finally, I became impressed with the futility of war. I learned anew that war creates more problems than it solves. Twice in one generation men have given their lives for peace. And yet, today the world is threatened with a third world war, more terrifying than any we've ever faced. We fought a war to stomp out Nazism. But Nazism is not dead in modern Germany. We're beginning to find out what we should have learned long ago from our own Christian heritage: you cannot shoot ideas out of man's mind with a gun. The battle is far more subtle. One modern statesman touched a profound truth when he said, "Obviously full-scale war is not a way out of trouble, but a way into more trouble."

When the world learns that lesson, when war is revealed in all of its destructiveness, in its corruption of the human personality, and in its futility, then mankind will be ready to search for peace. And man, given half a chance, is certainly more willing to promote peace on the basis of love than to prepare for war on the basis of hate.

I cannot help contrasting my hateful image of stereotyped masses of goosestepping Germans acquired during the war with today's feeling of brotherhood with German people learned through the warmth of one human personality in times of peace.

The train was in motion. As I looked out the window, I saw a charming, attractive German Fraulein, the same girl who had said, "Hello...Is your name Guy?....There's been a terrible blunder." Only this time there was no uneasiness in her approach. No, she was running, completely oblivious to the danger of lamp posts and baggage carts; running, with reckless abandon as fast as she could to keep up with the train as long as possible. Her arms were up over her head, her hair was streaming out behind and tears down her face as she cried, "Auf Wiedersehen! Auf Wiedersehen!"

The Price of the Best

In the pursuit of his goal to become a superior communicator, he vowed "never, ever" as a student to "refuse any speech invitation that he could wangle no matter how small the group." He followed this principle so scrupulously that he gave up one of his fraternity's annual formal dances to drive 120 miles to address seventeen people at a meeting of the Farm Bureau.

As a student in college, then, he was already sacrificing his pleasures to the study and practice of public speaking. This first formal effort in college oratory shows the kind of excellence such sacrifice produces. It is, in his own words, "probably the most perfectly polished and the least conversational speech in the entire collection. . . . It is an oration that I worked upon for the better part of a year." Although it is his first speech, it is a fitting final note to the collection of speeches presented here.

WHEN I was still in short pants I had an extra big case of hero-worship. I was a virtual puppy-dog to a fellow who was then in high school. His name was Donald Feury. Don must have had the patience of Job, for I was on his heels from morning until night. And whatever Don did, I wanted to do. And whatever Don said, I said. He had a favorite saying, however, that I couldn't swallow even though he was the one who said it: "You can have anything you want—anything—if you want it badly enough." I couldn't go along with that because there'd always been too many things I'd wanted but couldn't have. Yet I can still hear my hero pleading his case, "Yes, Guy, you can have whatever you want. Take it, but pay for it. The price of the best—is all the rest."

Since those early years, I have come to realize the soaring heights that can be attained when a person wants the best enough to sacrifice "all the rest." I think of Fritz Kreisler, a mediocre musician as a youth, willing to sacrifice "all the rest" to become the finest violinist in the concert halls today. Or I think of George Kell, the all-star third baseman of the Detroit Tigers. Kell refused to call it "quits" after being told he didn't have the "stuff" to make the high-school team. Instead, with a stubborn determination, he spent hours of sweating practice under a sweltering sun and inched his way up the ladder of baseball immortality. I imagine that every young fellow has dreamed of stepping up to bat in the last half of the ninth and winning a crucial game with a mighty blast into the centerfield bleachers. How natural it is to want to be able to do that! But only rarely does a man like George Kell come along who is willing to pay the price of making that dream come true.

What a chasm between what we want and what we're willing to pay for! You see, it's one thing to make easy idealistic choices about what we'd like to have but a completely different matter to be willing to pay the price of their fulfillment. Today, it's one thing for the nations of the world to proclaim, "We want peace!" But to pay the price of realizing that age-old dream, that's something else again. After World War II, the world glibly chose the pearl of peace but promptly forgot that it was a pearl of great price. As though peace could be wished into existence! As though it had no price-tag!

Today our emphasis is all wrong! Contrast our meager investments in planning for peace with our enormous expenditures in other areas. Private concerns spend $30 million annually to sell American women on cosmetics while our government spends a million less to sell the world on peace through the "Voice of America" programs. We contribute $16,076,000 to the United Nations to help it dispose of world problems but that is considerably less than New York City spends in the same time to dispose of its garbage! Is it not clear that we are far more deeply concerned with how to win a war *if* and *when* it comes than how to win peace now while it's still precariously here? It is my belief that we shall never

235

attain peace until we are willing to spend more, in time and talent, in energy and effort, in men and money, toward securing peace than we have in the past toward winning a war. None other than Dr. Ralph Bunche, in spite of countless frustrations and failures in his peace efforts, confirms this view with his confident assurance: "We *can* have peace when we are willing to work and pay and sacrifice for it!"

And yet today we have become faint-hearted about our goal. Already a few Americans, eager to make "negotiations" synonymous with "appeasement," have become advocates of a so-called preventive war. You've heard their oft-repeated cry, "Let's just drop a few atomic bombs and clean up the whole rotten mess!" "Just drop a few atomic bombs!" To them, this naive solution is so much easier than solving the problems of peace. It ignores the fact that an *idea*, like communism or democracy, cannot be defeated by material weapons alone and that the resulting chaos would not eradicate the world's problems but increase them tenfold. Another group—and its number is increasing daily—is saying, like the Wild West heroes of moviedom, "This world's just not big enough for both of us." Fatalistically, these people assume that war is inevitable! They argue that Russia's present aggressive attitude cannot be altered by anything we do! Nonsense! Human nature is not static! It is dynamic, constantly changing. A communist is not a block of granite, unmoving and unwavering. Stalin's communism is not Trotsky's communism, nor even Lenin's. Witness, too, the defection of Yugoslavia! In World War II, because it was to the best interests of both Russia and the United States, we cooperated to stop the Nazi war machine. Today it is to the best interests of humanity to stop the devastating consequences of another war. A blind man can see that! It is only in a world where frantic preparations for war have backed two mighty opposites into a corner that this simple truth becomes obscured. War preparation, *standing by itself,* is not the road to peace. Our planning to survive an atomic attack, important as it is, must never overshadow the far more important task of preventing one. In short, we desperately need a bold gigantic peace offensive, one which fires our imagination, captures our enthusiasm, enlists our loyalty, and one which rests upon a confident conviction that peace is possible in a world where God has meant good for his creation. This peace offensive goes far beyond the current MacArthur-Truman dispute concerned with the passive prevention of World War III; it assumes the initiative in the active promotion of peace.

Perhaps you ask, and rightly, just what concrete action such an offensive would assume. Let me briefly suggest a few areas into which our efforts might be directed.

Remembering that we are not likely to have peace or prosperity on this planet until everyone else has them too, we should concern ourselves with the three-fourths of humanity that is going hungry. In contrast to appalling conditions of hunger throughout the world, our grain elevators are filled with rotting produce. We should back by deeds our proclamations of humanitarian interest by putting our surplus produce into empty stomachs instead of into empty bins.

We must keep open the lines of communication between all peoples. To achieve this objective, we need exchange scholarships on a vastly expanded scale and a liberalized program of help for the world's sixty million refugees. We should sponsor attention-arresting foreign broadcasts that would genuinely deserve the name "Voice of America." Truly we have a cause that deserves to be heard, and we need have no fear of the world's verdict if we succeed in presenting the facts.

Another step in our all-out grand offensive for peace would be to help other people help themselves, something on the order of Senator Brian McMahon's proposal totaling more than $50 million over a ten-year period. Expenditures for plows, tractors, fertilizer factories, cement plants, roads, and hospitals would be immeasurable assets in our struggle for peace.

But you say, "Whew! This is breathtaking!" Ah, it is. But can anything less win the battle of peace? Remember peace has a price-tag on it! It costs! Twice in one generation we've been willing to sacrifice "all the rest" to win a war and seem reconciled to doing so again. Let us now match and overmatch these efforts in a far greater struggle—the cause of peace.

Idealistic? Yes. Impractical? Perhaps. But no more so than a mediocre musician becoming a violin virtuoso, a fourth-string third baseman becoming an all-star big leaguer. No more so than man flying like a bird or swimming like a fish. No more so than the splitting of the atom or the reaching of our fantastic production standards. In each instance the prophets of doom have said, "It can't

237

be done!" But always America answered with the spirit made famous by the slogan of the Panama Canal engineers:

Got any rivers you think are uncrossable?
Got any mountains you can't tunnel through?
We specialize in the strictly impossible,
Doing the things that nobody can do.

In winning our independence, in establishing a government by the people, in pushing westward, in building, expanding and growing, a cynical, unbelieving, skeptical world first said of our fledgling republic, "You can't!" But this great nation with its people united in purpose, united in a common fundamental faith, has answered, "We can."... And we did! Someday a nation is going to be willing to say, "We can" about peace, and be willing to lead, to struggle, to sacrifice, and to be heroes for that cause. I covet that place of honor for our beloved land and for this, our generation.

Every school in this contest has its Johns and Joes and Jims who "didn't come back." It is almost ten years now since they left the life they loved so well: exciting thrills of a homecoming weekend, bull-sessions in the dorms, mid-day snacks in the Student Union, and strolls across campus with their girl. Why did they go? Many times I've asked my servicemen friends that question. True, some said, "Because everyone else was doing it"; others, " 'Cause I had to." But typical of the vast majority were these responses: "I fought so that my kid brother would never have to do the things I had to do" and "to give my little boy the chance to grow up in a world of peace." Thousands gave "all the rest" for that kind of world. Dare we now make their hope an empty dream?

One unforgettable scene coming out of World War II vividly demonstrated the costly price men were willing to pay to make that dream come true. In the great island-hopping campaign of the Pacific, the tiny island of Tarawa barred our relentless push toward the heart of Japan. Because of a reef three hundred yards offshore, it was necessary for invaders to wade with their heads barely peeping above the waterline, presenting a target like sitting-ducks that mechanically revolve in the penny-arcades of carnivals. But the island's key position made her indispensable to American victory. A group of hardened leathernecks, armed with little more than a burning desire for victory and an unquenchable faith, determined: "If we must, we can; and we will take Tarawa."

The night was cool but the marine uniforms were soaked with sweat as the landing barges inched their way to the treacherous shore. The enemy were waiting, machineguns poised, and the Americans knew it. We shall never forget the ineffable heroism that drove the home-loving marines into the rain of deadly bullets. Wave after wave slipped into the icy water, straight into one of the bloodiest slaughters of the war until somehow a handful had miraculously gained the shore. The rest is history; when night fell, an American flag flew over the island labeled, "Unconquerable."

The list of heroes who gave their lives that day is a long one. But for me, one name looms forth. For one of them was my boyhood hero—Don Feury. I can almost see his gray eyes boring into my soul as he says, "See, Guy, you can take what you want—if you want it badly enough." Today I fancy Don and his comrades waiting on the other shore, waiting for us, the soldiers of peace to match their heroism, fully resolved that "all the rest" is "the price of the best."

Conclusion

THE CONGRESSMAN from the Ninth District in Michigan, Guy Vander Jagt, is a phenomenon in contemporary American politics. By a constant and conscientious repetition of simple, classic methods of communication which he learned in the classroom, he played an essential role in bringing the Republican party from the brink of disaster in 1974 to power and prominence in the government of the United States today. Over these difficult years, through the 70s and into the 80s, he helped Republicans stand up to the strength and sophistication of the liberal mass media; his work helped to thwart well-financed special interest groups in their attempts to control the national channels of communication; his was a guiding spirit and the rallying voice of the minority party as it faced a half-century tradition of Democratic majorities in the House of Representatives.

Without losing political friends or making personal enemies, he focused Republican communications unerringly on areas where the greatest effects could be achieved at the least cost. In this, he spearheaded a two-part political campaign. One part he directed toward specific live audiences through person-to-person speaking; the other part he aimed at a national viewing and reading public through mass media, financed and shaped by the National Republican Congressional Committee.

As chairman of the NRCC, Vander Jagt was positioned perfectly to fulfill this dual function in communication, and so, he played a significant part in the ongoing dialogue between Americans and their leaders, a drama which was steadily moving the country toward social and economic conservatism. It was he who

241

carried the messages between grassroots America and the Republican leadership in Washington, D.C. As this vital link held, as he listened and spoke, conservative ideas gained more and more potency around the nation.

Behind his successful use of television and print lay his finely honed skills in communicating with Americans firsthand. He judged responses, he listened, he responded to people as only a speaker who meets his listeners face-to-face can. He pushed himself to do this because he believed that an intelligent use of the mass media must be based on insights found in the give-and-take of direct contact with people to whom the mass media speak.

Although his efforts in the Congress were supportive of three different Republican presidents and spanned the Carter years between Ford and Reagan as well, he never really assumed a starring role in the drama of political change. His role was greater than that of a minor supporting character, less than a lead, more like that of a major supporting character upon whom the story pivots at key moments in the rising action. Just as the act of communication has been likened to the catalytic agent in chemical reactions, so Vander Jagt might be thought of as a facilitating agent in the productive political relationship between an expectant, at times demanding, public calling for their leaders to revive a conservative interpretation of the American dream and the leaders themselves.

His speaking and listening, both to the public and within the organizational structure of the National Republican Congressional Committee, set the stage for the Republican landslide in 1980. In 1982, again, in his staunch congressional support of President Ronald Reagan, he contributed to stemming a Democratic landslide which could have completely wiped out the Republican gains in 1980. The very likely possibility of such a reversal was avoided when, in tandem with the president, he was able to communicate to people a hope and confidence in the future, while at the same time repeatedly framing anew for specific as well as mass audiences the dominant theme behind Republican policies: the renewal of American strength, at home and abroad.

These accomplishments found him teetering from time to time on the verge of acquiring a national identity with the American people. At present, in 1984, he is known in Washington as having great influence, and his appearances on network television and in national magazines have added to a broadened image which was first dimly etched when he gave the keynote address at the 1980 Republican National Convention in Detroit, but he remains a secret to most Americans. He is still referred to by local broadcasters on the evening news as "Vander Gast." The average American, upon hearing his name, still wants to spell it "Vander Jack."

There is a lesson here, perhaps the most telling of all the lessons his speaking has taught the reader of this volume. Highly important communicators who contribute substantially to the democratic process in the United States are not always recognized when the products of that process are realized. Their works, however significant, may stay hidden; their stories, however classic, may remain unsung.

In a way, what is written here as a conclusion is really an afterthought, a postscript to a report in progress. Vander Jagt is fifty-three years of age with many years of potential service ahead, so no conclusions about his influence can be drawn. The future remains to fill in a final summary and evaluation of his life in politics.

His earliest speech, the last one in this collection, "The Price of the Best," it seems, is the most appropriate stopping place for now. As a student in college, he paid the price to become so persuasive as a speaker that the speech profession in higher education will probably never see his equal again. Although the arena of his activities is now immeasurably enlarged and his responsibilities are so very much heavier, he is still paying the price.

Notes

CHAPTER ONE

1. Interview with Congressman Guy Vander Jagt, November 30, 1982. He attended this reception and dinner for the freshmen congressmen on November 29, 1982.

2. Hedrick Smith, "Specialists Assess Reagan at Midterm," *The New York Times*, November 21, 1982, p. 31.

3. For a social scientist's view of this change in national outlook, see Daniel Yankelovich, "Hard Times and Presidential Luck," *Psychology Today*, November, 1982, pp. 8, 11, and 92. Also see Amitai Etzione's book, *An Immodest Agenda: Rebuilding America Before the 21st Century*, reviewed in *Time*, December 20, 1982, p. 85

4. For a detailed account of this tidal wave of "a return to the old-fashioned, traditional values and conservative philosophies," see Burton Yale Pines, *Back to Basics* (New York: William Morrow and Company, Inc., 1982), pp. 348. Also see Jack F. Kemp, *An American Renaissance: A Strategy for the 1980's* (New York: Harper and Row, 1979), pp. 207.

5. Peter McGrath, "The Crash of '80," *The Washingtonian*, April, 1981, pp. 122-25 and pp. 52-55.

6. *Washington Week in Review*, PBS-WETA, Channel 26, Washington, D.C., October 8, 1982.

7. Albert Shanker, "Will Voters 'Throw the Rascals Out'?" *The New York Times*, October 24, 1982, p. E7.

8. Haynes Johnson, "It's Politics but Elementary, Watson: The Dogs Aren't Barking," *The Washington Post*, October 24, 1982, p. A3.

9. *Ibid.*, p. 11.

10. Patrick Caddell, "Why the Democrats May Win Big: Last-minute swings and Reagan's unpopularity," *The Washington Post*, October 17, 1982, p. B1.

11. *Ibid.*

12. David S. Broder, "Conservatives Expected to Retain Hold," *The Washington Post*, October 31, 1982, p. A16.

13. Barry Sussman, "Poll Finds Voters Fearful of GOP Programs," *The Washington Post*, October 14, 1982, p. A1.

14. Interview with Linda DiVall, Survey Research Director, NRCC, November 9, 1982.

15. David S. Broder, "Giving Reagan a Chance," *The Washington Post*, September 12, 1982, p. 13.

16. Richard Wirthlin, "Newsmaker Interview," *First Monday*, November/December, 1982, p. B7.

17. This speech was carried by NBC and CBS at 7:30 P.M. ABC did not carry the speech as it was viewed by that network as political in nature.

18. p. 22.

19. When he appeared on this program, it was the fourth time in 1982 that he appeared jointly with Congressman Tony Coelho, his counterpart in the Democratic party. Their first meeting was on January 23rd with the National Association of Home Builders in Las Vegas, Nevada; the second was on September 30th before the National Press Club in Washington, D.C.; and the third was on the October 14th edition of the *MacNeil-Lehrer Report*. They met again on December 4th when each spoke at the Winter Dinner of the Gridiron Club held in the Capital Hilton, Washington, D.C.

20. He debated Gerald Warner, prosecuting attorney for Muskegon, Michigan, before an audience of 250 at 7:30 P.M.

21. Interview with Vander Jagt, October 19, 1982.

22. Interview with Vander Jagt, November 23, 1982.

23. Interview with DiVall, *op. cit.*

24. Wirthlin, *op. cit.*

25. *Ibid.*

26. November 5, 1982.

27. A cartoon copyrighted by "Benson" of the *Arizona Republic* which appeared on page sixteen of the November 15th issue of *Time* says it all. It is a picture of the president riding the GOP elephant on a very narrow mountain path overlooking a bottomless precipice. He is leading the elephant out of the "Democratic Landslide Zone" and saying, "Whew!" There are smaller rocks on the elephant's back, piled around the president, and pebbles are still bouncing down the mountain, suggesting what might have been. The "Stay the Course" bumper sticker, highlighted on the elephant's rump, boldly tells the tale. The GOP elephant made it through a very tight and dark place in November of 1982 with little room or time to spare.

28. John W. Mashek with Thomas J. Foley and staff, "The Democrats Surge Back," *U.S. News & World Report*, November 1, 1982, pp. 18-22.

29. Vander Jagt-Coelho Press Conference, "How Will the House Go in November?" The National Press Club, Washington, D.C., September 30, 1982.

30. McGrath, *op. cit.*, p. 122.

31. Much of this information is provided in a small brochure published by the NRCC in Washington, D.C. Another more detailed coverage with historical perspective is given in a booklet entitled, *One Hundred Years: A History of the National Republican Congressional Committee*. Each can be obtained by writing to the NRCC offices at 320 First Street, S.E., Washington, D.C. 20003.

32. Interviews with Wyatt A. Stewart III, director of finance and administration, NRCC, November 9 and 22, 1982. He has occupied this position since July of 1975.

33. *Ibid.*

34. Interview with Steve Sandler, director of communications, NRCC, December 17, 1982. Stockmeyer and Stewart both agreed on this point.

35. Interview with Steven F. Stockmeyer, December 2, 1982.

36. Speech of welcome to 1982 Republican candidates for the House in the White House Executive Offices on October 6, 1982.

37. Interview with Richard Richards, December 20, 1982.

38. This wording was chosen by Mark Shields, editorial writer for the *Washington Post*, speaking at the Godfrey Sperling Breakfast, November 3, 1982. No one in attendance objected.

39. Paul Taylor and David S. Broder, "Democrats Landslide May Never Slide," *The Washington Post*, October 17, 1982, p. A4.

40. Vander Jagt-Coelho Press Conference, *op. cit.*

41. *Ibid.*

42. Don Campbell, "GOP Fundraising Campaign a Study in Success," *The Tennessean*, February 14, 1982, p. 1B.

43. Morton Mintz, "Republicans Far Ahead in Harvesting Cash," *The Washington Post*, February 22, 1981, p. A24.

44. Steven V. Roberts, "In Era of Permanent Campaign, Parties Look to 1982," *The New York Times*, January 26, 1981, p. 22.

45. Elizabeth Drew, "A Reporter at Large, Politics and Money II," *The New Yorker*, December 13, 1982, p. 67.

46. Interview with Sandler, *op. cit.*

47. This same James A. Willders, for no remuneration whatsoever, was starred in an ad for the Democratic party in late 1982 attacking the Republicans for their inability to control unemployment.

48. This information was taken from a report which was provided by Elizabeth Kochevar, assistant director of education and training, NRCC: *Status Report: Education and Training Programs*, September 21, 1982.

CHAPTER TWO

1. This information was compiled from the congressman's 1980 schedule of appointments and speaking engagements.

2. Alan Ehrenhalt, "GOP Leadership Contest Pits an Orator Against Tactician," *The Washington Star*, July 29, 1980, p. A3.

3. Martin Tolchin, "Another G.O.P. Campaign: For House Leader," *The New York Times*, September 28, 1980, p. 4E.

4. Dennis Farney, "Oilcan and Sword: House GOP to Pick Between 2 Weapons," *The Wall Street Journal*, November 28, 1980, p. 1.

5. *The Post-Standard*, Syracuse, N.Y., December 8, 1980, p. 1.

6. Jacqueline Teare, "Vander Jagt loses; 15 who promised votes didn't deliver," *The Flint Journal*, December 9, 1980, p. D-4.

7. *Ibid.*

8. Robert Lewis, "Vander Jagt fills bill as 'the best speaker,' " *The Muskegon Chronicle*, May 9, 1980, p. 6.

9. Duplicate of a memorandum from Don Shea to Bill Brock and Ben Cotten, February 15, 1980, in the Vander Jagt office files.

10. An unplanned conversation in the spring of 1980 at the Faculty Center at Syracuse University, Syracuse, New York.

11. Jacqueline Teare, "Vander Jagt swamped by speech requests," *The Bay City Times*, Bay City, Michigan, August 17, 1980, p. 15C.

12. July/August, 1980, pp. 6-11.

13. Letter, Vander Jagt office files.

14. Bill Neikirk, "Vander Jagt's keynote is patriotism," *Chicago Tribune*, July 17, 1980, p. 8.

15. Karl Blankenship, "Vander Jagt gives keynote," *The State News*, East Lansing, July 18, 1980, p. 5; Robert Lewis, "Vander Jagt pitch fails to capture crowd's attention," *The Flint Journal*, July 17, 1980, p. A6; Randall Vande Water, "For Vander Jagt waiting was worth it," *The Holland Sentinel*, July 17, 1980, p. 1; and Robert Burns, "Keynote speech called best of the convention," *The Muskegon Chronicle*, July 17, 1980, p. 14. In this last article, the following persons were quoted as extremely pleased by the keynote: John J. Rhodes, George Romney, Robert P. Griffin, Melvin A. Larsen, Jack Welborn, Margaret Riecker, Gary Byker, Dr. Tirso Del Junco, and S.I. Hayakawa.

16. The July 17, 1980, edition of the *New York Times* on page B1 referred only to Vander Jagt as asking "voters to chart a new direction," and the *Washington Post* gave not a word to Vander Jagt's speech after he had given it. The July 28th *Time* noted in one sentence on page 15 the poetry which he used, and then *Time* quoted as a footnote one stanza of Van Dyke's *America for Me*. The *Washington Star* reprinted the text of the keynote address in full on page A5 of the July 17, 1980, edition.

17. *America in Search of Itself: The Making of the President 1956-1980* (New York: Harper and Row, 1982), p. 326.

18. Lester Kinsolving, "Vander Jagt: Wolverine Demosthenes," *Washington Weekly*, July 17, 1980, p. 3.

19. To put the importance of television in perspective, former President Richard M. Nixon said to Vander Jagt that just one of his own nationally televised speeches reached more people than all of Vander Jagt's after-dinner speeches put together. But the congressman's need for response and his faith in its importance constantly draw him away from the more impersonal machine-based media and toward the more personal situations found on the campaign trail.

20. Susan Preston, "Vander Jagt was Driving Force Behind GOP Capitol Steps Rally," *The Grand Rapids Press*, September 18, 1980, p. 9C.

21. Mary Battiata, "Jelly Beans and Bravos," *The Washington Post*, March 19, 1981, p. D3.

22. Letter from Gerald R. Ford to Guy Vander Jagt, July 27, 1980, Vander Jagt office files.

23. Congressman Stan Parris, statement at the committee meeting of the NRCC executive committee, H227, Capitol, August 11, 1982.

24. John Kasich (now Congressman John Kasich), Washington Marriott Hotel, Washington, D.C., September 14, 1982.

25. State Senator Ray Garland, "Introduction of Guy Vander Jagt," Fund Raising Dinner, Hotel Roanoke, Roanoke, Virginia, September 17, 1982.

26. *The Holland Sentinel*, Holland, Michigan, December 4, 1981, p. 4.

27. Jacqueline Teare, "State Democrats told to find a foe for Vander Jagt," *The Muskegon Chronicle*, December 10, 1981, p. B10.

28. Robert Burns, "Assistant Prosecutor may oppose Vander Jagt," *The Muskegon Chronicle*, December 29, 1981, p. 1A.

29. His vote totals and percentages as compiled by the congressman's staff appear below:

| | Vander Jagt | | Opposition | |
	Total	Percentage	Total	Percentage
1966	92,710	66.7	42,266	33.3
1968	111,774	67.5	53,886	32.5
1970	94,027	64.4	51,223	35.1
1972	132,268	69.4	56,236	29.5
1974	87,551	56.6	65,235	42.1
1976	146,712	70.0	61,641	29.4
1978	122,363	69.6	53,450	30.4
1980	168,713	96.5	—	—
1982	112,419	64.7	61,728	35.3

These figures collected over the years coincide with those compiled by Richard B. Scammon and, since 1976, Alice V. McGillivray in the *America Votes* series most recently a part of the Elections Research Center published by the *Congressional Quarterly*, Washington, D.C., 1966 to present.

30. "Biography of Congressman Guy Vander Jagt," a brief synopsis of his political career prepared by his congressional office staff in conjunction with the staff of the NRCC, August, 1980.

31. Debate with Gerald Warner, *op. cit.*

32. Interview with Vander Jagt, March 11, 1982.

33. "The G.O.P.: A Party in Search of Itself," *The New York Times Magazine*, March 6, 1983, p. 38.

34. Allen Brownfeld, "Is the Liberal Bias Real or Imagined?" *The Washington Times*, September 21, 1982, p. 11A.

35. Interview with James M. Sparling, Jr., administrative assistant to Guy Vander Jagt, March 11, 1982. Sparling made this point by suggesting that almost any senator can call a press conference and get general coverage from the large number of reporters who inevitably attend. On the other hand, for example, Congressman Daniel Rostenkowski, chairman of the House Ways and Means

Committee, is one of the most powerful men in the country, but no one except legislators and their Washington staffs seems to know it.

36. Unpublished manuscript, Vander Jagt office files.

37. Vander Jagt office files.

38. *Gridiron Club 1982 December Dinner Song Book,* used on December 4, 1982.

39. *The Syracuse Herald-Journal,* May 21, 1982, p. A9.

40. *You and Your Congressman* (New York: C.P. Putnam's Sons, 1976), p. 172.

41.An untitled speech to General Motors executives, Grand Rapids, Michigan, January 25, 1977.

42. Interview, September 28, 1982.

43. Conversations with Prof. William Schrier during the school year 1956-57.

CHAPTER THREE

1. While evaluation is necessary in political communication, it is not always accepted by rhetorical critics as a necessary function of criticism. The critic who views the critical role as that of a participant who enters into the communication being studied to experience what speakers and listeners are experiencing may seek understanding as an end in itself. Critics who attempt an evaluation of speakers, by contrast, stand at a distance as observers to achieve an objective perspective in order to compare the speaker with other speakers.

Each of these two approaches to criticism might be thought of as extremes on a continuum scaled according to the amount of the critic's personal involvement in the actual communication being studied. One approach results in experiential knowledge; the other results in empirical knowledge. The former is associated with the humanities, the case study, and classical rhetorical theory. The latter tends more toward the social sciences, the sample survey, and the modern scientific experiment where standards and criteria for evaluation would depend on contemporaneous forms of measurement.

Whether a critic chooses explanation or evaluation as the ultimate goal in criticism, both approaches result in products which have educational value. Further, to suggest that either of these forms of criticism should be developed in isolation from the other is to ignore the benefits which accrue from the support each can give to the other. Each should finally lead into the other, offering up its own special advantages for those given in return.

2. Taping conversations represents the best attempt to solve the problems of studying these private conversations, but tapes are not the complete answer. The problems associated with taping presidential phone conversations have proved that conclusively.

3. The author writes from his role as a participating observer here.

4. The congressman is still thinking through his stand on this issue. In a March, 1983, interview, he offered a different line of thinking that the point at issue should be state or federal control of crime and punishment, not pro-life or pro-choice. He believes that the Supreme Court decision to define life and murder for states exceeds the court's authority. The states' traditional control over these matters, if it had been permitted to stand, would have resulted in the best answers

being made standard around the country. In most cases in the past, states have gravitated to the best answers to such questions, making the best answer a more-or-less general policy.

The only argument he sees against giving states their traditional power over abortion is the one which is based upon discrimination against the poor. Assuming, for the moment, Michigan was pro-life and Florida was pro-choice, a rich woman from Michigan could go to Florida for an abortion, but a poor woman could not. His reply to this argument is that, for the short term, before states reach a generally acceptable answer to the overall question, women's groups could put money now being used to support both ends of the question into financial assistance to women who wish to make the trip from Michigan to Florida.

When he brings this argument up, however, both contending groups become angry. They seem to be so involved in a two-sided conflict, they are blind to a third idea which could possibly mediate the other two.

5. July 16, 1982.

6. The disinformation project was established to inform the media and certain Democratic congressmen about attacks that were being made on the voting records of Republican congressmen by the Democratic Congressional Campaign Committee. The Democratic congressmen who were informed were those who had voted with the Republicans who were being attacked.

7. Until July of 1982, the RNC door at 310 First Street, S.E., was the only entrance to the building which housed the RNC and the NRCC. A second door which was added specifically for the NRCC at 320 First Street, S.E., was christened on this date, July 13, 1982.

8. Interview with Richard N. Bond, deputy chairman of the Republican National Committee, on March 9, 1983.

9. This conclusion results from the author's close observation of the congressman's discussion leadership with both equals and subordinates in several different situations.

10. In 1982, each state with the exceptions of Nevada, North Dakota, and Hawaii was represented on the committee. These three states did not have a Republican congressman in the Ninety-seventh Congress.

11. Washington, D.C., September 21, 1982.

12. More recently, since 1980, Vander Jagt has become more willing to engage in question-and-answer dialogues in formal public situations, employing more indirective, even nondirective, designs on these occasions.

13. Vander Jagt-Coelho Press Conference, "How Will the House Go in November?" The National Press Club, Washington, D.C., September 30, 1982.

14. For an excellent example of an adaptation of materials used in person-to-person audiences to the more formal carefully planned interview for publication, see, "Newsmaker Interview: Congressman Guy Vander Jagt," *First Monday: The Republican News Magazine,* Vol. 12, No. 4, May, 1982, pp. 16-21.

15. There are other kinds or genre of formal political public addresses. These are not usually a part of congressional speaking. Rather, they are associated with presidential (and gubernatorial) addresses, e.g., inaugural and State of the Union messages.

16. PAC stands for Political Action Committee. Such committees were begun in 1974 when the Federal Election Commission was authorized by the Congress to control the contributions made to candidates for federal office. Any organization, labor unions, corporations, societies, and associations could establish such a committee. From 1974 to November, 1982, approximately three thousand committees contributed close to eighty million dollars to all political campaigns whose candidates accepted PAC money. This total developed in spite of the ten-thousand dollar limit any one PAC can give to any one candidate. For the first time in 1980, corporate and professional committees gave more than labor unions through PACs.

17. U.S. Congress, *Congressional Record*, 92nd Cong., 2nd sess., March 29, 1972, p. 10770.

18. Congressman Guy Vander Jagt, "The Great Lakes Coho Gamble," *Argosy*, August 1974, pp. 79-80.

19. U.S. Congress, *Congressional Record*, 94th Cong., 2nd sess., February 3, 1976, p. 2169; and July 1, 1976, pp. 21830 and 21837-8.

20. U.S. Congress, *Congressional Record*, 94th Cong., 2nd sess., March 30, 1976, p. 8569.

21. U.S. Congress, *Congressional Record*, 96th Cong., 1st sess., p. 17175.

22. U.S. Congress, *Congressional Record*, daily ed., 97th Cong., 2nd sess., August 20, 1982, E4045.

23. There are two kinds of media coverage: (1) that for which you pay as in an advertisement, and (2) that which is "earned." Having earned media coverage means that what you have done or said is newsworthy enough to be purposely sought and underwritten by the media themselves. Getting either of these two kinds of coverage is not easy.

24. *PBS Late Night*, February 22, 1983.

25. As early as 1980, the GOP was spending more than eight million dollars on media advertising per year, and almost half of that amount was used by the NRCC for radio and TV ads alone.

26. One of the few occasions in close, interpersonal discussion when Vander Jagt's design is directive is when a member of the committee argues against spending money for mass media advertisements. He invariably argues for it.

27. As on Channel 5, WTTG, in Washington, D.C., when a few seconds of his floor speech for the president's tax reform bill was televised at 10:00 P.M., August 19, 1982.

28. Memorandum from Paul Serrano, managing editor of *Eighty-Two*, to the author, July 16, 1982.

29. *Eighty-Two*, Vol. II, No. 9, June 9, 1982, p. 8.

30. August 13, 1982.

31. September 20, 1982.

32. *Grand Rapids Press*, July 11, 1981, p. 2A.

33. *The Indianapolis News*, August 23, 1982, p. 17.

34. Ralph Van Natta, candidate in the Second District, and Mike Carroll, candidate in the Tenth District, both spent the day with Vander Jagt to show support for Burton as well as to share in the publicity surrounding the congressman's visit.

CHAPTER FOUR

1. "A Story We've Got to Tell," delivered to the American Astronautical Society, Ann Arbor, Michigan, September 17, 1968.

2. "Frank Borman," delivered at the Mid-Year Convocation at Hope College, Holland, Michigan, February 19, 1970. It is included here in his collected speeches.

3. "Earth Day," delivered at the Calder Plaza, Grand Rapids, Michigan, April 22, 1970. It is included here in his collected speeches.

4. "Expect the Unexpected," delivered at the 52nd Annual Convention of the National Association of State Departments of Agriculture, Detroit, Michigan, September 20, 1970.

5. "Personal Tribute to Ambassador Cleo Noel and Deputy Minister Curt Moore," U.S. Congress, *Congressional Record*, 93rd Cong., 1st Sess., March 6, 1973, pp. 6405-6 and reprinted in the *Department of State Newsletter*, No. 143, March, 1973, pp. 10-11.

6. "Will American Free Enterprise Survive?" delivered before the Dow Chemical Management Seminar, Midland, Michigan, September 25, 1973, and "U.S. Business Abroad," delivered at the Third Annual Meeting of the Advisory Council of the Overseas Private Investment Corporation, Kennedy Center, Washington, D.C., October 29, 1973. The first of these is included here in his collected speeches.

7. "The United Nations," delivered at the Annual UN Day Dinner of the United Nations Association of Tulsa, November 10, 1973. It is included here in his collected speeches.

8. Delivered at the National Republican Convention, Detroit, Michigan, July 16, 1980. It is included here in his collected speeches.

9. Delivered in honor of Abraham Lincoln's birthday in Wayne County, Wooster, Ohio, March 18, 1976. It is included here in his collected speeches.

10. Delivered at a fundraising dinner for Congressman Jim Coyne, Trevose, Pennsylvania, October 18, 1982. It is included here in his collected speeches.

11. Delivered for the Washington, D.C. Chamber of Commerce Insider's Breakfast, October 6, 1982. It is included here in his collected speeches.

12. "How to Get the Job Done," delivered in Muskegon, Michigan, April 26, 1973. See "Excerpt from 'Beyond a Reasonable Doubt,'" in his collected speeches to note how early in his career he was pumping "new twentieth-century meaning and relevance into phrases that had been repeated so many millions of times through the centuries that their original impact had become blunted on the modern ear."

13. Unpublished manuscript, Vander Jagt office files.

14. "GOP Platform Reflects Plans of the House Republicans; A Program for the Eighties," *Congress Today*, July/August, 1980, pp. 12-13. This pamphlet is published by the National Republican Congressional Committee in Washington, D.C.

15. Interview, March 11, 1982.

16. Yet another analogy he considered was one Gloria Swanson suggested to him by phone on August 5, 1982. She believed that Republicans were facing a situation similar to the housewife who must postpone preparing a meal for guests because she has to clean up a horrendous mess in the kitchen first.

17. Statement made in the NRCC Executive Committee meeting on July 13, 1982, held in the fourth floor conference room of the NRCC offices in the Eisenhower Center.

18. "Remarks," National Frozen Food Association meeting, Washington, D.C., February 26, 1981.

19. Eugene B. McDaniel, Capt. U.S.N., with James Johnson, *Scars & Stripes*, Friends of Red McDaniel, O.W. Goodwin, treasurer, Dunn, North Carolina 28334.

20. "Why There Should Be More Business in Politics and Less Politics in Business," an undated speech manuscript from the Vander Jagt office files.

21. "Address Prepared for Delivery by George Romney of Michigan," Lincoln Club Banquet, Convention Center, Louisville, Kentucky, February 11, 1967.

22. Vander Jagt made use occasionally of the famous "How to Hug" story used so forcefully and humorously by McFarland when he was speaking as a representative of General Motors.

23. Letter, dated July 7, 1980, in the Vander Jagt office files. Several of Nixon's allusions to the years of President Carter were picked up and used by the congressman in his keynote address of July 16, 1980.

24. Letter, dated June 17, 1980, in the Vander Jagt office files. Congressman Bethune suggested that the keynote address should represent ideas which are *not expected.* "If you can portray our Republican principles as a new fundamentalism, you will convince the people that this is 'Day One' of the new Republican party."

25. Letter, dated May 30, 1980, in the Vander Jagt office files. Congressman Michel's suggestion centered on a "pitch for the state legislatures, where the redistricting for the new congressional seats will be made."

26. "Oilman's Prayer Breakfast," American Petroleum Institute, Chicago, Illinois, November 10, 1981, and transcribed by Clara Berger and Associates, stenotype reporters, Chicago.

27. The author sat at a table in the Patio unobserved as he watched and listened to these activities through a set of glass doors. Very few people have ever seen and heard Vander Jagt as he makes such preparations. He seeks complete solitude.

28. "Ford's Soothing Words Kept Vander Jagt's Spirits High," *The Grand Rapids Press*, September 20, 1981, p. 4D.

29. Philosophers have recognized the great difference between what *should be* and what *is.* Confusing the two has been termed by them the naturalistic fallacy. In communication, recognizing what is in fact reality constitutes a nondirective approach. Here, the communicator chooses to inquire into a situation, to ascertain its limits, to expose the network of elements and functions within these limits, and to attempt, perhaps, to lay bare the cause-effect relationships which account for the occurrences within that situation. If the speaker is objective in a treatment of these matters, personal values are separated as much as possible from the interpretation of the phenomena under study. Direction in communication, by contrast, means that the speaker has taken a "side" or a position on the idea being considered. The speaker has injected values into the situation, and, on the basis of resulting priorities, has closed off further inquiry in order to take a strong stand on the matter. At this point, the speaker chooses advocacy and becomes interested in what should be over and above what is.

30. The classic example in American history of the fire-eating advocate who was never heard from again after his public advocacy of an extreme position was Patrick Henry. Certainly others, e.g., Daniel Webster, Henry Clay, John C. Calhoun, and William Jennings Bryan, stand as examples of speakers with a definite point of view which they forcefully advocated who were denied that higher office which they all sought presumably because they had become too closely identified with an extreme position or one special group. In recent political history, 1964, Senator Barry Goldwater advocated an "extreme" position and lost by a greater percentage of votes than any other candidate in the history of presidential elections.

31. "The Three Rs," *op. cit.*

32. "A New Beginning," *op. cit.*

33. "A Nation in Prayer," the Annual National Prayer Breakfast, Washington, D.C., February 7, 1980. It is included here in his collected speeches.

34. In addition to the problem-solving design in the "Price of the Best," the student speaker revealed great skill with description in "Bonn Report." The fact that he has gravitated to advocacy results from his position as party campaigner, not from a lack of skills in nondirective designs. Often, it has already been pointed out, on less formal occasions, the congressman shows great facility with indirective and nondirective designs. All of this does not contradict his own personal preference for a more directive design even as a student at Hope College. It points up, instead, his professional willingness to do what has to be done to fulfill his responsibilities as a communicator.

35. *U.S. News & World Report*, November 29, 1982, p. 20.

36. Interview, March 8, 1982.

37. Interview, July 16, 1982. It is of interest to note how this self-criticism improved his work later with Coelho when they "debated'" at the National Press Club on September 30, 1982, and on the *MacNeil-Lehrer Report* on October 14, 1982. In these two situations, it was established by the master of ceremonies that each speaker was taking one side of the picture, so Vander Jagt was able to spar with Coelho in a good-natured way. Each speaker could develop a partisan case without fear of giving offense to the other by taking advantage of a situation where other designs might have been expected.

38. Interview, October 18, 1982.

39. "You Were Willing," February 21, 1979.

40. *Op. cit.*

41. Interview, March 8, 1982.

42. The author was present when Vander Jagt promised dutifully to undertake assignments given to him on this occasion. The author was also present when he proceeded to fulfill these promises.

CHAPTER FIVE

1. Deanna Black DePree, "Vander Jagt: West Michigan's 'other' Republican Potentate," *Wonderland, The Grand Rapids Press*, August 17, 1975, p. 8.

2. Televised interview with Dr. Robert Schuller, pastor, Garden Grove

Community Church, California, October 2, 1977, on "Hour of Power,' transcribed from audiotape.

3. Interview with Congressman Vander Jagt, March 9, 1981. Many of these personal notes originated in interviews with the congressman.

4. Conversations with Prof. William Schrier during the school year, 1956-57.

5. Letter from Mrs. William Schrier to Congressman Vander Jagt, July 24, 1980.

6. Letter from Guy Vander Jagt to his parents, undated, but during the school year, 1949-50.

7. *Cadillac Evening News*, May 31, 1950, p. 1.

8. John Corry, "One Day in the Life of Guy Vander Jagt (R-Mich)," *Harper's*, April, 1971, p. 71. His campaign manager used the slogan "Fly High with Guy."

9. Unpublished manuscript from the files of Congressman Vander Jagt. His many collegiate awards recounted here were corroborated by newspaper clippings found in his four-volume college scrapbook.

10. William Schrier, *Contest Oratory: A Handbook for High School and College Contestants and Coaches* (Metuchen, N.J.: The Scarecrow Press, Inc., 1971), p. 39

11. The Ciceronian canons, sometimes in almost unrecognizable modern terminology, have been made the basis for the art of speech-making in mos' textbooks in public speaking to the present day. They are: (1) invention, or developing the idea, (2) disposition, or organizing the idea, (3) elocution, or wording/symbolizing the idea, (4) memorization, or keeping the idea in mind, and (5) pronunciation, or delivering the idea. Cicero attributed general authorship of the idea to the speaker with the belief that each stage in an idea's evolution is within the speaker's control and therefore dependent on the speaker's mastery of the art of public speaking.

12. Essays from Congressman Vander Jagt's college scrapbook.

13. DePree, *op. cit.*, p. 8.

14. Letter from Guy Vander Jagt to his daughter, dated January 1973. Virginia Marie Vander Jagt was born on August 31, 1969.